Raising A
Mathem

ONE WEEK LOAN

Raising Achievement in Secondary Mathematics

Anne Watson

Open University Press

Open University Press
McGraw-Hill Education
McGraw-Hill House
Shoppenhangers Road
Maidenhead, Berkshire
England SL6 2QL

email: enquiries@openup.co.uk
world wide web: www.openup.co.uk

and Two Penn Plaza, New York, NY 1012–2289 USA

First published 2006

A catalogue record of this book is available from the British Library

ISBN 0 335 218 601 (pb)   0 335 218 61X (hb)
ISBN 13 PB 978 0335 218 608   HB 978 0335 218 615

Library of Congress Cataloging-in-Publication Data
CIP data has been applied for

Typeset by BookEns Ltd, Royston, Herts.
Printed in Poland, EU by OZGraf. S.A.
www.polskabook.pl

Contents

List of tables and figures

Tables

Figures

Acknowledgements

This book is a combination of several years of research and many hours of watching and talking with teachers. I have been influenced, consciously and subconsciously, by many people, so it is hard to produce a definitive list of those whose words, work and practice have helped me – but I shall try. Teachers and ex-teachers who have let me into their classrooms and their thoughts in ways significant for this book include: Khurshid Ahmed, David Askew, Anthony Broadley, Andrew Christoforou, Jackie Fairchild, Claire Fletcher, Rebecca Freeman-Moody, Simon Haines, Kate Hockridge, Sheila Hirst, Sara Howes, Linda Juul, Di Pettifer, Andrea Pitt, Andrea Rigby, Sarah Shekleton, Kevin Slater, Alec Swift, Sian Roberts, Rebecca Wadcock, John Warner, ... and several cohorts of Postgraduate Certificate in Education students at the University of Oxford.

Colleagues who have, wittingly or unwittingly, helped me think things through, given me new challenges to confront and new factors to consider include: Afzal Ahmed, Mundher al-Adhami, Thabit al-Murani, Mike Askew, Margaret Brown, Ann Dowker, Viv Ellis, Paul Goldenberg, Dave Hewitt, Yusuf Johnson, Donald Katz, Emily Macmillan, Candia Morgan, Mthunzi Nxawe, Stephanie Prestage, Malcolm Swan, Geoffrey Walford, Dylan Wiliam, Peter Winbourne and especially Els De Geest who worked with me on some of the research.

In particular, I thank Leone Burton, Steve Lerman and Ed Silver for agreeing to look at the outline for the book and some early manuscript excerpts, and especially Tony Harries, Pat O'Shea and Caroline Roaf, for reading in detail a draft version and then being encouraging yet usefully critical. Tony was especially helpful in suggesting some extra sources.

Some of the research was funded by the Esmee Fairbairn Foundation; the rest was funded either with small grants from the University of Oxford Department of Educational Studies or from my own pocket. All the findings, positions and implications in this book are totally my own responsibility.

For the Open University Press, Fiona Richman, Katie Metzler and Richard Leigh have been encouraging and hard-working throughout production.

I am upheld by my daughter Alice, who shares my passion for social justice and acts nobly towards everyone, and my husband, John Mason, who shares so many things including a sense of the deep relationship between mathematics, learning, and the human spirit. Finally, thanks to my daughter Kate, for whom my insights, hard-won in a personal struggle to undo the effects of a so-called privileged education, were always blindingly obvious.

... it will be necessary to resist the tendency to render easy that which cannot become easy without being distorted.

(Antonio Gramsci 1949)

To confirm the deepest thing in our students is the educator's special privilege. It demands that we see in the failures of adolescence and its confusions, the possibility of something untangled, clear, directed.

(Barbara Windle 1989)

1 Learning about school mathematics

This book arises from personal research and reflection on practice over about 20 years.

This opening sentence might cause several contrasting reactions for readers. I can imagine you thinking 'it is unlikely to be of relevance to me' or 'it isn't proper research then' or 'I don't need an account of your personal navel-gazing', for example. If you are still reading, it may be because you recognize, as I do, that all theorizing about mathematics education is to some extent a personal version by the author. Perhaps you have enjoyed reading about mathematics education when the author's voice is explicitly personal and the research is obviously guided by personal development. Personal knowledge is valid; it offers more opportunities for access, acceptance or rejection than depersonalized reports of research and practice can do. From Henri Poincare's reports of the power of intuition (Hadamard 1945) to short reports of exploration such as can be found in professional journals, we can relate personally to practitioners' insights into mathematics, research and teaching and *then*, once hooked, search for their value to us, and, if we want it, rigour.

Rigour, while being an essential feature of research which is intended to offer generalities, does not necessarily give rise to the pragmatic knowledge appreciated and taken up by practitioners. Indeed, the level of rigour demanded by the research world often fails to give authentic accounts of classrooms and learning, since these are complex places and processes with many ephemeral characteristics.

What I write is synthesized from 13 years of teaching in schools which served relatively socially deprived areas of cities, followed by 10 years of research, pre-service teaching, and professional development work in secondary mathematics. During that time I have been privileged to work alongside several significant thinkers. Anyone active in mathematics education could write their own list of influences, but it may be more usual to do this in acknolwedgements, not a first chapter, and I have included a list there as well. My excuse for doing it here is that it situates some central characteristics of this book. First, the claims I make are warranted in a number of ways: through systematic research of an empirical kind which has been scrutinized by the research community; through systematic thought of a theoretical kind, tested out with critical teachers and researchers; and through reflection and synthesis of a practical kind, validated through adaptive and effective use by critical teachers and teacher educators. Second, and more importantly, the fundamental beliefs and values on which my practice and this book are based are also espoused by people with whom I have worked, and whose own practice and research between them encompass everything I offer. These are colleagues who are themselves members of critical research communities, so when I make claims in this book which might challenge orthodox views, I do not make them from an isolated place but from the firm ground of community.

Peter Gates (2001), a mathematics educator with a strong critical commitment, was my first head of department in school, with Michael Fielding (2001), who places a very high value on students' voices, as our head of school. Barbara Jaworski (1996) and Jo Boaler (1997), both well known for their descriptions of empowering teaching, became colleagues through research, and Barbara was later a colleague at University of Oxford where Richard Pring, an advocate for the comprehensive ideal, was our director (Pring and Walford 1997). I followed Linda Haggarty (Haggarty and Postlethwaite 2003), now an insightful researcher, into teaching in a comprehensive school in Oxford where I worked alongside Caroline Roaf, whose work centres on inclusion and justice (Roaf and Bines 1989). I worked with Mike Ollerton (2003), a popular author and campaigner about teaching in heterogeneous groups, on an innovative assessment project for the Association of Teachers of Mathematics (ATM). I met John Mason (1988), a prolific author and thinker about many aspects of mathematics education, now my husband, and my friend Dick Tahta (1980) while doing some mathematics for pleasure. I have given as references what I see as significant publications, and these could provide introductions to their work for readers who may be mystified by these names.

Beliefs and values in this book

I often find myself evaluating situations in terms of how the least advantaged are affected by the decisions of others. In terms of mathematics teaching, the beliefs and values with which I identify are the following:

- Nearly all school learners are able to learn significant mathematics given appropriate teaching.

- It is the role of teachers and the education system to extend possibilities for human development. Understanding some key mathematical ideas is essential for realization of the full potential of the human mind. Thus there is a moral imperative for mathematics education.
- Mathematics qualifications act as a social discriminant through segregational practices in schools and on entry to employment. Hence, mathematics educators have responsibilities for social justice, with all school learners having a right of access to key mathematical ideas.
- Mathematics can be terrific fun; knowing that you can enjoy it is psychologically and intellectually empowering.

Without the first belief the next two are impossible to actualize. To do so would require redefining school mathematics to be easy enough for everyone to do within the existing assessment systems and teaching methods, selecting the content of mathematics according to limited visions. Without the last belief it is all a waste of time.

This book is not going to offer ways to raise achievement by tinkering with detail around the edges of statutory structures or normal practices; I will show that the roots of underachievement are within the normal practices of well-meaning teachers just as much as they are within systemic mechanisms. Ways to raise achievement are to be found at the heart of practice in classrooms and in school departments. In this book I question normal practice, trying to open it up and lay bare what it can do to and for underachieving learners. In the process, ways to change are revealed, so that practice can be reconstructed to enable more success for more students in mathematics.

Nature of mathematics

There are so many different views of what mathematics is that it is almost customary to start a book about teaching it with some definitions.

As I write, a new curriculum is being prepared for 14–19-year-olds in England. Never mind. If we all held off publishing our thoughts because new curricula are being prepared that purport to resolve all problems, nothing would ever be written. History shows that new curricula do not, by and large, solve problems. They merely shift the way in which the underlying problems of mathematics teaching manifest themselves. There will still be a shortage of good teachers, more attention on test results than personal development, an underachieving subclass of learners and an overbearing political interference in the process for some time to come – and these problems will still be international and countries' positions in international league tables will be scrutinized and criticized and teachers will be urged to 'do better'. But while I am pessimistic about the working context for teachers, I am optimistic about the underlying capabilities of learners and teachers to improve mathematics learning.

A curriculum is only a selection and arrangement of a subset of mathematical possibilities, chosen according to some political aims and purposes and enacted by schools and teachers according to *their* aims and purposes. So whatever the underlying definitions of a curriculum, what learners see as mathematics will ultimately depend on their perceptions of what teachers offer, what is given special value in their classroom and through assessment (sometimes contradictory values), and the folk status of mathematics in their communities. So, for example, some children believe mental arithmetic to be the most important part of mathematics, some see written algorithms as more important, some value test results of any kind, and others see mathematics as a subject in which you have to articulate what you think.

> My nephews were trying to explain some skate-boarding moves to me in terms of the subtle shifts they had to make to the board, their weight and feet. I asked them if they had ever explained it in this way before, and they said that the way they learnt was more active and physical, and they did not break things down in this way either in actions, thoughts or speech. I asked if there were any school subjects in which they could similarly express what they already knew, and one of them, after a lot of thought, said that the only subject he could think of where this *could* happen was mathematics. Even if this answer was especially constructed to appeal to their aunt, it is a sad indictment of their grammar school education that there was nothing else to say. I asked if he was encouraged to talk about his mathematics in his school lessons. I won't report his reply.

Paul Ernest's (1991) classic collection of views of mathematics which might influence policy and practice is a starting point for exposing a range of possible definitions:

- Utilitarian. School mathematics might prepare learners to function mathematically in society through using intellectual tools such as choosing, adapting, checking and devising methods, evaluating and acting on results.
- Democratic. School mathematics might prepare learners for citizenship through critical interpretation of situations such as making decisions, understanding statistics, comparing choices, becoming fluent with large numbers.
- Humanist. School mathematics might allow learners to develop every kind of faculty they possess to fully function in as many

aspects of humanity as possible, such as developing insight, creativity, puzzle-solving, curiosity, enjoyment.
- Academic. School mathematics might prepare learners for further mathematical study, in which case understanding, memory, rapid use of subsidiary skills, development of mathematical thinking, ability to work with abstract concepts of increasing complexity might all be seen as important.

I do not accept a deterministic view of human behaviour. Such views suggest the existence of mechanistic, predictable relationships between teaching and learning, and the predictability of the relative achievements of certain social groups. But it seems evident that in general people cannot do what they do not know is possible, or have not imagined as possible, or have not experienced as possible. A teacher who has *only* a utilitarian view of mathematics cannot help learners learn it academically, although some of his learners may do so independently due to other influences. I am not claiming that offering different ways to see mathematics necessarily leads to their adoption, but if they are not offered at all then they are not available as possibilities. Offering possibilities, even if they are not taken up, or not recognized, or interpreted some other way, is a responsibility of any educator. Consequently, seeking ways to extend one's own knowledge of possibilities is also an educator's responsibility. A teacher who has only a utilitarian view, but is also aware that there are others, has a responsibility to learn to understand them. Changing the ways of teaching, assessing and communicating with learners, so that they see mathematics as more than just utilitarian, is harder to achieve. Teachers often report that their students ask 'why are we doing this? I shall never use it when I leave school'. It may be a surprise to learn that there are teachers who never hear this question being asked, because they engage adolescents in mathematics by subsuming utilitarian purposes within a more holistic and intriguing approach to the subject.

Ernest's views of mathematics are not mutually exclusive; it is common to find teachers acting as if they espouse different views for different teaching groups, such as working academically with those who have previous high attainment, and working in a utilitarian frame with those who have previous low attainment. Much research about teachers' beliefs about mathematics seems to assume that views of maths and how it is learnt are fixed for each teacher, and that changing beliefs through more training leads directly to changed teaching. This seems too simplistic, and does not explain differences in teaching style, or response to learners, within the practice of individual teachers. For example, Norton *et al.* (2002) write about five teachers who use investigative methods with 'able' learners and 'show and tell' methods with 'less able', presumably because the 'less able' are less able to convince the teacher that they can participate in more sophisticated forms of mathematical interaction. To appeal to the teacher a learner has to use certain forms of language and behaviour, but she can only use the appropriate forms of classroom language and behaviour if she has had opportunity to acquire them, and encouragement to use them. Once having used them, a learner needs to have that use recognized and validated by the teacher. At any stage of this process teacher preference and bias can come into play to distinguish, fairly or not, between those that 'fit', those that will be able to acquire these forms of engagement, and those that do not and cannot.

As I said before, the relationship between teaching and learning is not straightforward. There will never be a guaranteed relationship between what a teacher says and does and what someone else learns. 'Simply because a teacher is teaching does not necessarily guarantee that the child is learning. And conversely, a child often learns when the teacher is not teaching' (Ainscow and Tweddle 1979: 22). There is instead a complex, delicate, multi-faceted and human relationship between teaching and learning.

Values

A belief that some children *cannot learn* algebra can be challenged by someone teaching them algebra, but a belief that some children *should not be taught* algebra cannot be challenged in this way. A teacher whose values include access, inclusivity and education for all might be excited by seeing a successful algebra lesson with learners whom she previously thought were unteachable, but a teacher who only values abstract mathematics as a tool for those who can afford to study higher mathematics at university is unlikely to be so excited and may dismiss the event as a 'waste of time'.

A young teacher was told by her head of department not to bother to teach her year 11 class trigonometry as they were predicted to get grades at GCSE which could be achieved without it. She disobeyed. The expected modal grade was D, with more learners getting below that than above it. The modal grade they achieved was B, and, apart from a few, the rest achieved C.

No one would say that this was only because they were taught trigonometry. It is more likely to be because they were taught with high expectations, which included trigonometry.

Values and beliefs are in complex relation; one's values about different learners could, but might not, alter if one's beliefs about what they were capable of achieving were challenged. The imposition of national targets for achievement does appear to have changed teachers' beliefs about what the 'average' learner can achieve. This has also changed the values teachers espouse in relation to making extra efforts with 'average' learners. It is possible for teachers to value low-attaining learners highly, and put a lot of time into working with them, and to believe that with enough one-to-one coaching they could learn harder mathematics, but not to enact this because they value social nurturing more than academic development.

Educational action which aims to *change* values and beliefs is therefore a tricky endeavour both in terms of likely outcomes and of ethics. Educational action which *challenges* values and beliefs with evidence or alternative views, or which offers more possibilities, runs fewer risks, but may not lead to immediate change. Indeed, the challenge may not even be noticed, since practitioners are adept at interpreting alien ideas to fit their present ideas. For example, the suggestion in the Mathematics Framework (Department for Education and Employment 2001) that there should be three levels of differentiation in mathematics lessons may have been intended to mean *three and only three*. However, when it is applied nearly everywhere to classes which are already differentiated by setting, schools offer $3n$ levels of differentiation, where there are n hierarchical sets.[1] Another example is in the adoption of materials designed for cognitive acceleration in mathematics (Adhami *et al.* 1998) by one school for use with their already high-attaining groups only. The project and materials had been designed for use by all learners, to show that better learning is pos-sible with teaching styles which encourage deeper and more flexible thinking. This particular school failed to understand this fundamental challenge, and used the materials for enhancement only.

What is school mathematics?

Each of the views of mathematics listed by Ernest suggests different ways to describe the purposes of learning mathematics. Because of the varied functions of mathematics and the many possible levels of understanding, there are also many paths by which learning can progress. In the present context, therefore, one cannot say with clarity that a learner 'has learnt' some mathematics until one is precise about what is meant by 'learn' in the context.

For teaching purposes one might require a variable definition of 'learning'. Bjorkqvist (1997) uses 'dynamic assessment' to describe how teachers interpret learners' responses to teaching and make pedagogic decisions accordingly. In dynamic teaching situations teachers find out what learners know in breadth, in the context of some task, rather than just whether they

---

[1] Mathematics teaching groups in the UK are usually organized according to a hierarchical notion of achievement, similar to what is called 'tracking' in some other countries.

have acquired a particular nugget of factual or procedural knowledge, or whether they are keeping up with the pace of events, during a lesson.

Even more interesting would be to find out *how* they are making sense of their experiences as a sequence of lessons proceeds. Too much focus on the learning objectives of individual lessons, while at least making sure that a lesson is about some mathematics and not just about the next page in a textbook, can limit everyone's attention to short-term, easily measurable progress without finding time to discuss long-term conceptual development.

A university mathematician, well known for his imaginative approaches to elementary mathematics, tells the story of his most memorable school maths lesson as a school student. The teacher entered the room, carrying the learners' marked exercise books. These were slammed down on the desk, a treatment he repeated to the chair, which broke. He then sat on the desk, legs swinging, saying in a contemplative way: 'This won't do at all, not at all. Now then, who can tell me – what is a number?'

What followed was discussion over several lessons about meaning, image, knowledge, experience, number sense and, through that, mathematical sense. We can be fairly sure, however, that at least one of the learners had completed the now-ignored homework and met its overt learning objectives satisfactorily.

A more complex view of school mathematics

Rather than being merely a sequence of assessable techniques, I see mathematics as sequences of: objects and their properties; classes of objects with their associated properties; generalizations about classes; abstractions and relations which become objects for more complex levels of activity. These can be represented by a variety of symbols which can, like abstractions and relations, be further manipulated in their own right. However, mathematics is abstract and can only be communicated through language, symbols, diagrams, models or applications; hence learners and teachers always have to work mathematically for themselves, to translate what they know into communicable terms, and to interpret each other's attempts at communication as part of any teaching, learning and assessing situations.

What is it that we hope learners will develop through this web of communication? Krutetskii (1976) studied gifted mathematics learners for many years in the Soviet Union and concluded that good mathematicians were those who could:

- grasp formal structure;
- think logically in terms of spatial, numerical and symbolic relationships;

- generalize rapidly and broadly;
- curtail mental processes;
- be flexible with mental processes;
- appreciate clarity and rationality;
- switch from direct to reverse trains of thought;
- memorize mathematical objects.

A few learners bring these faculties to their mathematics learning whatever the lessons are like, whatever the assessment methods are like. This suggests some stimulating questions for teachers and curriculum planners. What would it be like if all learners were taught to act in these ways in mathematics lessons? For example, how might you 'teach' learners how to 'switch from direct to reverse trains of thought'? This kind of question makes nonsense of the belief that each lesson should have a stated learning objective which is communicated to learners. To have individual lessons with 'switching to reverse trains of thought' as an aim would do little to embed such thinking throughout learners' mathematical engagement, but it would make sense for a teacher to have this as an underlying, medium-term aim running through several lessons, and to be explicit about it. Similarly, it makes no sense to confine integral features of mathematical thinking, such as proof or symbolic manipulation, to lessons which have them as stated objectives. Subtle methods of teaching are needed which focus on learners' ways of being, rather than what they know.

In a recent report from the Third International Mathematics and Science Study (TIMSS),[2] countries' ways of differentiating teaching were compared (Hiebert *et al.* 2003). Overwhelmingly, both high-achieving and low-achieving countries teach all learners the same curriculum in the same ways. A few countries teach different curricula to different groups. England, however, claims to teach the same curriculum to all learners but through groupings which enable different learners to be taught in different ways. I suppose to outsiders reading our national curriculum documentation it may look as if this is the case. In practice, however, most teachers would agree that in secondary school different groups are not taught the same curriculum. It is, however, an interesting idea. Suppose all year 10 groups were going to be taught trigonometry at the same time, to the same level, but those who could already 'switch from direct to reverse trains of thought' were going to have one kind of teaching, and those who could not were going to have a different kind of teaching. What would the lessons be like?

---

[2] See http://isc.bc.edu/timss1995i/TIMSSPublications.html (accessed 5 August 2005).

Organization of school mathematics

But this can seem like the stuff of dreams. To be manageable, school mathematics is usually seen as hierarchical so that learners need to understand ideas in a particular order. For this reason mathematics classes in schools in the UK are almost universally organized according to perceived ability or past achievement, and the curriculum available to learners is varied according to the set they are in (Ofsted 1994). In order to select who should be in which group, teachers have to make decisions very early in the learner's career. Mathematics setting can take place as early as Year 1 of primary school, for instance. Because such decisions lead to some learners having limited access to the curriculum, whatever is said in the TIMSS, setting decisions can deeply influence learners' futures. It is therefore important to know how such decisions might be made, because they are merely management decisions for the school but have high-stakes outcomes for the child.

The assessment of school mathematics relies on the assumption that learners' knowledge is describable and assessable. Teachers and assessors are required by law to behave as if the mathematical knowledge of others is knowable, communicable and definable. School procedures function as if it is possible to describe fully the current and future state of learners' knowledge. Teachers believe that they can make those decisions, and critique assessment procedures according to their own judgements.

Two teachers were expressing dissatisfaction with the assessment procedure which relies on a child's performance on one day.

One said: 'A child who *should* get level 3 really ought to be given it, even if they are having an off-day'.

The other said: 'And a child who gets level 3 by a fluke should be given a high 2'.

These two statements, both of which went unchallenged, show a belief that the teachers are the ones who really know whether a child is 'really' level 3 or not, and that levels should describe a general state over time, rather than a consistent level of performance on every occasion.

Social justice

I define social justice as practice which ensures that one person's progress should not be heavily dependent on one other person's judgement; that disadvantages are identified and acted upon; that no one who is a member of a systemically disadvantaged group should be further disadvantaged by an educational system; and that existing disadvantages receive compensatory

attention. As views of social justice go this one is not very radical. It is essentially based on John Rawls's (1972, 2001) theory of justice in that fairness
requires us to select schemes under which the least advantaged are better
off than under any other scheme. Using 'higher mathematics grade' as a
measure of advantage, given its marketable qualities in employment, a
socially just grouping system would be one in which disadvantaged
learners did better than under any other system. Rawls examines closely the
question of who should make decisions about such groupings. He argues
for 'realistic utopianism' (2001: 4), in which no one acts as if they have
bargaining advantages based on aspects such as 'social class; native endowments; opportunities to develop those endowments; good or ill fortune and
luck; periods of involuntary unemployment' (2001: 55) or family income
(2001: 44). Too often this is not the case where schooling is concerned.

> A mathematics department which had regularly enabled disadvantaged learners to
> achieve well at GCSE, through heterogeneous grouping and activity-based teach-
> ing, was encouraged to introduce textbooks and setting by the headteacher who
> wanted to attract middle-class learners to the school and was supported in these
> requests for change by Ofsted inspection. A parent living in a nearby middle-class
> area, and who had children coming up to secondary-school choice, was heard to
> comment 'School X will have to go to streaming now they have more middle-class
> children'. This is indeed what happened.

This anecdote exemplifies a classic muddle in lay thinking about
achievement, social class, setting, and teaching methods. On one side, there
is an assumption that class is related to achievement and potential, so there
has to be differentiation in the school system to attract, or cater for, such
differences. On the other side, there is an assumption that exploratory
teaching styles are always related to heterogeneous groupings and vice
versa. Although I shall mention setting and tracking in this book, I shall try
to avoid this latter confusion. My focus is on ways to teach low-attaining
learners in whatever kinds of teaching group they are positioned. In my
research, such learners were usually positioned in two main ways: either
they were in mixed groups with teachers who tried to classify students
according to some notion of ability and thus treat them differently, or they
were already separated into groups of students with similarly low past
attainment.

Since I am writing about achievement within a state education system
I am going to accept that the system exists, and that my role is to explore
how disadvantaged groups might benefit more within it. Thus more radical
ideas such as deschooling society, or creating alternative schools, while they
appeal to me in principle, do not offer useful ideas for those working in education as it is, except in isolated cases. Similarly, another radical line of
thought would be to construct a curriculum which is about the curiosity of

adolescents, and immerses them in meaningful problems, both global and local, or offers specially designed curricula for special groups of learners. A further solution would be to support learners to work on their own problems and questions. These too have some appeal, but I am persuaded by Antonio Gramsci's argument that all people, by rights, need to be educationally prepared to participate fully and hence be empowered in the world as it *is* and not as it *might be*. For Gramsci (1971), and for me, this includes the opportunity to learn the 'high culture' of school subjects. In this way they can participate in, and even be agents for, change. Thus those who already know least about mathematics are not necessarily best placed to decide what it is they need to learn. For example, learners who have been taught algebra badly and hate it are not in a position to see the potential intellectual and economic power which an algebraic view of mathematics might give them (Mason *et al.* 2005). Discussion between teachers and learners, in which each pays full attention to the other's knowledge, might enable what Tony Harries calls a 'common mind' to develop for such decisions (personal communication, July 2005[3]).

Some may argue, on grounds of social justice, against teaching the subject at all for the part it plays in the production of weapons of destruction, the way it services global companies, and the way it operates in schools to select certain groups for success. But there are several ways in which even a conventional mathematics curriculum can contribute to fair access to the social goods and opportunities of society, even potentially to critical change:

- by equipping people to take a full part in ordinary life;
- by equipping them to make mathematically based decisions about more complex aspects of life such as voting, investments and tax;
- by allowing them to understand information about society;
- by providing a knowledge base on which they can build further in order to get certain jobs;
- by providing access to higher-paid jobs which may have no connection with mathematics;
- by preparing the way for them to gain enjoyment from participating in mathematics as a human activity;
- by providing intellectual tools to argue, challenge and change society.

I prefer to focus on the potential of mathematics to map epidemics, to predict climate change, to inform people about social and economic

---

[3] Developing algebraic thinking from learners' own questions and curiosity is possible, as the work of Brown and Coles (e.g. 1999) shows.

injustice, and to provide evidence for arguments about social change as well as to provide personal and social uplift. It is because I know mathematics well enough to see these potentials that, as a teacher, I might want to teach as much of it as possible to everyone, and not allow their current horizons and choices to limit the development of tools which will allow them to see further in the future. I am suspicious that a learner-guided curriculum could trap learners into narrow worlds and narrow views. This would also be true of a purely 'functional' curriculum.

Underachievement

In the earlier statement I made about beliefs and values I allowed for the possibility that some learners in mainstream schools might never under any circumstances be able to learn mathematics. After many years in teaching and working with teachers and observing lessons, I do not know if this is true. Until policy-makers and researchers take the achievement of those who currently fail in school mathematics seriously, I do not think anyone knows what *real* limitations might exist. I am not talking about those who fail to learn because they have been put into a bottom set with a teacher who does not give them anything worthwhile to do; I am not talking about those who might be said to have a condition called dyscalculia, because there are many areas of mathematics which do not require calculation skills and a calculator can substitute for those they lack. Instead I am wondering how many people in mainstream schools are *truly* unable to recognize pattern, to generalize, to imagine, to reason about shapes, to connect ideas to symbolic representations, to do the approximate numerical and spatial reckoning which they need to function in the world, and so on. How many would never, whatever kind of teaching they have, be able to do the things Krutetskii described as habits of gifted learners?

In the UK we do not do very well at helping *all* learners learn mathematics and get valuable school-leaving grades in the subject. At the time of writing (August 2005), in common with many other countries, even generally high-achieving countries such as Japan, about 50 per cent do not even get the valued grades at 16+. Even those who get good grades may not be able to do what others expect of them. Employers and universities regularly complain that entrants with good grades cannot apply their mathematics to non-standard problems, and cannot start anything which is unfamiliar or for which the end is not in easy sight (Smith 2004).

National test scores throughout school, whose usefulness can legitimately be challenged by employers and universities, appear to rise but the performance of our learners in international tests does not invite confidence (Hiebert *et al.* 2003). It is always possible to argue that international comparisons ignore cultural features, such as the following:

- the highest achieving countries also seem to have the least diverse populations;
- England has special circumstances because of social diversity;
- we have a more awkward number system than some high-achieving countries;
- we spend less per capita on education than some countries;
- historically we bestow a low cultural value on mathematics;
- we have many high-income alternative careers to teaching for mathematics graduates;
- working conditions for teachers are harder than in some other countries.

All these are true, but so is the inescapable fact that the system of grouping which we use in school replicates society as a whole, so that learners from already disadvantaged groups are most likely to find themselves gathered together in the lowest sets for mathematics, hence with the least possibility of being empowered and enfranchised through mathematics. Differences within countries between different social groups overwhelm differences between countries (Postlethwaite 1999), and the more selection and differential tracking a country has, the wider is the achievement gap between rich and poor students (Programme for International Student Assessment 2004: 29).

We exacerbate differential achievement by continuing to separate learners for different treatment, in spite of consistent research evidence that most learners do better in heterogeneous groups (Hallam and Toutounji 1996; Suhknandan and Lee 1998; Boaler *et al.* 2000; Wiliam and Bartholomew 2004), and compelling anecdotes, such as the trigonometry story, which show that so much more is possible. The biggest challenge is how to break inevitable underachievement which comes from categorizations arising from well-meant 'segregation' and ascription of levels to students.

It is so hard to accept that a teacher can thoughtfully, reflectively, intelligently, benevolently practise in a way which can disadvantage and limit learners. It has been known for decades that the decisions teachers make about the curriculum they offer certain learners, the way they talk to certain learners, what they praise them for and what they expect from them can limit or extend the possibilities open to learners throughout their time in the mathematics classroom, not just at examination times (Brophy and Good 1974). Because of the intimate relationship between teachers' expectations and learners' achievements, social justice is an issue in informal as well as formal mathematics assessments.

Raising achievement

When I started the research trajectory on which this book is based I was firmly committed to the notion that teacher assessment of the work done in the normal course of classroom life was the fairest and most valuable way to credit learners' achievements (Bell and Wheeler 1968; Dearing 1994). Through this intimate knowledge, the theory goes, a teacher can devise ways to teach and adapt the curriculum to suit each learner. Learners need not be constrained by the unusual demands of timed pencil-and-paper tests which, in any event, could only test recall of facts and procedures and accuracy under pressure. Additionally, if all achievements during schoolwork can be credited when demonstrated, and that record of achievement never taken away, then more learners would do well in mathematics and higher levels of motivation would result. Teachers might also discover that more learners have the potential to study mathematics to higher levels. Teachers would carry the responsibility of finding ways for learners to express their thinking including those who could not, for instance, decode a textbook or produce neat written arguments. I no longer believe that this approach, teacher autonomy over decisions which affect individual futures, is desirable and unproblematic.

This book starts with the research story of how I came to understand how teachers' casual judgements can either embed social inequity, or be liberating and empowering, but are never neutral. It continues with stories from subsequent research which show that there are other ways to be, and that students can be rescued by teachers who maintain integrity with mathematics as it is, and learners as they are, and vision about what might be.

The message in this book is that to raise achievement in secondary mathematics for all, including the most disadvantaged students, a radical change in the usual approaches to teaching, assessment and grouping for such students is required. At the heart of this change there needs to be a belief that all students can learn mathematics, and freedom within the system to enact this belief.

In the next chapter I shall explore the notions of 'ability' and 'understanding' because teachers are usually concerned that learners should 'understand' and a common belief is that what they are capable of understanding is related to their 'ability'.

2   Abilities and understanding

When I use the term 'underachievement' I do not mean to measure achievement in terms of predictions from baseline scores or assumptions about intelligence and population norms. Instead I think about achievement as the exploitation of the human mind to understand and enjoy mathematics. Thus any learner who wants to study more at any time and is still actively learning new mathematics is achieving, and any learner who rejects it and/or fails to learn is underachieving. I accept that my definition is hard to measure, but measures such as test results and enrolment in higher courses can give some indication of the presence or absence of my kind of achievement.

In this book I am not replicating the substantial research results about the negative effects of setting on achievement of the most disadvantaged students, although these are part of the overall story. Instead I am going to explore the micro-systems of assessment and teaching by which so many underachieve, whatever kinds of group they are in, and thus suggest how the divisive results of mathematics teaching might be put right, whether learners are separated according to past attainment or not.

Teachers' judgements

To try to understand why teachers trust segregation into different groups to provide appropriate learning environments for all, I will start by examining what characteristics teachers talk about when describing their students' mathematics.

The unfairness and bias which can be introduced into the education system by processes which rely on the outcomes of teacher assessment and evaluation have been known about for some time. By no means the first to raise this issue, Derek Blease (1983: 124) points out that

> Teachers are led to believe, through their professional training, that
> they are able to make accurate judgements about children. They

occupy a status in society whereby it is thought legitimate for them to make such judgements. In the heat of the moment they may more readily accept their own first impressions or the judgements of others without question – myth becomes reality.

These informal judgements, as well as influencing one-to-one interaction, contribute to decisions about grouping, setting, and differentiated provision; poor judgements can therefore lead to wrong decisions in all these respects. Ken Ruthven's (1987) study of ability stereotyping is pivotal in that he shows that teachers' classifications of mathematical ability, and judgements of learners' global cognitive states, are constructed from personality or even class-related traits, with very little attention to mathematical activity or mental acts which are specific to mathematics. Where there is attention to mathematical activity, it is overgeneralized (p. 243).

In mathematics, Jens Lorenz (1982) found that teachers' perceptions of children were linked to behaviour, so behaviour became linked to learner achievement, and personality traits served as explanations for success and failure. Personal characteristics and general classroom demeanour have also been shown, in the work of Arnold Morrison and Donald McIntyre (1969), to be more emphasized by teachers than learning achievements:

> Although scholastic assessment is a dominant concern, teachers spend a far greater proportion of their time observing, evaluating and acting upon indications of ongoing social behaviour and upon forming impressions of the more or less persisting personal traits of learners. (p. 200)

They warn:

> The very confidence that some teachers have in their abilities gives them excessive faith in the quality of their measures and evaluation. This can lead in turn to failure to recognize some of the factors affecting evaluations of learners' work and to faulty conclusions about the extent and nature of difficulties being experienced by individual learners. (p. 206)

At the very least poor judgements could lead to misapplied help. As Lorenz (1982) points out, help is dependent on what the teacher has already decided a learner can achieve. Yet teachers' judgements are 'subject to all those prejudices, stereotypes, distortions ... to which all people are exposed when they only have their common-sense to rely on' (Ingenkamp 1977: 81).

One would expect that these studies would influence the way teachers' judgements are incorporated into school regimes. However, when the current regime of assessment and testing was introduced into schools, scant attention was paid to the potential for bias. The Schools Examination and Assessment Council (1989) comments very briefly on the importance of checking for bias: 'Has opportunity been taken to discuss assessments with colleagues?' (p. 43) and 'Teachers need to be aware of the ways personal interest or bias is sometimes brought into the assessment' (p. 58) and further, 'Try to approach observation of the assessment task without preconceptions about the child's performance' (p. 39).

As with most top-down professional guidance, whether teachers did this or not would be dependent on local factors and on knowledge of why this advice had been given and how to carry it out. Indeed, Robin Nash's (1976) observation is that superficial categorizations made by teachers tend to 'stick' and points to the staffroom 'community of knowledge' which perpetuates them through informal conversations, so that checking one's assessments with colleagues may not provide an adequately critical environment. I shall return to this observation in Chapter 5.

We could hope that these concerns no longer apply in our more assessment-aware times, but Mairead Dunne (1994), working closely with a few teachers within the then current assessment regimes, explored how their notions of ability developed. She found that cultural and class factors, and views of mathematics, had a far greater influence on their understanding of learners' mathematical ability than their supposed knowledge of what goes on inside a child's head. Mike Askew and his colleagues, also working within the current regimes, found that 'differences in learners' abilities ... were more often described in terms of personal qualities, particularly confidence, than in terms of mathematical abilities' (Askew *et al.* 1993: 14).

The questions lurking beneath all these comments are whether it is *ever* possible to know what goes on in a learner's head, and what it is we are really saying when we claim to have assessed a learner. Any teacher reading this will be aware that she *has* to make judgements in order to operate at all, and that many times her judgements are helpful and well founded. It is not the making of judgements in itself which leads to problems of social injustice, but the way these are gradually embedded into the life opportunities of different learners through the assessment system, the way learners are grouped in school, and the habitual ways in which the profession responds to those who are considered 'strong' or 'weak'. This is why Broadfoot (1979) argues powerfully that assessment methods are inherently biased to discriminate against lower classes in order to retain elitism, and that this bias is accepted as the 'common sense' of education. Thus, while every teacher is working with goodwill and trying to act fairly, the systems in which she works, apart from some individual maverick cases, determine different futures for learners from different social classes and social groups. One way this acts itself out is through the availability of statistics which show how students who enter secondary school at certain 'levels' generally achieve certain GCSE results. Instead of using these as historical feedback about past teaching, some teachers use them as targets so that a zero residual (maintaining the past level of results) is acceptable and any positive residual (improvement) is worth celebrating. The status quo is not radically challenged by this approach, so students who have been to primary schools which are less well equipped, with less imaginative teachers and lower expectations, continue to be subject to lower expectations.

Furthermore, we imagine that teachers diagnose different needs for learners and apply different treatments accordingly. In practice this does not happen, because we do not yet have the knowledge and language to discuss how to teach learners who do not (to use the example from Chapter 1) 'switch to reverse trains of thought' or 'grasp structure' (Krutetskii 1976) and need to incorporate this flexibility into their thinking. Instead, the socially invented labels of 'less able' or 'low achiever' are applied to the learner and this allows teachers to expect less learning without having to feel guilty about it.

This sounds harsh on teachers, and for this I apologize, because I do not think teachers individually are responsible for this. It is the habits of the profession, and the ways in which mathematics teaching operates within a more complex system, which maintain these practices and attitudes.

Teachers' notions of ability

Between 1994 and 1997 I set out to find out for myself how teachers were constructing their concepts of mathematical ability through tape-recording interviews with 30 teachers about their use of informal assessment methods with learners from Years 6 and 7, the years which straddle the move from primary to secondary school. Here I shall report their ideas about the mathematical abilities of their students. The literature suggested that 'ability' would be constructed in terms of behaviour or personal characteristics, but I wanted to find out if it is possible, by probing more deeply, for teachers to be more mathematically specific about learners' work. After all, there is no point in authors berating teachers for making judgements based mainly on social features of classroom life if that is the only possibility for informing practice.

Data from a relatively small sample[1] cannot, of course, provide a robust representation of what all teachers believe, but that was not my aim.

---

[1]   The sample was largely opportunistic, but was well balanced between primary, middle school and secondary, different local education authorities, and different lengths of teaching career.

My aim was to identify the parameters which teachers noticed in their normal work; to find out what they thought worth mentioning; to try to see learners through their eyes, understanding what was in the foreground of their perceptions as they interacted with learners individually or *en masse*.

As I analysed the content of the interviews I found that many of the transcripts contained the concept of 'ability' in some form or other. In other words, in the context of telling me about learners' mathematics, teachers would make more general judgements about characteristics of the learner which they saw as determinants or predispositions acting in a more or less constant fashion throughout the learners' mathematical learning. To tell me about a learner's mathematics they often told me about past perform-ance and potential, as they saw it, in terms of national curriculum levels. This was not a surprise; ascribing national curriculum levels 'correctly' is seen to be an important professional task. Similarly, the language of accountability and target-setting for schools, classes and individuals is used widely and future test results act as a central motivational device for teach-ers and schools. Teachers were keen to talk about how they made sense of these requirements. However, I felt that merely describing levels according to a hierarchical scale did not convey anything much to me about someone's learning potential or disposition. To hear that a learner has moved from level 3 to level 4 without knowing if this was the result of copious practice, or deepened understanding, or achieved against a background of domestic strife or peacefulness, says nothing about what is commonly called 'ability'.

As one of many approaches to the data I analysed both direct and oblique references to learners' general learning characteristics to obtain a broader picture of what the teachers regarded as contributing towards a child's success, or otherwise, in mathematics. This included comments about the attributes, skills, attitudes and characteristics of learners who were 'good' at mathematics, and also any other characteristics which were listed by teachers as being desirable or essential to the successful learning of mathematics. I did this by rereading all the data many times, selecting aspects just described, and compiling and analysing a separate text of all the utterances.

The main features that teachers described were:

- what learners brought into the current teacher–learner relationship;
- behaviour displayed when learners were working on mathematics;
- emotional factors which the teacher observed or inferred;
- intellectual and mental activity.

In the discussions that follow,[2] I use the word 'ability' when teachers used it to describe specific abilities, such as an ability to be accurate, or an ability to give examples. Where it appeared to be used to suggest a global tendency, a general 'mathematical ability', I have substituted other phrases.

At the start of the teacher–learner relationship

Teachers were concerned about what learners bring with them at the start of their teacher–learner relationship in terms of:

- prior knowledge and experience;
- retained knowledge;
- mental images;
- attitudes to the subject;
- preferred ways of working;
- sense of achievement, or of lack of success.

Those things which seemed likely to affect the teacher's initial judgements of a learner were:

- the view expressed by the previous teacher;
- the view that the new teacher has of the previous teacher's work or style
- past experience of groups or learners seen as 'similar'.

Thus the teaching relationship starts with assumptions, givens, prejudices[3] and predispositions on each side.

Behaviour while learning

From this starting state the first things the 'new' teacher was likely to notice and comment on were, as has been the case in other studies, behavioural. Some of these are easy to observe and seductively easy to interpret, in that teachers are in the familiar territory of interpreting non-verbal signals between human beings. Teachers see who appears to pay attention and who, apparently, does not; who behaves in ways which convey interest and who appears bored; who talks a lot and who stays silent. Such behaviour leads teachers to make inferences about underlying ability, yet the possibility that

---

[2] Early versions of the discussions that follow appeared in Watson (1995, 1996a).
[3] I do not use 'prejudice' to mean anything more than 'prejudging'. It could apply to positive as well as negative judgements.

different interpretations can be made is glaringly obvious – for instance, whether a learner who talks a lot is seen as enthusiastic, hyperactive, disruptive or demanding.

One teacher thought it important that learners should 'desire to know', should be curious and want to understand. Another felt that the will to push forward, to ask for help or ideas in order to progress, not just when stuck, was a good indicator of 'ability'. This desire for learners to 'push on' presupposes that the learner knows how to do this, and does not believe that her task is only to do what the teacher suggests. In a negative summary of a learner one teacher said 'She spends too much time on the minutiae rather than pushing herself on', thus valuing progress over a learner's desire for accuracy. Yet the learner's desire for accuracy could be a habit developed with a previous teacher.

Both the more and less desirable characteristics of behaviour are influenced by the past. 'Learned helplessness' (Peterson *et al.* 1993) is a good example of this. There are often those who will do nothing without being personally reassured that their interpretation of a task is correct, or without it being simplified until it is more structured and/or less challenging than its original version. This helplessness can appeal to the nurturing instincts of teachers and classroom assistants and it is tempting for adults to gain the easy satisfaction of giving the requested help rather than the harder satisfaction of encouraging independent willingness. Thus dependency is nurtured, rather than independence. In mathematics this temptation is particularly acute if there is more emphasis on getting an answer, no matter how, than on understanding and application.

Over the whole sample, teachers seemed to value a progression in learners' engagement from

- providing the external appearance of expected learning behaviour,
- doing the work offered, and
- showing a personal desire to finish the work

to

- having internal goals and personal drive to work on mathematics.

All of these are learnt behaviours in the sense that they depend on the perceived effects of previous behaviour and the norms of previous classroom experience. They are therefore strongly related to the starting state of the teacher–learner relationship, and thus to the past. I began to wonder if teachers were telling me about what, in their view, were fixed characteristics of their students or whether they saw their task as helping learners progress through increasingly independent kinds of engagement. After all, if patterns of behaviour which learners bring into secondary school have been influenced by prior experience, then they can be further influenced by new expectations.

Emotional factors

The next set of factors I identified reveal the teacher's interpretation of the emotional state of the learner in various mathematical learning situations. It is important to note that these were mentioned in response to being asked about a learner's mathematics since it indicates that the teachers were skilled in interweaving affective and cognitive aspects of learning. They talked about the following:

- Reactions to being right or wrong, such as: 'He has pride in being right'.
- Reactions to being stuck: 'She'll ask very quietly and politely "how do you think I could do it?"'.
- Reactions to different types of activity, especially open versus closed activities: 'If they have to do some work where they have to work things out themselves they own it more and they are trying to create something instead of doing something that already exists. I think there is a hurdle that is removed.'
- Sense of self-worth: 'One little boy wrote "I am a bit silly and a bit slow". Well that would need tackling through his work and not through the label he had been given. To take that away would be a starting point for his working.'
- Confidence: 'I think mathematics is a bit of a confidence trick. I believe you can do almost anything you can believe you can do, most children can too.'
- Liking challenge: 'When I set work for the brighter learners they generally get on and finish it. They like more of a challenge.'

Again these are heavily influenced by what has gone before, and the present teacher may never know why a learner's emotions are as they are. I am going to leave the relationship between affect and cognition in this rather uncritical state. However, since engagement and motivation are widely seen to be essential for learning, it is possible to see emotion and learning as inseparable concepts (Damasio 2000). For now I shall point out how the connection, as seen by teachers, could be a strength if they choose to work on the learner's ability to learn mathematics through developing positive emotional responses. However, it could also be a weakness if the teacher responds to confidence only by offering harder maths, and to lack of confidence only by offering easier maths.

Intellectual and mental activity

In contrast to the comments from other writers reported earlier, there were several comments about learners' 'ability' in mathematics which were based on observations and interpretations of mental or intellectual activities. It was in this area that I hoped to find more detail about mathematics, rather than general intellectual skills. I categorized these according to subheadings developed by the ATM for assessing extended mathematical explorations (Southern Examining Group (SEG) 1988): communication; attitude; planning; implementation; understanding; knowledge.

Communication

Reading fluency was frequently linked to mathematical achievement, especially where teaching was mainly from written resources. Some teachers linked the two with no explanation but others did elaborate on a link, one teacher saying that 'ability to overcome hurdles of reading textbooks' was crucial. Possibly what is being described here says more about the appropriateness of the teaching method than the learners' mathematics.

Learners' facility to communicate their own ideas verbally was considered very important, otherwise the teacher had no 'window into their minds'. All claimed to encourage discussion.

No teacher claimed that the standard of written work is itself an indicator of mathematical competence, although one teacher thought that an ability to write creatively and the ability to spell and punctuate perfectly were analogous to creativity and precision in mathematics, and another said that 'linguistic ability is not far from mathematical ability'.

One teacher recognized that some learners who are very good at mathematics may produce high-level but very terse arguments which need careful interpretation by the teacher. He felt as a reader that he, the teacher, might miss the sense of what was going on. That this teacher articulated his own sensitivity so clearly, and no others did so, suggested to me that it is possible for teachers to *imagine* that they recognize ability when really they are recognizing how well they can personally follow a learner's arguments, or how far the learner's articulated understanding coincides with their own (Morgan 1998).

From these aspects of communication only the use of precise, terse and/or shorthand arguments seems specifically, conventionally, mathematical although communication skills are, in many obvious ways, central to classroom learning. I am avoiding any claims that mathematics *is* discourse since for the pedagogic purposes of this book it makes more sense to me to regard mathematics as a body of knowledge enacted as a set of practices into which learners are inducted. Those practices include mathematical communication, and the use of symbolic forms, including words, through which mathematics is always represented – but no one talked of these.

Attitude

Some teachers talked of learners who were interested in mathematics, who responded broadly and deeply to mathematical stimuli, who responded positively to teachers' attempts to extend their thinking, who could think on their own, who looked for patterns and other recognizable structures and who understood the concept of 'trying'. It was noted by one teacher that his 'low-ability' learners had responded much better when offered a mathematical situation to explore than when offered someone else's thinking to follow in a book, so it is possible that enthusiastic engagement is as much task-related as it is a personal characteristic.

While many of these attitudes could be applied to any subject, an interest in pattern and structure is particularly relevant to mathematics. Also, since much mathematics teaching is still concerned with replication of techniques and answering other people's questions, the observation that learners respond better to exploration has specific power for mathematics.

No teacher talked about any learners having a mathematical perspective on the world, or being willing to mathematize even when this was not directed.

Planning

Organization of work was often the first thing mentioned about individual learners, along with being methodical. Some teachers said that being methodical is a sign of mathematical ability. The ability to collate relevant information and decide what mathematics to apply in open situations was mentioned many times. If this means mathematizing a situation by describing it in mathematical terms and applying maths to its resolution, then I would say that was specific to mathematics. However, I suspect that learners usually know, because of the classroom context, that it is mathematics they are supposed to be doing, and very often they also know what mathematics they are supposed to be applying. This makes problem-solving situations less good as opportunities to observe mathematizing capabilities than they might be if they were less contrived. No teacher talked of planning as prior consideration of mathematical possibilities. No teacher talked about choice of method as showing an understanding of efficiency or power.

Implementation

Over and over again, teachers said that they wanted learners to 'think', and in particular to 'think for themselves'. This might imply that there are times when they do not think, or think on behalf of other people, and that a general instruction to 'think' might make a difference to achievement! It was as if there was deep frustration around, in that teachers knew what kinds of thinking they wanted learners to do, valued it when they saw it, but did not know how to describe it except in vague terms. Often generic problem-solving skills were described as if they were mathematical abilities. In some schools students are given a sequence of actions to perform (try some examples, put your results in a table, check your results, and so on) which is supposed to provide a frame for thinking. This approach removes the central activity of deciding what to do and how to do it on mathematical grounds.

Once a piece of work has been started, teachers considered it important that learners move from one process to the next themselves, can apply mathematics correctly, can get right answers, can approximate appropriately, can develop a range of strategies and processes, can work creatively, can think and can take jumps which are longer than step-by-step approaches. I was interested that this kind of comment was made by most of the teachers, since a constant criticism from employers is that young employees cannot do these things when they start work (Smith 2004). Perhaps the problem is in the words 'can' and 'cannot', for these imply global capability rather than behaviour in a particular context. Thus, teachers may say 'this student can approximate correctly' when all they know is that the student did so on a couple of occasions. Conversely, they may say 'this student cannot work creatively' when all they know is that they have seen no evidence so far. That teachers remark on these skills when thinking about Years 6 and 7 shows that they regard them as important, so what happens between Year 7 and school-leaving age? Do teachers regard such propensities as fixed, or leave further development to nature, or does the assessment system make it hard to spend time on developing such skills further?

Understanding

Teachers said that a good mathematician could be interested in finding out why things are the way they are, but also described skilled performance of techniques as a mathematical ability too. Several teachers drew attention to this difference. One Year 6 teacher suggested that GCSE may be a test of the latter rather than the former and that a learner might succeed in school mathematics through performance rather than through understanding.

Another aspect of understanding mentioned was that learners should make links with other knowledge and concepts, and could make specific and general statements about the situations they were working with. The interconnected roles of generalization and exemplification are central and significant in mathematics.

In this study I did not explore what was meant by 'understanding', but I shall return to this in the second part of this chapter.

Knowledge

Memory for mathematical facts and formulae was considered useful. Teachers also mentioned quantity of work or pace of work as a good indicator of ability. Some said that it is important for a learner to create their own knowledge, and this I took to mean that they should be able to make conjectures and statements as a result of mathematical experiences.

Summarizing mental activity

In analysing the teachers' descriptions of mental and intellectual activity I hoped to find characteristics which might be specifically mathematical, rather than general classroom norms, social and communication skills and other fluent adaptive behaviours. Ways of thinking mentioned by the teachers which I thought were specifically mathematical were:

- using terse or shorthand arguments;
- showing interest in pattern and structure;
- seeing and expressing situations mathematically;
- being able to string processes together;
- applying mathematics correctly and appropriately;
- developing mathematical strategies;
- making multi-stage jumps;
- having useful images of, for instance, numbers;
- memorizing mathematical facts and formulae;
- having mathematical ideas;
- generalizing mathematically.

These coincide remarkably with the characteristic behaviour (called 'psychological abilities') generated in Krutetskii's research about gifted mathematicians, mentioned in Chapter 1, namely: to grasp formal structure; to think logically in spatial, numerical and symbolic relationships; to generalize rapidly and broadly; to curtail mental processes; to be flexible with mental processes; to appreciate clarity and rationality; to switch from direct to reverse trains of thought; and to memorize mathematical objects.

Some of the teachers' comments reflect Krutetskii's descriptions closely. They span his descriptions of giftedness and his non-obligatory aspects of mathematical ability. About half his descriptors match the teachers' ideas loosely. However, although the teachers' list makes useful reference to specific thinking processes associated with mathematics, it is compiled from infrequent utterances. Whereas behavioural and emotional factors were mentioned by nearly every teacher, and there was agreement across the sample about what these were, the mental activities listed above were usually only mentioned by one, or at most two, teachers in the sample of 30. The teachers who offered anything only offered one or two ideas about useful intellectual or mental factors, and only seven of the teachers contributed to the list at all. The only exception to this was the almost ubiquitous mention of general 'problem-solving' capability, without saying what was encompassed by this.

So teachers' working views of mathematical learning were predominantly about behaviour, emotion and general mental activities, as had been found in previous research, yet some teachers did have an awareness of, and a language for, identifying abilities which were more specific to mathematics. In general, however, all of us, including me as interviewer, appeared to lack ways of discussing specifically mathematical aspects of school work.

Obstacles to improving the quality of mathematical activity

Many times during the interviews, however, I found myself wondering whether I was hearing as much about opportunities to learn and teaching methods as I was about learners' abilities. One obvious instance of this was where ability to read a textbook was mentioned as an important issue. If the problem is technical reading skill, then why is a textbook being used at all? If the problem is comprehension – making sense of diagrams, worked examples and written explanations – then are learners taught how to do this? I also found myself wondering more generically: if a given mental or intellectual activity is valued, what opportunities do learners have to observe such activity, learn about such activity, practice and use such activity, appreciate the results of such activity? From the interview data, this kind of question arises about opportunities to:

- verbalize ideas;
- discuss mathematics;
- take a mathematical perspective on a situation;
- engage in extended mathematical exploration;
- consider mathematical possibilities when planning work;
- recognize what is worth memorizing, and know ways to do this.

In a few interviews I asked 'what kinds of activity would help X, Y or Z do better in mathematics?'. The replies were thin. One teacher suggested: 'If he concentrated more ...'. Another said: 'He could check his work more often.' A third exclaimed, with her hands flying up in a gesture of hopelessness: 'Where do you start? With her background!' She then said of a high-achieving student: 'She cannot do any more than she is – she is wonderful.'

None of them talked about what a teacher could do to make a difference. It was as if the teachers valued certain kinds of activity, but did not see that teachers could effect whether they happened or not. The mention of background by one teacher could be dismissed as an assumption about the determinism of social class, yet there is a telling finding in the report prepared by the National Foundation for Educational Research (NFER 2003) to highlight lessons for England from the TIMSS. International comparisons of achievement around the lowest benchmark appeared to show that:

> Mathematics teachers' perception of student ability, needs and attitude as a limiting factor to how they teach was a strong negative predictor of attainment in all aspects of mathematics. Interestingly, if the range of student background, number of students and resources were seen to be limiting, then students were likely to do better.
>
> (NFER 2003: 284)

My interpretation of this is that teachers who see themselves as compensating for weaknesses in the system, or who see students as socially and economically disadvantaged, are more likely to make a difference to attainment than those who see low-achieving students as the architects of their own misfortune, or as deficient in some abilities. This echoes findings by Brophy and Good (1974), in that a minority of teachers, while having rather negative views of some students' achievements, nevertheless saw it as their job to work very hard and positively to improve matters. While Carol Dweck (1999) shows us that if students believe that they are fundamentally incapable they lose faith in doing anything to influence their own attainment, Susan Hart *et al.* (2004: 25) points out that a belief in fixed ability is disheartening for teachers too since they cannot then find ways to make a significant difference. Thus notions of fixed ability generate despondency in both teachers and students.

Making global judgements

The word 'ability' is endemic throughout mathematics education as a reason for differences in achievement, and it is used to make distinctions between learners. Imagine it being used to describe black learners' relative underachievement, 'black learners are less able at mathematics than white learners', or to describe the relative underachievement of economically poor learners, 'economically poor learners are less able at mathematics than rich learners'. We would rightly find such dismissive statements abhorrent, yet schools which separate learners according to a notion of fixed ability often find that their 'top' groups contain a predominance of middle-class white learners. Teachers then talk of their 'more able' and 'less able' learners in terms which they would never use if they were talking about racial, class or gender groups.

Setting

It seems to be easier for schools to embrace research which divides learners, such as separating boys and girls (Independent 1998) or treating differently those who have different 'learning styles' (Revell 2005), than research which points to the merits of heterogeneity. As I write, there have been suggestions that some Afro-Caribbean boys might be taught separately (British Broadcasting Corporation 2005) and many argue that this is divisive. There is a limit, therefore, to how much separation is acceptable. A class consisting entirely of Afro-Caribbean boys would be the visually obvious kind of separation which we might find repugnant, even though separate treatment might be compensatory in Rawlsian terms. Nevertheless, we create classes in our schools which consist of already disadvantaged learners in less visually obvious terms; we often give them the least well-qualified teachers and hold the lowest expectations of them. In these cases, separate treatment is not compensatory at all.

When learners are put into particular sets, tracks or streams to be taught mathematics, or selected for particular schools, a statement is being made about the potential for learning which teachers have identified for such children. This decision is often clothed in language about 'providing an appropriate level of challenge and support', 'taking learning needs into account', 'provision for gifted and talented learners' and 'working from what the child knows already'. Teachers feel that learners whose attainment level has been lower than average should not be daunted by being expected to do work which is too hard or to grasp concepts too quickly; those whose attainment levels are high should not be bored by being given work which is too easy, and should be 'stretched' to their full potential. Hidden within these arguments are the assumptions that measures of past attainment are good predictors of limitations and possibilities, and that teachers can ascertain learners' needs accurately. The whole rhetoric of 'learning needs' suggests a 'diagnosis and treatment' model of education, in which some students are seen as deficient and thus have to be normalized or removed from mainstream expectations. Teachers are seen to be capable of knowing the 'needs' of someone else, but these 'needs' are defined in terms of the societal and political aims of education, not as personal needs at all. So, taking past achievement and work habits into account, segregating learners into different groups is seen as allowing teachers to provide lessons which they consider to be appropriate for each learner. Sadly, this often means that the low-attaining groups are often taught in ways which avoid, rather than confront, difficulty.

I am increasingly incredulous that schools continue to separate learners in this way when research points in a different direction. At the time of writing, the UK government is even considering measures to *increase* the degree of separation practised in secondary schools. Research which shows that learners such as those I am focusing on in this book do better in non-segregated groups does not tell us why this might be so. It is possible that this result is not due to grouping alone, but that teachers of heterogeneous groups use eclectic pedagogy, or have established a culture of communal learning, while teachers of 'low' sets have lowered expectations and use limited kinds of teaching and limited kinds of tasks. The only consistent results about the benefits of setting, nationally and internationally, are that the very brightest learners might do better if taught separately, while those below average generally do worse (Slavin 1990; Hallam and Toutounji 1996; Sukhnandan and Lee 1998; Wiliam and Bartholomew 2004). But the teacher glimpsed in Chapter 1 whose learners did very much better than predicted because she taught them hard mathematics was teaching within a system of setting, so de-setting cannot be the only way forward. The overall message is far from clear. Different studies come to different conclusions about those learners described as 'average' and there are different effects according to what kind of school they attend. For example, learners who are on the borderline for grammar school selection, and manage to get into such schools, tend to do better than similar learners elsewhere who attend comprehensive schools – and much better than those peers who fail to enter grammar school (Schagen and Schagen 2001). This could be due to having better-qualified teachers in grammar schools, but could also be due to being immersed in an environment which has higher expectations of all learners.

Problematizing 'ability'

I found myself increasingly conscious that, as a profession, we lacked ways of talking about teaching learners to become better mathematicians, although some teachers could recognize strong and useful mathematical behaviour when we saw it. This lack leads to several rather negative outcomes:

- Acceptance of varying ability to learn mathematics, treating this as innate because we do not teach in ways which alter abilities. Thus, we continue to talk about 'less able' and 'more able' as givens, rather than as outcomes, of education (McDermott 1993, Hart et al. 2004).
- Separating learners out into groups for different treatment according to test achievement because we do not have a shared language for talking about their mathematical proficiency and potential. Thus, learners who respond differently then get taught differently, which embeds their different responses and thus confirms the original diagnosis of difference (Nash 1976; Ruthven 1987).
- Failure to recognize good mathematical thinking from some learners because we have conditioned ourselves to certain expectations from certain groups (Houssart 2001).

- Reproducing existing divisions in society because the way we separate learners turns out to relate to their social status. Thus, those
  who are less able to adjust to the expectations of school mathematics to start with, because of language, emotional, social,
  cultural, domestic or dietary differences, continue to benefit least
  because they are placed in groups of learners which are similarly
  impoverished in relation to the dominant culture and norms
  (Gillborn and Youdell 2000; Ireson and Hallam 2001).
- Being vulnerable to outside influences which offer 'quick fixes' but
  are not as helpful in mathematics as they might be elsewhere. Thus,
  global techniques for the development of thinking skills, or for
  stimulating brain activity, or for identifying different 'intelligences', are imported into mathematics lessons without any
  change in the fundamental goals of such lessons or ways in which
  teachers judge success.

This may sound intemperate, yet each of the above points is well supported
by other writers and their research projects, or by easily accessible facts. That
we treat 'ability' as given is shown throughout educational literature and
discourse which refers to 'low ability' and 'high ability' learners as if these
are stable identifiable qualities, independent of task and context, and
without need for further definition. Robert Sternberg (1998) takes educa-
tionalists, psychometricians and others to task about the nature of ability
in an eloquent elaboration of abilities as being developmental, so that all
we ever can say about them is that they provide a snapshot in time, rather
than a means to label individuals.

The easy take-up of 'quick fixes' grafted onto unchanged teaching
methods and goals can easily be seen in schools which have adopted formative assessment strategies but still stick to rigid programmes of study,
rather than responding to learners, and schools which adopt cognitive
acceleration strategies, but not for all classes and not with a concomitant
underlying change to how mathematical activity is assessed. Similarly,
schools which identify learners as 'verbal, aural or kinaesthetic' to inform
their teaching (Coffield *et al.* 2004), often fail to develop programmes of
study which enable all learners to develop the full range of 'intelligences'
which would improve their learning of mathematics. Also, some schools
which insist on the use of a three-part lesson format, as recommended in
official guidance, do not seem to mind if the main part of the lesson always
consists of content transmission.

It was, of course, naïve to expect teachers to describe mathematical
abilities, since there is little agreement even among researchers about what
these might be in generic terms, or even if specifically mathematical
abilities exist. Howard Gardner, in his attempts to clarify different kinds of
intelligence, talks of logico-mathematical intelligence as encompassing

problem analysis, mathematical operations, pattern detection, and deductive reasoning (Gardner 1983). Any mathematics teacher reading this will see immediately that what is required to learn mathematics (rather than what is inherent in its structures, or expected of working mathematicians) is far broader than this. For example, it is well known that aesthetic response (Sinclair 2004) and intuitive response (Fischbein 1987) are also components of expertise in mathematics.

What 'understanding' means

In retrospect I see that my disappointment about these interviews was due partly to a frustration about the forms of discourse we have for talking about learners' learning. The language of the National Curriculum is at times very vague – such as asking that learners should 'understand equivalent fractions' (Qualifications and Curriculum Authority (QCA) 1999: 59). At other times it sounds specific enough to be amenable to simple testing – for example, 'understand that "percentage" means "number of parts per 100"'' (QCA 1999: 59) might be tested by asking what 'percentage' means.

   Since this study was done I have tried to become more articulate about the kinds of activity which learners might display and which teachers might encourage. When we try to use the word 'understanding' precisely it becomes problematic, as it can take slightly different meanings. Statutory requirements and curriculum documents suggest that there is a state called 'understanding' and we can know when it exists and when it does not exist. Teachers often use 'understanding' to contrast with 'performance', seeing a difference between following a procedure and knowing how and why the procedure works. Even if we exclude decontextualized manipulations from any claim to the word, we still have a plethora of meanings all of which are important in doing and learning mathematics: understanding as a state; understanding as making meaning and connections; understanding as choice and performance in a context; understanding as knowing the mathematical canon; understanding as overcoming inherent obstacles; and understanding as a potential.

Understanding as a state[4]

A distinction between procedural learning and learning about connections and relationships can be useful when shifting from seeing understanding as a fixed state to understanding as dynamic growth of knowledge. However,

---

[4]   Earlier versions of some of the ideas in this chapter appear in Watson (2002a, 2002b).

this distinction, variously described as 'surface v. deep' (Marton and Saljö 1976) or 'instrumental v. relational' (attributed to Stieg Mellin-Olsen by Skemp 1976), fails to take account of the fact that mathematical procedures consist of strings of simpler procedures. Connecting and relating mathematical ideas includes using known techniques, facts, and their fluent performance, which could be described as knowledge. Thus, relational knowledge may depend on acting instrumentally with less complex ideas, and surface knowledge includes subsumed relational knowledge of previously learnt procedures. To apply value-judgements to distinguish between 'relational' and 'instrumental' knowledge is, to my mind, a mistake. Often it is enough to know how to carry out a method and to understand that the method works. What is missing from a totally instrumental approach is a growth of underlying meaning that explains why the new procedures work and also justifies the answers we get.

It is commonly recognized that there may be ways in which understanding can grow in any new situation when you look at the topic differently, even when you are skilled with a technique. We hear statements such as 'I never really understood addition of fractions (or calculus, or graph-plotting, etc.) until I had to teach it!' By this, we are not saying that our learners should be taught to see fractions as we *now* see them, because the way we see them in order to teach is the product of many years' use and recent reflection. The insights gained when we come to teach them cannot be gained by a learner meeting them for the first time. What is really being expressed when we recognize the excitement of 'really understanding' is that we want learners to appreciate, from the start, the exciting and unfolding nature of understanding, rather than just being told what a fraction is.

Understanding as making meaning and connections

Richard Skemp (1976), described 'instrumental' understanding as the application of rules without reasons and 'relational' understanding as knowing what to do and why. The latter kind of understanding can range from the purely pragmatic – 'it works in these circumstances; I can check by other means' – to the purely logical – 'given these axioms and these rules of logic, this will always work'. In between these two is a plethora of other kinds of relations, such as relations between different representations, or different contexts, or different stages of dynamic processes. To make sense of 'relational' understanding we need to ask 'relate to what?' and the answer might be within mathematics, or outside mathematics, and might be universal or highly situationally specific. We cannot give relational understanding to others; they have to develop it for themselves, over time, in a range of experiences.

Examples of relational understanding using representations

Using representations

I know that $(a + b)^2 = a^2 + 2ab + b^2$ because

i   I can produce a layout which justifies the answer, rewriting it as $(a + b)(a + b)$ and multiplying everything in the second bracket by everything in the first bracket; also because

ii this diagram justifies the answer:

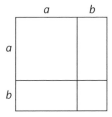

Using contexts

'Half of two' of anything gives you one of the things. For example, half of two shoes is one shoe; half of two pizzas is one pizza. Therefore half of two-thirds must be one-third.

Using dynamic processes

A chord of a circle supports two angles at the circumference, one acute and one obtuse.

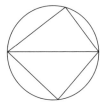

If I drag the chord across the circle parallel to itself there must be a point where both angles are equal. In addition, this is the point at which they change from being acute to obtuse or *vice versa*, so they are both right-angles.

Learners can make individual connections which may be obscure to others. A teacher cannot give meaning to a learner, nor make the connections for the learner. Often it is not until some connection a learner has made is seen to be inappropriate that teachers find out what has been 'understood'.

TEACHER:	What is 10 per cent of 230?
LEARNER A:	23
TEACHER:	Why?
LEARNER A:	Because I moved the decimal point one place to the left.
TEACHER:	So what is 20 per cent?
LEARNER B:	2.3
TEACHER:	How did you get that?
LEARNER B:	I moved the decimal point two places to the left.

Learner B is trying very hard to make connections and does this by looking for patterns and extending them.

Understanding in context

'Understanding' could be taken to mean that a concept can be used in either a mathematical or 'real world' context. This requires the learner to know the instrumental and illuminative powers of the particular concept or technique, and to recognize that it might be brought into play in a situation. For example, a learner may be able to factorize all kinds of quadratics expressed in the form $ax^2 + bx + c$ but fail to recognize that $4\sin^2 x + 4\sin x + 1$ is also a quadratic and might be usefully factorized. The learner's knowledge of quadratics is therefore shown to be dependent on recognizing what it looks like, rather than on analysing structure. Similarly, a learner may be able to multiply all kinds of numbers, but fail to recognize that multiplying is the way to deduce real measurements from a scale diagram and might resolutely apply repeated addition to the problem instead. The relationship between what can be done in one focused lesson and what can be brought into use later or elsewhere is much more complex than 'use in a context' might imply, and the shift between them is a focus for major research on transfer.

A well-established head of science, introducing himself to the new head of mathematics said: 'Are you the new head of maths? I am the head of science. What are you going to do about teaching them ratio?'

I replied, nonplussed: 'Hello, my name's Anne.'

At the time of this interchange I thought the head of science was just rude; later I realized that he was expressing serious frustration which had to be resolved somehow, and he had an overriding interest in students' learning. When teachers find themselves saying 'Come on, you did this last week, you should know this!' they are expressing frustration not necessarily at lack of memory, but at learners' failure to recognize the power, place and purpose of what they did last week. Said like this, of course, the issue becomes one for the teacher to resolve – what was it about last week's lesson which led to learners being able to do whatever it was at the time, but not draw on it later when it is needed?

Understanding as knowing the mathematical canon

Edwina Michener (1978) talks about understanding as knowing what examples to reach for, and knowing what to do with them. For example, if the word 'polygon' is used, we hope that learners will recall what this means. If they have learnt a formal definition they then have to construct something which fits the definition. By the time they have done this, the lesson has moved on and they may miss whatever the teacher has said next. Michener points out that experienced mathematicians have examples to hand with which they can test out what is being said, so 'polygon' triggers a particular polygon which can be used as an illustrative case. For learners who have an example to hand, the lesson continues to flow smoothly so long as they can manipulate their example in the appropriate way. There can be clashes here; for example, if my handy polygon example is a quadrilateral, but the teacher is talking about something with an odd number of sides, I am going to be a bit puzzled. I will need time to rethink my example image in order to make sense of what is being said.

What teachers do to help learners is, of course, to draw a diagram. This means learners never have to build up their own bank of diagrams because one is always given. The learner is expected to know that this week's polygon, which has five sides, is in some way related to last week's polygon, which had four sides. If the connections are not made, it is easier for learners to give up attempts to build their own images and rely on teachers for diagrams. In this way, learners' knowledge about different polygons becomes teacher-dependent. Understanding 'polygon' as a label for a set of certain shapes is hard to develop if you have a learnt definition on the one hand, and a set of disparate experiences on the other, and cannot see how to link them.

A socio-cultural perspective would see learning mathematics as entering a discourse in which one connects these different experiences because that is the accepted practice; one learns how to talk about them and connect them by being immersed in an environment which makes such connections. But a teacher cannot make connections for a learner; all the teacher can do is provide opportunity, encouragement and affirmation for such connections to be made.

One way which is very effective is to ask learners explicitly to make such connections through building their own examples (Watson and Mason 2005). In this approach it is recognized that 'good' mathematics learners voluntarily build up their own banks of examples, but others may need to learn explicitly that this is a useful thing to do. A teacher might ask learners to draw examples of polygons so she can see how flexible their images might be; she then might ask them to draw polygons with odd numbers of sides, and to talk about how they can alter their diagrams, if necessary, to get new ones. In future she might ask learners 'what is it useful to do when you hear a new definition?' and, gradually in this way, learners become encultured into developing their own example spaces to illustrate mathematical concepts.

Understanding as overcoming obstacles

Learning mathematics sometimes feels like overcoming a series of obstacles. In the UK it is much less common than it used to be to hear learners being upbraided for not concentrating, not watching what was on the board, not listening, not working hard enough. By and large teachers now know that learners are trying to make their own sense of mathematics, but that there are errors which are so commonly made that they must arise inherently from the mathematical concepts rather than from learners' individual recalcitrance. These obstacles include inherent difficulties in the subject. Anna Sierpinska (1994: ix) sees understanding as overcoming inherent obstacles and says that these arise from 'unconscious, culturally acquired schemes of thought and unquestioned beliefs about the nature of mathematics'. Often these have presented difficulties in the historical development of mathematics, provoking intellectual and philosophical argument, such as the introduction of negative and imaginary numbers. For learners, there are more frequent obstacles such as recognizing that multiplication is harder than repeated addition; misunderstandings based on common use of language, such as believing rectangles are regular polygons because they have a name; and overextending ideas which only work in a restricted domain, such as putting zero on the end of numbers when multiplying by 10. In other words, some obstacles are to be expected, and taken into account when teaching, and when learners do not make the expected, common, errors we could say that they understand. For example, if a learner knows that adding two fractions does not involve adding tops and bottoms, we could say that there was evidence of understanding because a well-known obstacle has been overcome. Similarly, if a learner knows that multiplying decimals by 10 is not always achieved by putting an extra zero on the end, a well-known obstacle has been overcome.

Understanding as potential

If we want a learner to know how to use a ruler, then showing her how to use a ruler correctly in a range of ways and contexts, some starting at zero and some not, some being left to right and some not, some shorter than the ruler and some not, may suffice. But wanting a learner to know multiplication is a much more complex problem.

Understanding, however it develops, can be seen as the potential to act mathematically. I shall illustrate this by using the seven times table as an arena to generate four kinds of potential for action: procedural learning, contextual learning, relational learning and transformable learning. I have called each type of action 'learning' to make the point that it is how learners act on what is offered to them that determines what it is possible to learn. With this perspective, 'understanding' means seeing that one can act procedurally, contextually, relationally and/or transformatively in the given situation.

This exercise was given to a year 9 class of very low-achieving learners to help them with the seven times table. Learners were given a sheet on which they could fill in answers to four columns of calculations. Here is an excerpt:

$5 \times 7 =$	$7 \times 5 =$	$35 \div 7 =$	$35 \div 5 =$
$6 \times 7 =$	$7 \times 6 =$	$42 \div 7 =$	$42 \div 6 =$
$7 \times 7 =$	$7 \times 7 =$	$49 \div 7 =$	
$8 \times 7 =$	$7 \times 8 =$	$56 \div 7 =$	$56 \div 8 =$

Procedural learning
To recall and use multiplication facts one has to be able to know them individually, rather than only have derivation methods to generate them. This worksheet is physically structured to encourage recursion (term-to-term), filling in the columns vertically by adding 7 or whatever simple pattern gives some right answers. For the learner to focus on individual facts a different physical layout would be essential, such as one in which '6 × 7' cannot easily be related to '5 × 7' except in the learner's head. The table may be completed, but it is possible to fill in this sheet without learning anything new, and without even noticing anything about the answers. The layout does, however, offer the possibility of forming relationships along the rows, and this idea will be revisited in Chapter 6.

Contextual learning
This exercise is purely about number relationships which could be applied in contexts, but it is highly likely that some contextual knowledge of

number facts might come first and answers be treated as abstract number facts. For example, a learner might know that 3×7 is 21 from playing darts, or that 7×5 is 35 from handling money. Here the learner is being asked to give some answers *in the context of* thinking about the seven times table – we do not know if they could give answers in a more varied context, or in a context from outside mathematics. 'Good mathematicians' are able to sort out whether they are supposed to be working as if within a context, or if they are supposed to be abstracting from a context. A famous example is that of planning a coach trip by deciding how many 51-seater coaches are needed for 111 people. The correct answer is not 2.176...; it is expected that learners will say that three coaches are necessary. However, when a learner says that two coaches plus a minibus are necessary, because she has actually organized such a trip and knows how these things are done, is she right or wrong? She has interpreted the question as being about booking coaches, not about doing mathematics, and may be penalized (Cooper and Dunne 1998, 2000).

Relational understanding

Learners' concentration on vertical relationships may lead them to ignore both commutativity and the relationship between multiplication and division, but some 'good mathematicians' may see this and not mention it unless it seems important to the teacher. Intervention by the teacher could direct the focus towards horizontal patterns by separating one line from the others and asking 'What do you see? Where do the same numbers appear?', then offering '7×23' as the start of a line and expecting learners to complete it. Rather than wait for some 'good' learners to spot these relationships, therefore, a teacher could encourage more learners to look for less obvious patterns. I call this process 'going across the grain' (Watson 2000) to distinguish the horizontal view of the layout from the vertical one ('with the grain') which has led to its easy generation.

Transformable, generalized and abstract learning

This worksheet has generalizable features which would allow a learner to transform the whole exercise into one about another times table, using visual and kinaesthetic senses to maintain the patterns and place the new numbers. A spreadsheet could be used to explore what stays the same if 7 is changed to 17 (do the patterns stay the same? do final digits stay the same?). Further, the four forms for each multiplication fact can be expressed algebraically, and learners asked to transform between them. For example, learners can pose questions of the form '$112 \times 34 = 3808$, so what is 3808 divided by 34?' in which large numbers play the part of generalities, or 'If $pq = m$, what does q equal?' when it is agreed that letters are easier to handle than large numbers. Again, a teacher can prompt these shifts rather than leave it to individual learners to make them alone.

What teachers mean by 'understanding'

The teachers I interviewed typically offered some interesting views of understanding, such as: 'I know they understand when: they can say it to me in their own words'; '... they can tell me how they did it'; ' ... they can use it in context without being told'; ' ... they use it without prompting'; '... they can answer a question which comes at it in a slightly different direction' (Watson 1998).

All of these indicate that teachers want learners to have enough of an overview of techniques and procedures to be able to shift into another representation, generalization, or transformation which allows use in unfamiliar ways, explanations, general descriptions and applications. These are skills which Tommy Dreyfus (1991) has described as components of advanced mathematical thinking.

Flexible views of ability and understanding

Once we try to talk more precisely about 'abilities', rather than 'the ability', required to learn mathematics we find teachable qualities and behaviour being discussed where before there was just vagueness. There have been many examples in this chapter in which being more precise about the ways in which learners see and do mathematics suggests things teachers could do to encourage more learners to behave as the 'good' maths learners do.

It is fruitless to expect adolescents to see far enough into the future that they will be motivated to learn maths because it might one day be useful in their employment, or that several years hence they might get a passable grade in some examinations. For the learners who are the focus of this book, the vision of a passable grade is even more foggy than for most. Taking the erratic emotional and social lives of learners who end up in low-attaining sets into account, it is necessary to focus on short- and medium-term ways to enhance their self-esteem and sense of self-worth through doing mathematics. However, lack of self-esteem is an obstacle to their doing anything worthwhile, because they have failed, or been made to feel failures, in the past. Lack of self-esteem prevents risk-taking and lack of risk-taking prevents growth of self-esteem. For many learners answering any mathematical question, even in the privacy of their own exercise books, is a risk. Because of this cycle, approaches to teaching which only focus on self-esteem by giving praise for anything and everything, and those which only focus on motivation or effort, are likely to fail because learners will not be able to use the feedback they receive to improve their mathematical activity.

Those who work with adolescents as youth-workers, drama teachers or PE instructors deal with this apparently unbreakable cycle regularly. What would be the mathematical equivalent of helping a frightened learner to put on a life-jacket and cross a river on a rope, or enabling a shy learner to put on a mask and act out a drama? In mathematics, we commonly deal with these situations by altering the task, such as making the rope into a secure bridge and holding both elbows as the learner walks across, or giving the learner a backstage task helping another teacher, because we cannot easily find the equivalents of life-jackets and masks to support the learner's own resources. This change of task, the simplification of mathematics, does not help learners to develop the ways of thinking which would help them learn harder mathematics.

Looking again at the kinds of understanding which could be the aims of the educational process, several of them require the learner to take some sort of risk: making meaning and connections; choosing what to do in a context; overcoming inherent obstacles; transforming; generalizing. Learners who are only offered mathematics as if understanding it is a fixed state, or as if the canon of knowledge can be learnt through non-risky activity, have been given limited horizons. The task of teaching mathematics to low-attaining adolescents is therefore the task of finding the life-jackets and masks which enable them to take intellectual risks with mathematical material, and grow in self-esteem and confidence as a result. This fits well with the natural way in which the teachers I interviewed had blended learners' emotional and intellectual approaches to the subject. It also fits well with recent thinking in cognitive science which recognizes no affective and cognitive distinctions: thinking and learning are emotional activities just as much as they are cognitive; the neural activities involved in what we recognize as thinking, emoting, learning are of the same kind.

Developing and applying flexible views of ability and understanding

Because it is considered normal in professional circles to talk of 'ability' and 'understanding' as if these ideas mean something, it can be hard to change to a more flexible approach, particularly for those working in isolation to improve their practice. Tiny changes in language help, not only as reminders to take a different viewpoint but also as a signal to others that different views are possible. Changing 'can't' to 'don't' is such a change, as is changing general statements to specific ones. For example, changing 'these students cannot concentrate' to 'these students do not concentrate in my lessons' opens up an opportunity to think about devising new strategies for extending their concentration. Similarly, changing 'do you understand X?' to 'what do you understand about X?' signals a shift from *students telling you about something you know* to *you listening to what they know*. Obviously such shifts take time to achieve, and require a new mindset in practice, but the first step is to appreciate the importance of deliberate change.

Another strategy which can contribute to flexibility is to plan in each lesson to focus on promoting a particular kind of understanding, and helping learners develop a particular kind of ability. These can become lesson objectives which can be used instead of objectives about performing techniques or vague uses of 'understanding'. 'Learn how to find the hypotenuse of a right-angled triangle' can be recast as 'understand more about the relationship between the three sides of a right-angled triangle' and 'get better at spotting right-angled triangles, identifying their sides and applying Pythagoras' theorem'. This recasting of objectives recognizes that each learner has a different starting place, and that the development of understanding and ability is a personal journey, rather than a sequence of finite hurdles.

In the next chapter I will show how teachers' knowledge of mathematics and learners, and their understanding of learning, combine to inform the judgements they make about individuals.

3 Teachers' judgements

Throughout this book, all the research was done by working *with* teachers, rather than working *on* them, or using them as objects to provide data for my research. The interviews in which teachers describe what they do were collected after a day's work together which gave us some shared experiences to discuss. Later in the book there are other kinds of research based on providing situations in which teachers can articulate their ideas, or gain support for changes in practice. I believe that by reporting what real teachers do, or say they do, the sense I make of it will be more accessible to other teachers and educators than if I wrote from a purely theoretical standpoint, or from one which summarized behaviour without examining the reasons for that behaviour.

But it will not have gone unnoticed that I am deeply critical of many common practices in mathematics teaching, and I might be accused of using the goodwill of teachers, and pretending to work with them, in order to vilify certain practices. I might be thought to misuse their good intentions and criticize them. Of course it would be wrong and unethical to act in this way, and I try to steer a different path. One of my aims is to understand why teachers act in the ways they do, and to identify qualities and actions which, within that general understanding, serve to perpetuate or challenge the negative effects of such practices. If, in addition, I can identify situations in which the negative effects reported in research do *not* accrue then I can report those too.

In Chapter 2, I outlined how teachers talk about their students' mathematical abilities. I also elaborated the complexities of talking about mathematical understanding in any meaningful way. We lack a common professional language about mathematical learning which allows fair and useful distinctions to be drawn between different kinds and stages of learning. It is easy for teachers to label learners by claiming they are 'more' or 'less' able and to treat them differently according to the label. Given that this approach to teaching mathematics is ubiquitous in the UK and is perpetuated by well-meaning professional teachers, I have to ask myself whether there is something wrong with the research which shows clearly that these groupings are detrimental to the most educationally vulnerable learners, and at best unfounded for many others. In order to understand why teachers willingly do this, I need to understand more about teachers and teaching. It is not enough to look only at the effects on learners, or at what teachers say. One teacher with a class of 30 learners is not in a position to know each one intimately and to adjust her teaching precisely to the responses of each individual, so she acts in ways which reflect the responses of the whole group. The views of the teachers were collected and analysed with care, so that the use I make of the results is founded on robust data and robust analysis.

Finding out about practice

My aims in conducting the 30 interviews mentioned in Chapter 2 were:

- to produce plausible, coherent descriptions of how teachers went about assessing their students' mathematics, validated by checking the data to ensure it was as complete as possible in a naturalistic, situational kind of truth;
- to produce a theoretical view of teachers' judgement-making, which might be applicable (even if not generalizable) to other teachers;
- to use these outcomes to understand more about the fairness and justice of teachers' judgements.

I knew that teachers may not tell me what they actually do, but might give accounts of what they would like to do, or what they want to be seen as doing, or what they thought would impress me, or what they thought they ought to do. Their accounts would therefore tell me about the range of what they know of as possibilities. This tells me what practices they can choose from, subject to local circumstances, energy, practical considerations and their own theoretical assumptions and interpretation of statutory demands. Knowing what is possible, so that one might recognize opportunity, is as much a part of practice as reflective development. To know what is possible there has to be input of knowledge, or observation of others, or reading, or professional development, or even that kind of competitive edge which leads some to say 'I could do that!'.

Anonymity is vital when attributing remarks or actions to particular teachers. Hence everything reported from the interviews is to be seen as a generality in that it is a possibility within mathematics teaching, rather than that it is an example of one particular person's practice.[1] This approach

---

[1] You may have gained the impression that this only happens when I want to criticize practice, but several publications containing advice about good teaching have also arisen from observations of real teachers' practices (e.g. Watson and Mason 1998; Watson *et al.* 2003b).

simultaneously protects individual teachers from being associated with something they may later reject, but also opens a worrying can of worms.

For example, it would be worrying if one teacher said that she assumes children from middle-class backgrounds are more likely to work neatly than those from working-class backgrounds. A response to this might be that she needs some further training, or to be brought face to face with some counter-examples, if we think that this belief must have a detrimental effect on her working-class learners. By the time this assumption has been written about in the dissemination of research, with her identity masked, she may have worked out for herself, based on experience, that her assumption is not universally true. Equally, she might still have this view but use it to give compensatory teaching to working-class learners so that they are 'as neat as' middle-class learners. However, if we see this teacher as representing a generality – that it illustrates the possibility that some teachers believe that middle-class children are more likely to work neatly than working-class children – then we have systemic trouble on our hands. We do not know who these teachers are; how they came to have this belief; what they do as a result of this belief; what happens to their students because of this belief; and so on. Rather than think about how an individual teacher might be encouraged to question this belief, or even how groups of teachers with these views can engage in professional development about learners' written work, we have the more serious question of whether and how the *system* compensates working-class learners whose teachers may have lower expectations of them. By protecting individual teachers from identification, we have to engage with political questions. At any one time there will be teachers who believe this, and act in certain ways as a result. While accepting the roles of training, reflective practice and experience, we also need to change the system so that future teachers do not fall into these habits at all, or, if they do, there is compensation somewhere else for those who are judged as inferior.

In the previous chapter I quoted one teacher who used a learner's background as a vehicle to avoid talking about how the learner could become a better learner: 'Where do you start? With her background!' Rather than dismiss this as the utterance of one teacher, I can use it to pose two general questions. Do we know enough about helping learners from underprivileged backgrounds to become better learners of mathematics? How do we compensate students who have been seen as problematic because of their backgrounds?

The more teachers I interviewed, the longer the list of aspects of their informal assessment practices became. Each teacher had her own particular subset of possible practices to report, and ways to report them, and I realized that generalization was impossible; there were too many factors to take into account. I also realized that loosely structured interviews, while allowing a very broad agenda, did not necessarily provide comparable data on related issues. For instance, one teacher talked of her own recent experiences of learning mathematics to illustrate her view of mathematics, but I found few opportunities with other teachers to raise their own learning as an issue. I found, however, that I could develop a broad picture of possible practices so that comparison would be pursued by actively looking for hitherto uncollected descriptions during future interviews – constantly searching, probing and prompting. I reasoned that the research would be 'complete' when I was hearing nothing new about practice. Even so, the completeness is *situated* within my sphere of research, at the time of the research and in my interpretations; it may not adequately describe practice in five years' time, or in the independent education sector, or in a society which values groups over individuals.[2]

Eventually, after careful, thorough, repeated and critical coding and analysis of the data, I arrived at eight categories of practice of teacher assessment:

- Assessment systems: how different schools and teachers organized assessment practices, data collection, reporting to parents and so on.
- Teachers' attitudes: how teachers' own views, knowledge, stated theories and beliefs affect how they comply with and interpret the system as they see it.
- Teachers' actions: how teachers' attitudes and institutional systems are compromised and combined in order to emerge as practice; what teachers actually do.
- Teachers' justifications for what they do to assess individuals.
- Learners' predispositions: how far individual learners are seen to be able to comply with and fulfil teachers' expectations.
- Interpreting learners' observable mathematical activity: how teachers make inferences about what they see, hear and read of learners' mathematics.
- Influences on interpretation: justifications for teachers' interpretations based on expectations, beliefs, knowledge.
- Teachers' voiced doubts about judgements: re-emergence of conflicts between teachers' beliefs and systemic demands which have not been resolved in practice.

In the literature from the 1970s on teachers' expectations, several studies showed that the expectations teachers had of learners were often

---

[2]   This process related most closely to *naturalistic enquiry* (Lincoln and Guba 1985) in which it is taken for granted that the researcher will have her own views and perspectives, but will rigorously search for alternative interpretations when building theory from the data, and acknowledge her own sensitivities.

realized through a self-fulfilment process. If a teacher believed that a learner was 'not very bright', then the tasks given to the learner, and the kinds of interaction offered, would be geared towards the achievement of low-level goals, thus producing the low level of achievement which the teacher expected in the first place. In the most infamous of these studies, teachers were informed by researchers that certain learners were stronger or weaker than others and, hey presto, at the end of a period of teaching the learners were tested and it was found to be so (Rosenthal and Jackson 1966). The trick was that these descriptions were assigned randomly to learners. The teachers had effectively 'created' the learners' characteristics which they had been informed existed. The ethics of this study were, from at least the point of view of learners and parents, appalling and other aspects of the study, such as the teachers' assumption that what they had been told had some academic credibility, have also been justifiably criticized. But the central finding, that achievement can be created to fulfil expectations, has not been challenged.

Research into links between teachers' behaviour and student achievement is brought together by Jere Brophy and Thomas Good (1974), who provide a powerful and critical overview of the literature relating teachers' expectations to student achievement. By drawing on at least 50 studies both in naturalistic and laboratory settings, they show how even the minutiae of classroom life can serve to discriminate between learners from different social or racial backgrounds, and between those of real or imagined levels of prior attainment. Teachers' differing expectations are displayed to their students through, for example, not waiting so long for answers from those they believe to be 'low' and from those they believe to be 'high', and when similar answers are eventually produced they lead to different kinds of feedback, depending on who gives them (p. 331).

This argument has been considerably fleshed out in the intervening years, particularly in the socio-cultural literature, which describes classroom life in terms of communities of practice and learning as becoming enculturated, more or less successfully, into those practices (Lerman 2004). Thus, if the practices of the mathematics classroom are that techniques should be practised repeatedly and valued through their production of right or wrong answers, this is how the learners will view mathematics and how they will construct their personal goals. If the practices of the classroom are to enquire, conjecture, justify and produce discursive arguments which are valued for their chains of reasoning, this is how learners will view mathematics and construct their personal goals. In mathematics education the literature making these arguments is well established and needs no rehearsal here.

So what is new in my analysis? What is new is the *detail* of how teachers managed to reach conclusions about individuals, and that they held these so strongly that they might disagree with test results and use their own assessments instead to make decisions which would affect learners' futures. Also new is that this process is challenged with examples from UK classrooms where interaction and inquiry are now the norm,[3] in contexts normally using formative assessment within structured assessment regimes. In other words, I will show that even in an environment in which teachers use a range of informal assessment strategies as common practice, there is the potential to misunderstand learners. Most of the examples I use come from observations made in 2002–4, showing that the concerns of the 'expectations' writers in the 1960s and 1970s have not gone away. Other examples come from observations made in the mid-1990s when teachers were aware of a range of informal and formal practices from recent in-service training. If anything, concerns about self-fulfilling prophecies are exacerbated in recent times by systematization of multiple assessment opportunities, so that judgements may have to be made so closely together in time that there is no chance for anyone to show significantly altered potential between assessment points.

What makes the data in this chapter timelessly useful is that the teachers being interviewed and observed were all aware that assessment was an integral aspect of their work, and that they would use whatever information they could to help them decide how to teach certain individuals and groups. They were knowledgeable, expert and skilful. Perhaps their knowledge was particularly strong, and that is why they agreed to talk to me. Whether this is true or not, their practices included a wide range of ways in which teachers learn about their students' understanding. As Black and Wiliam (1998) show, use of this information is crucial for effective teaching, but in this chapter I want to look at a slightly different use – how it can be used to build up mental pictures of individual learners. The difference between these two uses is that Black and Wiliam's approach is a temporary snapshot across several learners at one moment in time to inform teaching decisions, while the 'knowing the learner' approach is longitudinal as the teacher adds fresh evidence to an existing view of a learner over time, ending up by feeling able to say 'this student ought to get an A' or 'that learner will be lucky to get a G'.

Evidence and judgements about learning

Within the category of teachers' actions there were seven types of raw material, or evidence, which were collected, sometimes systematically but usually informally or casually, to make judgements about individuals. They were:

---

[3]   Similar to the 'reform' curriculum advocated in the USA.

- oral evidence through the teacher overhearing conversations or commentary by learners or through formal and informal pedagogic dialogue;
- written evidence in the form of exercises, tests, rough work, notes or writing about mathematical exploration;
- actions observed by the teacher while watching the learner do practical activities or other work;
- unprompted use of mathematics while working on other mathematics, or in another context;
- behaviour and body language, as seen by the teacher;
- knowledge of the child as a learner or in other respects;
- views about mathematics held by the teacher.

The first four types listed are widely recognized as raw material for judgements but the last three are obviously problematic, implying interpretation of the teacher's perceptions. I found that the deeper I probed into how teachers used all these aspects, the more I found vague phrases such as 'professional judgement', 'gut reaction' and 'in my experience', or talk of 'feelings'. As a teacher I would have used and accepted these phrases uncritically; as a researcher I began to question their meanings and use. If teachers' judgements about individual learners contribute to decisions about setting or examination entry, then perhaps there could be more precision and less personal interpretation involved in these processes. But since teachers' judgements influence all classroom decisions, they have had a hand in creating, as well as assessing, the manifestations of learning. At what point in the cycle indicated in Figure 3.1 do teachers try to challenge the way in which different learners are being constructed through their teacherly actions?

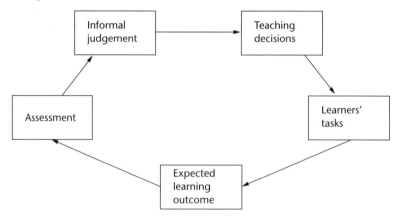

Figure 3.1 A teaching and assessment cycle

Oral evidence

Oral evidence, though highly valued by all the teachers, is time-consuming to organize. Language difficulties, diffidence or fear might prevent some learners from offering it. It is rare to overhear useful remarks in a busy class-room, although such remarks often give insight into a learner's thinking before they are able to record what they think on paper. Oral evidence does not give hard copy to support a teacher's judgements, so that over reliance on oral evidence may leave the teacher vulnerable to criticism. Most teach-ers said that they use oral interactions to make sure a child understands or to find out what led to errors in written work; some teachers said that they would be unwilling to believe a learner understood unless they had heard the learner explain 'in their own words'. However, teachers' reported reliance on oral work can be seen in the light of Basil Bernstein's work (1990) on how middle-class learners are at an advantage in school because the elaborated codes of language are what they might be used to at home, while working-class learners are expected to communicate at school in a way very unlike the restricted codes that might be used at home. Whereas the way I have described this theory relies on a very stereotyped view of language use inside and outside school, it does prompt a closer look at lan-guage forms in mathematics classrooms, leading to the realization that 'explain how you did something', a common requirement in teacher–learner discourse, is a rare form of speech outside school in any social grouping. Hence, reliance on learners' ability to use this form is expecting a keen awareness of different discourses as well as any mathematical ability. We could look to Lev Vygotsky (1978) to support this reliance on oral work by claiming that language is both the act and expression of thought, and knowledge is mediated in interaction through speech. Oral work would therefore give teachers access to how their students are thinking mathematically as well as influencing such thoughts. Teachers in my sample were not, in general, saying this, however; they were seeing speech as the means to report mathematics already done and understood.

Written work

Written work was regarded as a safe and reliable form of evidence which can be held up to scrutiny. Many teachers commented that they wanted more than 'right answers' in order to be convinced that learners understood the work; they wanted oral evidence, or written workings and explanations as well. However, there was also wide recognition that many learners had considerable difficulty in recording in writing what they could do mentally or practically. Assessment based on written work has to be seen in the light of research resulting from increasing use of coursework in public examinations. Many writers (MacNamara and Roper 1992a, 1992b) have shown that learners can be very selective in what they write down, so that written work represents a highly edited view of their mathematical thinking. Sometimes this is an attempt to produce curtailed, terse, classical math-ematics, but it can also be due to a failure to appreciate what is important, a 'right-answer-only' ethos or the representation of abstract or intuitive thought on paper. Furthermore, Candia Morgan (1996a, 1996b, 1998) has shown that teachers can vary widely in their interpretation of what written work represents.

Observed actions

Observed actions provide no permanent record of achievement. Organizing observation in a busy classroom is difficult but such observation can reveal that the learner is using particular methods, such as counting, instead of using number bonds. Observation of actions depends in part on the teachers' notions of how mathematical activity *might* be observable. Sometimes this is clear, such as when one sees a learner use a ruler correctly and read off a measurement accurately. Other times it has to be interpreted, as when a learner is trying to make a cube from six squares and may appear to us to be doing it in an obscure way, but nevertheless succeeds. Other times, there is little to interpret; the learner who is gazing motionless at a problem may or may not be thinking about it, and the thought may or may not be productive. On the other hand, avid writing may not indicate anything useful is being done. How the teacher interprets the actions can be influenced by many factors. In these examples interpretation depends on what the teacher expects to see mathematically, what the teacher expects from the particular learner and what the teacher expects from learners in general. It also depends on what is noted by the teacher. What is noticed is affected by preconceived impressions; how teachers interpret what they see depends on the existing impressions of learners' 'ability'.

Unprompted use

Unprompted use of mathematics was highly regarded as a form of evidence, but difficult for teachers to plan for and only of use on rare occasions. There were different views about how long after being formally taught a topic one could regard its use as evidence of 'knowing'; it was generally implied that there had to be some sort of time gap to be sure that the learner had internalized the concept or method and was not relying on short-term memory alone; estimates varied from 2 weeks to 6 months as appropriate gaps. During the whole of my research, which took place in about 30 classrooms over 3 years, there were no reports of incidents of unprompted use, although most teachers mentioned it as something to look out for. Of course, tasks have to enable and encourage learners to bring other mathematics into use, and the classroom ethos also has to support learners in this regard.

Problems in using data

For the final categories, interpretations of behaviour and body language, and knowledge of the child clearly depend on individual teachers' perspectives, rather than on anything purely mathematical. The existing view of the child informs future interpretations, since what is done is seen as typical or atypical of that child.

The teacher's view of mathematics as an influence on judgement is central, since it guides what is seen as achievement, and what is not. In the previous chapter, meanings of 'understanding' were described which were so different that one teacher could say that learners understand something while another could, just as legitimately and carefully, say that they do not. When learners move from primary school to secondary school a common complaint is that primary teachers claim that their students 'understand' something and secondary teachers claim that they do not. The change of teacher, school, confidence, and nature of expected mathematical discourse can all conspire to deskill both learners and teachers.

While analysing the data I became less immersed in, and more critical of, assumptions about shared language and meaning. Words such as 'confident', 'less able' and 'potential' became words I wanted to query, rather than words I accepted (Watson 1996b; Burton 2004). Their use appeared to affect teachers' judgements and, hence, the mathematical and social progress of learners. Since the meaning and use of such vague words affects learners' futures, my take on social justice urged me to examine them more closely. I began to hear circular arguments such as 'he lacks confidence so he has low self-esteem so he does not make the effort so he cannot understand' without knowing whether the teacher could, or did, take all stages of the implied cycle into account in her teaching. Or cycles such as 'Mike is level 2 so cannot do division', where not doing division may have been both a reason and a consequence of 'being level 2'. I found that I longed to hear teachers talking about mathematics instead of 'levels', 'ability' and so on. I decided to analyse some of the data about teachers' actions from the point of view of the development of mathematical understanding.

Teachers' informal assessment practices

I selected some of the informal assessment practices which appeared in the data to illustrate how they might contribute to the continuing construction of the teacher's view of a learner over time. Here I am trying to get to grips with how learners become identified as 'low attainers'.[4] It is by understanding how this process operates that I can pinpoint elements of the process which might be justifiably queried in terms of social justice. The tool I used to question each process is mathematics; I sought alternative mathematical interpretations for incidents and methods. For every assessment method reported here I will create possible scenarios which would problematize the method by showing that other interpretations are possible. However, for many such methods I do not have to create scenarios from scratch because I saw examples which illustrate possible problems during my observations.

Ethically, if there are alternative possible mathematical interpretations of learners' mathematical work, then the onus for justifying an assessment judgement arising from such work ought to be on the assessor who decides which interpretation to use. However, teachers often have to make responses and decisions instantly, without the time for critical reflection or systematic searching for other possibilities.

Learners creating examples

A strong feature of all the teachers' work was that they looked for places where they could give learners some choice, so that they could then see what choices were made. They reasoned that the choices made gave them information about how the learner could deal with complexity and whether they were happy to challenge themselves or were satisfied with taking an easy option. Some teachers regularly asked learners to make up examples for themselves, particularly in arithmetic.[5] However, the teachers differed in their interpretation of choices. I will illustrate this by describing what was said about arithmetical choices.

In arithmetic, the teachers had a sense of hierarchy of difficulty which more or less coincides with that in the published national curriculum. Roughly: addition, subtraction, multiplication and division are in order of difficulty, with strong relationships between the first two, and the first and third. Although mathematically we could say that division relates strongly with subtraction – indeed, it is by repeated subtraction that we calculate the results of division – these were not linked by teachers or learners with the

---

[4]   I now try to avoid labelling learners in this way, but have in the past used this term myself.

[5]   See Watson and Mason (2005) for a full acount of possibilities here.

same strength. Within each of these operations bigger numbers, decimals and fractions are seen to be a progression, and combinations of operations are seen to be harder the longer they get! Let us consider a typical exemplification prompt:

The answer is 5, what is the question?

When learners are asked to make up examples, they usually start by making up ones similar to those they have already been given, and then, when urged to make them harder, change the size of the numbers at first and then the number of operations, and then start to include multiplication and division. There does not seem to be an understanding that the *order* of operations often contributes more to complexity than does the *number* of operations. An opportunity is often missed to emphasize that order matters so much that eventually we need to use brackets to communicate this. A teacher who offers big numbers as hard examples, such as $1665 \div 333$, will have learners who offer big numbers as hard examples and are then praised for so doing. A learner who offers big numbers to a teacher who looks for special examples, such as 1×5, may get no praise and may become disgruntled. A learner who works with special examples but whose teacher does not recognize them as special may also become confused and alienated. Furthermore, if a teacher does not recognize the order of operations (such as $5(8 - 7)$) as more mathematically complex than the number of operations (such as $2 + 2 + 1 + 4 + 2 - 6$) then learners are hardly likely to do so either.

Some teachers pointed out that making apparently simple choices could mean that learners were being lazy, or were lacking confidence, or were not able to do harder work, and that by interacting with them they could find out the difference between these reasons. But one teacher, Sharon, claimed that some learners chose apparently easier options because the underlying structures of mathematics are sometimes easier to see if the numbers or contexts are easy. For example, if I am exploring subtraction and I can choose my own examples, then subtracting two digit numbers from 100 can tell me a lot more about how subtraction works than, say, choosing to subtract 43 210 from 98 765. She had noticed that some of her students would choose small and rather special numbers to work with and others would choose large numbers which they might not use successfully.

Research into what happens when learners make up their own examples suggests that there is usually a very close relationship between their creations and what has been presented in textbooks or by the teacher (Ellerton 1986). This is not at all surprising. It is too much to expect learners to have insight about the nature of speciality in mathematics without access to the overview of the teacher, or to expect a teacher to have such insight if she only has a textbook to rely on. Typically textbooks reduce mathematics to routines rather than using special examples to expose structure.

But choice is more complex even than this, because even having a teacher who explicitly uses special examples may not be enough for all learners to recognize this as a useful habit and to use it. A special feature of Sharon's teaching was her own use of such examples, and hence, some of her students might think of using similar examples, and she would be sensitive to the value of their use. But not all her students used them – they have to grasp *why* they are used (and this might be hard) and to decide *when* to use them (and this too might be hard) and to be able to construct their own (and this too may be hard). Rather than labelling some learners as 'unable to use special examples' the teacher can make this a focus of her teaching, trying to alter their ability to use special examples.

Making these choices does not have to be left to chance uptake by learners. One teacher used the strategy of asking learners to tell him their favourite example, and then switched this to asking for what they thought would be *his* favourite example when he realized that they were dependent on him for knowledge about what 'harder' meant in mathematical terms. I saw him explicitly working on one learner's expectations by saying: 'You were giving me examples like that last term, isn't it time you moved on to using multiplication a bit more?'

If the learners' use of special examples, whether deliberate or not, is not recognized by the teacher then it may not be developed. In a lesson in which pairs of learners were asked to make up calculations for which the answer is 5 one pair offered, among other examples, this sequence:

$$5 + 0 = 5$$
$$0 + 5 = 5$$
$$1 \times 5 = 5$$
$$5 \times 1 = 5$$

The teacher's view was that they were using easy examples just to pad out their work. This may have been true; but a mathematician's view might be that these examples are somehow essential, the basic examples from which all arithmetical structure springs. I could even claim that without these examples being included, the rest of the activity is incomplete, since they demonstrate the additive and multiplicative identities and the commutativity of those operations. Nothing was said about them in the lesson, however. The teacher did not use, and maybe did not see, possibilities for the direction of the lesson in these examples.[6]

---

6   While writing this section I had to change this example from being based on 6 to being based on 5; using the 'find' and 'replace' facility illustrates powerfully how elemental and well structured these relationships are.

So far I have described possible differences within only one feature of teachers' practices and already many possible differences have emerged. Do they matter? On one level there is no difference: the teacher is asking for examples and learns, from what is said, what the learners know as possible. But what they know as possible has come from the teacher, and she is likely to recognize what she already sees as valuable, which is what they are trying to mimic anyway. All this is inevitable. On another level it matters enormously, because her mathematical expectations constrain everything which happens. As a mathematician I know that special cases are eventually more important than big numbers in understanding mathematics algebraically, but I also know that practice and familiarity with a range of numbers are important for confidence throughout arithmetic. Also big and awkward numbers can sometimes be used to create an awareness of structure simply because doing actual calculations with them is too hard. I also know that shifting to seeing multiplication as the central operation in arithmetic is crucial in secondary mathematics, so that being praised for producing an example using addition may not help learners to make that shift. And I also know that asking learners what first comes to their minds does not tell me the full extent of what they know, because if I am asked for examples of concepts I do not necessarily choose the most complicated one I know. Learners may need prompting to delve deeper and show more of what they know.

So while creating their own examples can provide *some* information about what is known, probing the *extent* of what is known tells more, and this may depend on what the teacher sees as important.

A further concern about the practice reported above is that making up questions which give 5 as an answer may not be connected in any obvious way to developing a generally questioning attitude to mathematics.

Marking written work

I shall apply a similar kind of critical analysis to what the teachers said about marking written work. Morgan (1998) has provided a detailed account of the potential inequities and other aspects of grading extended written work, but in this chapter I am going to focus on written work generated during classwork and homework, usually of a fairly traditional type, and how teachers use it to judge what their students can do.

A point which was made strongly by all teachers was that there were gaps between learners being able to *do* mathematics and to *write* about it coherently. This gap was seen to operate at all levels, and was a particular issue with learners for whom English was not a first language, or who were diagnosed as having dyslexia or dyspraxia.[7] It was claimed so universally

---

[7] I try to distinguish between 'having dyslexia' and 'being dyslexic' so that I am labelling behaviour rather than people.

and strongly by teachers that I call it 'the do–write' gap, imagining that it is seen as similar by all teachers.

All teachers, especially those of younger learners, described how much more could be learnt by asking what written work represents, but said that there was never enough time to do this for everyone. No one wanted to describe achievement in terms of written work alone, but the teachers often said that since learners would, in the end, be assessed on written mathematics it was reasonably fair that this should have higher priority as they approached formal national testing.

Many teachers tried to find time to write detailed notes and comments on learners' work, such as giving worked examples, or cases with which to test arguments, or ideas for further questions or alternative methods. As I write, familiarity with research which claims that comments without grades are more effective than grades or comments with grades (Butler 1987) is spreading and more and more teachers are changing to this process.[8]

Written work is seen as multi-purpose. Although marking written work was given high priority by teachers as a source of assessment information, with or without supplementary conversations or interchange of comments, it was also the case that most teachers used a range of self-marking or peer-marking strategies as well. Sometimes this was fairly formal, such as asking the whole class to discuss errors in an invented test script which included all the errors they had made individually. Other times it was informal, such as marking their own work, or swapping books and ticking the right answers. No one questioned whether this last procedure is of any use to anyone, and, if so, of *what* use, although it was generally claimed that learners like to know if they are right or not. However, since many were observed to be changing answers as they were marking work, even if it was not to be seen by anyone else, some learners must perceive it to be about something other than knowing they were right. Self-assessment of written work only makes sense if the criteria for success are clear, hence, for extended written accounts of exploratory work, with their complex and interpretable criteria, self-assessment is rather hard, but for right and wrong answers self-assessment is easy to initiate.

Some teachers asked learners to check their own calculations with a calculator; one said that she only ever gave them tasks which could be checked by using some kind of inverse procedure and expected them to self-check throughout. The main contribution teachers' marking makes is that, in the comparative peace of her own time and place, she takes it to indicate about ways forward.

---

8   It is interesting to speculate why some teachers and schools, knowing of this research, are still giving marks or grades. Smith and Gorard (2005) show that superficial adoption of this strategy, without an accompanying complex pedagogy, is not necessarily effective.

Identifying correctness is only the start of assessment. For example, the statement made by some learners that the straight line joining (2,3) to (3,4) is $y = x + 1$ is certainly correct, but does not show whether they understand:

- whether all points on the line show the same pattern;
- whether there are any other lines, straight or otherwise, which can go through these two points;
- whether they have mechanically applied a procedure to generate the formula;
- whether they have spotted the relationship between x and y values and expressed it consciously as a generality;
- whether they have used a graph plotter to generate the equation;
- how y varies as x varies.

In contrast, a student who makes a statement that this line is of the form $y = x + c$ may have known that the gradient was 1, or may be floundering without any real understanding, or may merely be copying something from the internet. We do not know: to assume some knowledge would be generous, to assume none would be unfair.

A more dramatic illustration of the unfairness of judging written work alone comes from my own teaching. A learner had been asked to find the derivative of $\sinh x$ and handed in only the correct written answer, with no working, as

$$\frac{(e^x + e^{-x})}{2}$$

I had to discuss it with him to see where this had come from, and he said that he had expressed $\sinh x$ in terms of e in his head, differentiated it easily in his head, and written down the answer, then checked by integrating in his head. He told me that he sees the exponential formulae for all trigonometric and hyperbolic functions in his head (and told me what they are) so was mystified about why I might expect him to write them down before differentiating, since 'only changes of words and signs' are required. His 'working' was to write down what he saw, changing the necessary symbols as he went. He had, he claimed, 'shown his working'.

In all these cases, more is needed if we are to say anything about a learner's understanding. A bald judgement of right or wrong is inadequate. In the absence of more information, what can be done if teachers are expected to make some judgement?

In two of the practices described earlier, the methods of addressing 'wrongness' are explicit: the discussion of an invented script and the self-checking use of an inverse function. The second has an in-built respect for mathematical structure and, in Sharon's class, has to be used for correct *and* incorrect answers in order to verify them. As a mathematician, the teacher who only uses tasks which can be self-checked using inverse procedures is not only making work easier for herself (although this is how she described it) but also offering the idea that, as Gerard Vergnaud and others have stated, mathematics contains its own validations and is the authority for itself (Hiebert *et al.* 1997; Vergnaud 1997). The difference between knowing you are right because you have checked it by another method, and being dependent on a teacher or textbook to find out if you are right, may be of central importance to adolescents, particularly those who, as Jenny Houssart describes (2001, 2004), may be able to see mathematics better from the back of the class than the teacher can up close to the board.

Thus written work, even when competently presented, may not tell us about understanding. Similarly, the layers of understanding revealed, or hidden, by written work may depend on teachers' knowledge of, and recognition of, the possibilities.

In the following example, taken from a low-attaining secondary class which was struggling with algebraic representation, a learner wrote this when asked for a generalization of the use of brackets:

$$-193 \ (101 - 99) = -386$$

Would this be a generalization or not? One could argue that to give this example the learner had to have a sense of structure and was using 'large' numbers as place-holders stating 'it is true for any number'. Also, the use of negative signs shows awareness of possible difficulties involved with brackets. Furthermore, this is either specially constructed to make some very subtle points about dealing with brackets, or was constructed to make the arithmetic easy. Recognition of its value depends on the normal practices in the classroom, what is or is not acceptable. A teacher for whom generalization is seen as synonymous with symbolization may not even notice all this, although mathematically it is very interesting. The teacher who was presented with this, Bob, used it as a starter for a subsequent lesson, adding:

and $-193 \ (101 + 99) = -38\ 600$. Make up more like it and explain.

Somehow, by thinking about written work I have slipped back to talking about making up examples – here being a request to give a generalization. But in a sense all written work can be seen as examples of what the learner understands about mathematics. Seen like this, the task of marking becomes one of assessing what is understood, even about the nature of mathematical questions. Thus, marking for 'correct answer only' is a powerful way of expressing that correct answers are in the nature of mathematics, but paying attention to method confirms that methods are important instead, or as well. The problem for teachers is to find the time to adopt the second approach, and the sensitivity and extra time to be as creative as Bob found time to be.

Still using mathematical thinking as a perspective for critical analysis of practice, I notice that Bob asked for more examples 'like it' before giving an explanation, thus suggesting an inductive or empirical approach to generalization rather than using this example as generic. But to decide what 'like it' might mean, learners will already have to decide what are the unchanging features and hence start to have a view about what is general.

In classes with a high proportion of low-attaining learners, teachers have to negotiate the tension between following leads offered by unexpected answers, of which there may be very many, and 'covering' the curriculum. My view is that there is no point in doing the latter without doing the former, since confusion about how to match their own understanding to the teacher's understanding is one of the many characteristics of low-attaining learners. Learning a sequence of unrelated topics festooned with unresolved questions is hard. In contrast, however, learning more mathematics is also important if they are to attain better grades in high-stakes examinations.

Verbal prompts and oral assessment

Having acknowledged how important one-to-one discussion is to teachers in deciding on the underlying meaning and value of written work, I shall now look at what differences and problems might arise in oral situations, and how teachers prompted classroom talk about meaning. Many teachers saw a 'gap' between being able to do mathematics and being able to talk about it. This is particularly interesting when juxtaposed with the view that thought is the same as language (often attributed to Vygotsky 1978), and that mathematics is a discursive practice (Sfard 2002). This 'do-talk' gap is not necessarily related to the do-write gap, since communication in written symbols is the mathematical convention, but being asked regularly in class to explain your methods may be very hard for some. It would be possible to have learners who can do maths, can write maths symbolically and correctly, but who cannot explain what they have done and how they did it. I myself have taught mathematics graduates who function very well symbolically with, say, rational functions but who are unable to speak about the procedures they follow beyond reading out loud what they have written – it seems to be beyond words for them, and indeed this was an influence on the creation of algebra as a condensation of abstract elements and their relationships. A neat test of this is to ask people to subtract 97 from 101, which most manage instantly, and then describe how they did it. The methods reported are most often *post facto* constructions of methods which take much longer to think through and talk about than it took to produce the answer.

Almost all the teachers in the study talked about how one-to-one interactions were the most reliable of the methods they used to gain oral evidence of knowledge, and some added that they often overheard remarks made between learners which were also of use. The favoured strategies were:

- asking questions which addressed the same topic but in some slightly 'twisted' way, such as asking 'what shapes can be made which have four right-angles?' rather than 'what angles does a rectangle have?';
- getting learners to explain something in their own words, rather than mouthing back what the teacher has said;
- prompting narrative talk, such as 'tell me everything you know about ...';
- setting up discussions between learners.

Each of these strategies was used by at least half the teachers, but some hedged their enthusiasms with comments about language weaknesses. Two teachers commented that different racial groups may have different levels of confidence in verbalizing their knowledge or their lack of understanding.

One teacher said that 'for those with English as a second language it is easy to forget what a difficulty it is ... if they are not comfortable with the language on a basic transactional level then ... ' She tailed off, and then added: 'I am also sure there are children who are quite gifted mathematically and can make intuitive leaps, so for them the explanation doesn't really exist because they haven't gone through the process, they've just "seen" it.'

In this insight, she had expressed two possible gaps: one gap between what can be seen and what can be spoken, and one between what can be said in a personal language and what can be expressed to the teacher. None of the teachers explicitly referred to those who may not be 'gifted', who *do* have English as a first language but still find it hard to communicate complex ideas verbally, and yet this is the case for many who end up in lower sets for secondary mathematics. Explaining mathematics, as every teacher knows, can be very difficult and often teachers choose to describe what to *do* rather than explain a concept. Becoming able to give reasons for what we do is part of learning to be a teacher – perhaps it is also an explicit part of becoming a mathematics learner. Even if these complications are sorted out somehow, there is still a problem with interpreting whether what is said is mathematically correct, or partially correct, or the product of serious but flawed thinking, or nonsense! For example, a learner who claimed that the shaded portions of these two circles amount to 'two-sixths' had a valid point to make.

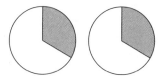

The teacher dismissed her idea as incorrect, yet it offered an opportunity to question what was being considered as the 'whole' here. Indeed, this observation reminds us that there are many conventions we expect learners to absorb implicitly in mathematics.

A learner who claimed that the sum of two odds must be odd because the sum of two evens was even, may have had some understanding, misapplied, of the symmetry of mathematics. Of course, one counter-example showed he was wrong, but his attempts to argue by symmetry are surely praiseworthy. Schmuel Avital and Edward Barbeau (1991) show that many undergraduates use symmetry arguments erroneously, so a low-attaining secondary learner is making a common mathematical error here which is not, in itself, a sign of inadequacy. A teacher who does mathematics enough herself to know how easy it is to make false arguments based on symmetry is more likely to notice the attempt to make a structural argument than one whose personal experience of doing mathematics is limited.

I know of a learner who was told that he needed three points to plot a straight line – the teacher claimed that the two he had used were not enough. Mathematically, and on graph-plotting software, two are absolutely enough, but did the learner know this, or was he seen as failing to heed his teacher's practical advice to plot three as a self-checking measure? These last two incidents show another value of verbal interactions, which is that if a teacher is not experienced enough with mathematics to recognize *all* that is good mathematically in what learners do, then verbal interaction at least leaves the door open for learners to explain their thinking – but the teacher has to be able to hear what is being said.

In an A-level lesson, a learner suggested that, when fitting a straight line to some experimental data, minimizing the total distances between each point and the straight line, might be useful. As observer, I saw her as being part-way towards constructing least-squares regression for herself, but the teacher proceeded to ignore this and give 'the' formula for the regression line with no connection explored between this approach and what had just been said. Here, a teacher failed to hear and use what had been said, even in an area of mathematics she knew well.

In another A-level lesson with the same teacher, a learner explained resolution of forces by showing, using a diagram, that the horizontal and vertical force components have to be fractions of the original force, and those fractions are obtained from the ratio of sides to the diagonal of the rectangle. This was accurate and gave the class and the teacher new insight into this diagram, without having to refer explicitly to sine and cosine. It was then easy for another student to exclaim: 'but that is the sine and cosine!' In this class, the teacher had listened and allowed the learners' thinking to contribute to the lesson.

If picking up learners' ideas, arrived at by some legitimate thinking, is hard to do consistently even when the teacher has a great deal of knowledge and the learners are articulate and high-attaining, then it is not surprising that it is inconsistent in low-attaining classes, with inarticulate learners, and teachers with less personal mathematics. I have included these last two examples to show that these issues of interpretation can occur at any level of mathematics, and can be very discouraging and puzzling for thoughtful learners if teachers do not recognize what is being said. How much more discouraging is it for learners who find it hard to get anything right anyway, and who have to struggle to express their thinking?

Fortunately we have a good range of ways to express mathematics – words, symbols, diagrams, models, numbers and arm-waving – so teachers can always ask for further explanation or, if things are still obscure, ask the learner for a worked example. Sadly, however, none of the teachers suggested that asking learners to draw diagrams might be helpful.

Diagnosing errors

About a third of the teachers reported that diagnosing errors was a central way to learn about their students' understanding. Some of them used commercially produced diagnostic tests to identify very particular misunderstandings and then planned their teaching carefully to address those places. Where errors are clearly informative, as many common errors can be, this procedure offers possibilities to rescue underachieving learners and help them to get back on track with mainstream work. The research work of Ann Dowker (2005) on early arithmetic provides good examples of this, where the ability to be very specific about confusions in arithmetic, and time to focus on specific concepts, can empower teachers to make a significant difference to the learning of individual learners. Her work even shows improvements in measures which have sometimes been used to indicate innate intelligence. Some of the teachers I interviewed took a diagnostic-treatment approach to the whole of their mathematics teaching, and their record books showed a massive amount of detail about who had done what successfully on which day, after how many attempts. More commonly, teachers use the errors which arise in given exercises to inform their general planning for a class, such as deciding to spend more time on a topic, or to return to it later.

What was missing for me in these accounts was any mention of how incorrect answers might actually reflect something about the teaching situation, such as what examples had been used, what representations, what language, what had been emphasized and so on. Instead the focus was on *what* learners did wrong, rather than *why* they did it wrong, and a belief that this had to be put right by more teaching and more exercises, rather than by different teaching. In some primary schools, learners were seen to be deficient but curable, and they did return to mainstream classes. In secondary schools, learners are more likely to be seen as deficient and incurable.

Every year, the Postgraduate Certificate in Education (PGCE) students whom I teach collect notes about errors they see being made by school learners. Eventually these are brought to a session to be discussed, with the aim of learning more about types of errors and reasons for making them. Every year I am heartened at the way PGCE learners rapidly abandon judgemental comments about 'silly errors' and begin to look for ways to explain how mathematical errors are manifestations of respectable thinking. They identify general causes of errors, and begin to think about what teachers might do about them. Their conclusions over the last few years have been that it is important to find out if errors are:

- random or repetitive, and in what circumstances they occur;
- general conceptual errors, or errors relating to particular cases;
- based on weak recording skills, or misuse of equipment;
- based on inappropriate generalization, or using rules adapted from elsewhere;
- based on unhelpful images of the concept;
- based on faulty memory.

These conclusions are very similar to those offered by Avital and Barbeau (1991) in their writing about mathematics undergraduates.

Each of these points suggests that teachers might take an inquiry approach to errors rather than just dive in with more teaching. More questions might be given which are designed to find patterns in how errors are made; the concept might be offered in a different way; learners might be observed at work, or be asked to talk about what they are doing and why; errors can become the raw material for lessons, to be discussed and challenged with counter-examples. The development of specific descriptions of learners' actions empowers teachers, because it gives them aims for lessons, aims for class discussion and aims for one-to-one intervention. These aims could be seen instead as levers for teachers' attempts to rescue low-attaining learners and allow them to use and develop their proficiencies; they are the life-jackets and masks which enable full participation.

Thinking about this has brought me to an uncomfortable place, for in many mathematics classrooms I see adults other than teachers helping low-attaining learners to do maths. I often overhear learners being shown how to do a calculation and then having to mimic the method for themselves. Language like 'put this here' or 'change the sign there' or 'take this from this' is frequently used. Yet these are the learners who make the most errors, which is why they are being helped. If learning mathematics was merely about copying methods or repeating some kind of inner instructions, such as 'take the denominator to the other side and multiply', then these learners would not be failing. The difference between the idealistic issues raised by the PGCE students and common practice for the most vulnerable learners is not just a big gap – it is a fundamental philosophical difference about the nature of learning and doing mathematics. Of course, when the PGCE students become teachers they will know that it is impossible to work at that level of detail for all students all of the time.

Why do errors matter? If they matter because we like learners to get things right, then the kind of support which helps them get right answers is fine. But if they matter because they provide a window to learning and understanding, then they are also holding up a mirror to teaching and a more useful response is to develop teaching, rather than to repeatedly retrain learners.

Fortunately, there are some simple-to-adopt strategies which enable a shift to be made from reteaching to reflecting on current understandings. Learners can be given examples of different kinds of answer, or different kinds of reasoning, and asked to work out which ones might be correct and why, and which might be incorrect and why. If giving reasons is too hard, they can be asked to suggest advice for the person who gave the wrong answer, or the wrong method. A fairly common method is to give the range of answers as if they were generated by another group of students, such as 'my last year's class' or 'students in my cousin's school' or 'I found this in a book but it looks wrong to me, what do you think?' This can be followed with 'make up a way of explaining this to someone so that they don't make the same mistake' – and the outcome of this task can be audio-recorded to save writing problems, or developed, perhaps as an animation, on an interactive whiteboard. In the last chapter of this book a teacher called Molly shows how to use this kind of strategy effectively as a common practice in her classroom.

Making sound judgements

In this chapter I have looked in detail at how teachers form judgements about individuals, and have begun to question the equity of some of these practices. A crucial characteristic of sound judgement is open-mindedness and a further one is self-doubt. However, rather than being frozen into inaction by worrying about the effects of making wrong decisions, a practical way forward would be to look for at least one alternative interpretation in every situation which leads to negative views of individual learners. Even questions about sight, hearing, sleep and nutrition might change one's view of a learner. More subtle, but equally important, would be questions about the learner's view of what has been offered in class, and how this view relates to what they already know about, or what they have seen before.

In the next chapter I bring out some clear differences which can lead to different decisions being made by different teachers in similar situations.

4 The impact of differences in practice and belief

I have already tapped into the research literature to tease out differences in views about mathematical abilities, and in how teachers' judgements are made. In this chapter I outline major differences in what teachers said about the influences they drew on to inform their judgements. I cannot go so far as to say that these are 'beliefs' or 'values' because that would involve claiming that what is said in an interview has some truth-value as a window to the teacher's mind. The furthest I will go is to claim that what the teachers said indicates possibilities of which they are aware, and which they chose as relevant for an interview with me.

The dimensions of practice in which major differences appeared were:

- perception of what is fixed and what might change;
- teaching practices;
- assessment practices;
- perceptions of learning styles;
- desired learning outcomes;
- views of mathematics;
- past personal experience.

Perception of what is fixed and what might change

The effects of home or socio-economic background were given as a reason for underachievement by some teachers:

I am now working in a deprived area socially and we are experiencing only 40 per cent at level 4 compared to 85 per cent at my previous school. Now working with different children is different, ... it depends where they are, it depends on the child and on their background the sort of work you can do with them.

Other teachers had high expectations as a norm and did not mention background as relevant:

I believe you can do almost anything you believe you can do. Most children can too. The children who've got problems are usually the ones who think they can't do it and aren't prepared to have a try at it.

For about a third of the teachers motivation, interest, boredom, confidence and preferred learning styles were treated as 'givens', but a few teachers regarded it as part of their job to affect these through their expectations or teaching styles: 'It's essential to have very high expectations and firm perimeters as the norm.'

Various theories about learner confidence were expounded, but they conflict. Many teachers indicated that lack of confidence is a barrier to success, for example 'the children who lack confidence cannot take huge jumps', but a few others suggested that confidence is a product, rather than a cause, of success:

I think it's because it's challenging and yet they are able to do it, and when they do it they feel pleased and get a feeling of satisfaction ... they know and need to know whether the answer is right or wrong and they get immediate feedback and satisfaction.

Clear inequities in teachers' treatment of learners, and teachers' reasons for it, can arise, possibly with those who exude 'natural' confidence surviving but others needing more confidence not being given the means to obtain it, for instance frequent opportunities for authentic success.

The influence of the teacher's existing knowledge of a learner is important. Several teachers commented that they would react differently to different learners doing the same thing because they had formed judgements about them in advance. For instance:

I respond in different ways to different children using a sort of mental dossier I have and I think definitely if I was asked the same question by a few children in the class my answers would be different ... at the back of my mind is what I think the child can cope with as a next stage.

There are strong expectations that learners will follow patterns of learning behaviour, and that the teacher can get to know these patterns thoroughly enough to spot when an incident is a manifestation of the normal, and when it is an aberration. One teacher, for instance, felt that he would usually know whether an error was evidence of misunderstanding or a 'slip-up' because of who had made it. The tension here is whether real changes in learning behaviour will be interpreted openly by a teacher who already has a clear opinion of a learner, and whether different teachers will interpret similar behaviour in different ways. Further, would a teacher who acts as if certain learning behaviours are fixed offer opportunity and scaffolding for changing such behaviour?

Teaching practices

There were different interpretations and practices about the tension most teachers felt between having to cover the curriculum at a pace and providing enough time for reflective understanding. This led to different decisions about how much of the curriculum was covered, and in what ways. Most teachers talked about placing learners in different groups and offering different levels of challenge while expecting different outcomes. Several also commented that it was easier to recall those at the extreme edges of achievement in any group than what was commonly referred to as 'the grey mass in the middle'. However, their own teaching actions have partly acted towards generating similar behaviour in most learners who conform to some notional norms about learners (they will listen, sit still, be polite, put hands up if they have something to say, etc.). Meanwhile the existence of such norms means that those who 'do not fit' are more noticeable than if everyone acted differently. The teacher's notional norms include some idea of appropriate standards for learning.

There are two tensions here, one between seeing learners as individuals and seeing each learner as a member of the group; the other between maintaining or improving standards based on past norms, and willingness to establish new norms with each group. Teachers showed contrasting views about past norms, some seeing them as a target: 'Year 6 children ... I took them for a few years and am comfortable with what I expect.' Others see them as a yardstick: 'I consider the work done so far to be of a good level, better than last year, better than the year before that, but not better than the year before that.' The first teacher teaches the same lessons every year, the second responds to learners' learning, so their classes have significantly different curriculum experiences.

A further difference in teaching practices is that several teachers said that if learners were stuck, they would offer similar examples and similar explanations, while four teachers said they actively searched for different approaches and examples. One of them said: 'One thing I want to do is find things a different way. Trying to come to the topic from a different angle.'

A marked difference here is between teachers who offer the learners fresh chances to fill in the gaps of a message previously received (and which they may not have understood) and teachers who trust learners to construct their own meanings and hence offer variety of tools or metaphors to aid construction.

One of the most startling examples of contradictions embedded in teachers' actions was that they acknowledged that working from written texts is difficult for many learners, and that teachers have to mediate frequently, very often the difficulty being with the text and not with the mathematics: 'just from the way it is set they find the booklet incredibly difficult. It is quite complex: the numbers get difficult, the language gets difficult.' Yet the same teachers often continue to use texts not just as sources of questions and ideas but as a major teaching medium.

Teaching practices can therefore advantage or disadvantage different groups of learners in several ways, those described here being whether students are expected to fulfil certain norms based on other students or not, whether students are given time to understand or not, whether they are given support based on 'filling gaps in a message' or 'further information to construct meaning', and, where the main teaching medium is written text, whether they can read it fluently or not. All of these practices could lead to valuing the preferences of one group while making learning harder for other groups.

Assessment practices

Time was a huge problem; teachers frequently said that assessment of individual learners required time to be done accurately, and time was not realistically available. Most talked of the time it takes them to 'get to know' learners, and though this varied from a few weeks to a whole term, there was a shared sense of time almost wasted before you can 'get it right' for individuals. A significant number were, however, more interested at first in how learners work, especially in investigative situations: 'from the way they tackle it and the way they go through it I make a guess at roughly the kind of work they can cope with'.

These teachers tended to give practical tasks as an assessment tool, believing application to be the ultimate demonstration of understanding. However, many other teachers gave practical work *first* to motivate the topic and to provide the enactive way into learning, followed by more abstract work, rather than the other way around. It is possible that some learners are disadvantaged by teachers' different views of a relationship between abstract and practical concepts.

Several others wanted to find out 'what learners already know' by using specially designed assessment tasks or tests. For example, one asked learners to subtract 10 repeatedly from 359. She was looking for those who could spot and use a pattern, and for those who could or could not cope with 309 – 10. Although nearly every teacher distrusted tests as 'not the

be-all and end-all', many talked of their students in terms of their overall performance on in-house tests, rather than about closely targeted diagnostic
questions.

Teachers tended to operate a judgement system in which they found
out as much as they could about individual learners and then subjected that
knowledge to a sense of norm for the age group or for the teacher's past
experience. In general, teachers talked as if it is possible to find out what
every learner knows, and that they have to behave as if this were so. About
a third of the sample mentioned the subjectivity of their judgements. A few
regarded subjectivity as unfortunate and unavoidable, while most of the rest
accepted that they could only ever be subjective and hence judgements
would be different for other times, places, circumstances and teachers. For
instance: 'We all have different ways of doing things so when he [another
teacher] thinks a child may have achieved something I might not think
they have.' Or again: 'It's very imprecise because you don't know the ins
and outs of what each child can achieve, you're just trying to build a picture
of what's achievable in given circumstances ... It's not scientific.'

The difference in credence given to test results, to performance in practical tasks, and to the subjectivity of teachers' judgements could lead to
different learners whose work is similar being seen differently by different
teachers, according to the teachers' idea of good assessment practice.

Perceptions of learning styles

Roughly a third of the teachers said that learners have different preferred
styles. For example, they said that some learners are goal-oriented and
dislike having to explain or explore before moving on to something else,
some prefer a conformist approach and linear progress through textbooks,
some aim for mastery, some aim for discovery and deeply connected understandings, some need to see how a concept could be useful. In contrast,
teachers used words like 'imagination', 'flair' and 'intuition' to describe
good learners of mathematics. Teachers seemed concerned to ensure all
understood and saw the achievement and display of understanding as an
exploratory, discursive and reflective practice which, nevertheless, could
cause frustration in some learners. Their professional experience led them
to make the same kinds of distinction between learners that Dweck made
over several years of research (Dweck 1999), that is, between those who
pursued completion of finite goals and those who saw learning as incre-
mental, effortful and progressive.

One teacher commented that 'thinking for yourself' and the desire to
take cognitive leaps can be a constraint if all you are required to do is follow
exercises in a textbook, and such exercises took up the bulk of her teaching,
but in general there was more concern voiced about those who could not

work in unstructured, relational or creative ways, than about those who could not work in structured or instrumental ways. Almost half the teachers commented on this when talking about individuals or about the whole teaching group, for example: 'I think a child would do much better at maths if they really feel they could mess about with it.'

All the teachers I interviewed claimed to espouse similar views about reflective learning, but I noticed when observing that a significant number of teachers use tests, SATs and GCSEs as targets to motivate their classes, some even going so far as to state how test questions should be done in ways which have little to do with understanding the underlying concepts. For example, one class was told that if a question said 'how many' this could be interpreted as 'divide' and 'how much' as multiply. (It is relatively easy to make up questions for which these interpretations are inappropriate.)

If it is true, as an emerging consensus claims, that 'messing about with maths' is the best way to learn, then it matters whether the teacher offers that as a way to learn or not; it also matters whether those who cannot work in these ways are helped to or not.

Understanding took priority over rote learning and 'tricks' for all teachers when discussing reasons for what they do, yet 11 teachers talked of giving step-by-step approaches so that learners would not find work too daunting, while four others suggested that *all* learners are capable of cognitive leaps and that step-by-step teaching works against this. Confidence either grows with smooth passage through step-by-step approaches, or with successful risk-taking and cognitive leaping. A related tension is between teachers who are happy to 'push' learners (though the way they select learners for pushing would be interesting to know) and those who talk of learners being 'ready to learn'.

This study was done before an explosion of information reached schools about differences between visual, aural, kinaesthetic and various other 'learning styles', but in many of the interviews the main distinction drawn was between intuitive and rational processes – the emphasis was on how learners processed a wide range of experiences, rather than how those experiences might be correlated with certain kinds of presentation.

Desired learning outcomes

One difference in desired outcomes was the perceived importance of learners' own methods. Almost everywhere in the data these are valued by the teacher, with an associated distrust of the ability of traditional layouts to indicate understanding, but traditional layouts are taught and given higher status by teachers because they believe these to be required for assessment, and because future teachers might expect learners to know them.

One teacher volunteered that conventional layouts are systematic records which can aid understanding and therefore have a useful teaching purpose.

The tension here is hard to tease out. Clearly teachers recognized differences in ways of learning. Clearly also teachers have adopted the shared aims of understanding, explaining and valuing own methods, as expressed throughout Cockcroft (1982) and the National Curriculum (QCA 1999). But these aims cause problems for some learners, especially those who find writing about their mental processes hard, and conflict with a per-ceived aim of producing traditional algorithms and the external goal of doing well in tests. Most teachers wanted to follow up written work, whether correct or not, with one-to-one discussion, but some teachers worked in reverse order, that learners talked first and then wrote down what they had said. Whatever the order, 'showing working' was universally important in the sample, as it provides teachers with a diagnostic tool and evidence for their judgements, but does this requirement devalue intuitive approaches, which are encouraged elsewhere in mathematics?

There were also differences between acceptance of learner jottings, own methods, diagrams, non-standard recording methods and neat, well-pres-ented traditional work. Examples of teachers' utterances about this include:

> I do ask them to show their working out to see where the answer is from … I would then give them something more complicated … I would try something where they would have to think a long time and then write something down.

> All the time I am introducing new work like trig I would expect them to follow my methods or at least if they are not doing that they should be getting them all right. So I suppose I do expect them to that extent to be like me.

Written work may or may not, therefore, represent what really went on for the learner. Quality of written work may be confused with good presen-tation, and very messy work is not always a demonstration of failure to understand. Thus, different judgements can be made about the mathemat-ics represented by written work (Morgan 1998). Some teachers said that learners who understand are able to communicate their understanding; others said that these are separate stages and communication does not nec-essarily go hand in hand with understanding. Some teachers may encour-age learners to explore what can legitimately be left out of a mathematical argument in order to shorten it, others may want every detail explained. All these differences show up in what outcomes are valued or not valued in dif-ferent classrooms.

Teachers also recognized that their own notion of a desired learning outcome, and whether it had been achieved, would be different from that of other teachers. This was revealed in a general distrust of the records of other teachers: 'I don't take much notice of them because of the differences in primary schools.'

Each teacher felt competent to assess, and could justify their assessment decisions, but would not accept the assessments of others without some confirming practice of their own (Gipps 1992): 'Teachers … are notoriously resistant to using others' assessments of children … it is really wasteful if the assessment information, including teacher assessment, is of good quality' (p. 281).

My observations of professional meetings held in school to moderate assessment decisions showed no such conflicts and distrust between those at the meeting, but they did show doubting comments about assessment practices of teachers who had left and of teachers in feeder schools. This could be a defensive search by vulnerable, accountable, teachers for absent scapegoats.

Views of mathematics

Whereas some of the differences in desired learning outcomes were about how learners communicated their learning, others related to the teachers' views of priorities in mathematics. For instance, the following were differently valued by different teachers: development of methods and written formal methods; *ad hoc* problem-solving skills and replicable mathematical skills; remembering rules and adapting and using rules; investigative skills and working through texts; making abstract leaps and producing practical solutions.

Even with similar views of mathematics, teachers may interpret evidence differently because their idea of how mathematics should be represented may differ. If the ultimate aim of an activity is an algebraic expression in correct form, other forms of that expression (diagrammatic, verbal, unconventional algebra etc.) may or may not be valued, depending on the teacher.

For some teachers, mathematics was a way of dealing with 'real world' situations, so that their lessons and assessment tasks were often cast as contextual problems, but situations may generate their own specific mathematics which is more appropriate so the desired application of a technique from outside the context may not happen. For example, buying wallpaper was seen as an area problem, where in reality one buys so many 'drops'. For this reason, one teacher may dismiss a method as a 'trick' where another may see it as a legitimate method applicable only to a particular situation.

For others, learning mathematics was seen as a growing body of competence in which learners have to reject earlier, more naïve, notions. For example, measuring the length of a hypotenuse should not be done by someone who now knows the relationships between the squares on the sides of a right-angled triangle – yet in 'real life' a variety of *ad hoc* and measuring methods might be used. Thus, a learner who chooses to use simpler methods where they are available and appropriate may be seen as less sophisticated than one who always uses the 'latest' method. A learner who 'sees' the answer to a simple linear equation may not be valued as highly as one who uses a method to find it. Yet there is a strong argument for praising the first more highly for being able to make mathematically informed choices of method than the second.

Within the community, therefore, there are differences in views about order and value in mathematical learning so that a display of understanding may lead to different assumptions, made by different observers, about what else the learner knows.

Past personal experience

Some of the interview teachers seemed to be assuming implicitly that those who could follow their expectations, or communicate in a way they understood, or respond well to them in class, were the 'able' ones. I asked one teacher, a highly qualified and articulate mathematician, what he meant by the 'good' ones and he said 'The ones who always answer, and have the right answers'. That approach, would not, however, work in the classroom of Nora, who believed that struggle and discomfort are part of learning, because that was the way she learnt mathematics. Nora told me: 'I want to give them a challenge and know that they would try in that situation. ... at the end he will say "phew! that was hard" but he really likes doing hard work' and 'There are those who are happy to work at challenging work but not step-by-step. ... I kept pushing and pushing and pushing and he is now thriving on it.' Of her own mathematics she said: 'Oh, I did struggle! Well if you struggle with something you have to think much harder about it so if you are successful in the end you feel more satisfied and feel you have learnt something.'

Nor would a 'quick answer' method work in Lilian's classroom, because Lilian knows from her own experience that one can make leaps into the abstract that are very different from what everyone else is doing and that one can be ridiculed for so doing. Lilian had told me that when she did a painted cube task:

> I didn't do a table of values, I went straight to a formula and people were looking, creeping up to look at it, and I was using a table to confirm a formula, which no one else did. My son who is doing GCSE said I was a screwball; how could I write a formula if I haven't got a table? ... He thinks I am mad.

So teachers' own experiences as learners can give them different views about what kinds of learning are possible and valuable.

Concerns about differences in practice

While many differences in practice are relatively benign, simply illustrating a range of practice and 'good ideas' which might be shared around the community, there are several points of tension and contradiction in the practices of mathematics teachers which could affect learners' future because they all contribute towards assessment decisions. It would be highly possible for the same learner producing the same work in different circumstances with different teachers to have her work, and her future, assessed differently (see also Watson 1997, 1999).

I have identified significant and influential differences in:

- approaches to communication issues which may advantage or disadvantage certain groups;
- diagnosis of the root causes of some difficulties which may depend on fortuitous observations, or on the mathematical knowledge of the teacher;
- approaches to testing, and knowledge about bias in testing, which may lead to unfair assessments;
- perception of how learners can change which may lead some teachers to accept what other teachers work to change;
- teaching practices which encourage different ways to work with mathematics;
- assessment practices which could lead to different outcomes;
- learners' natural ways of working which may or may not be engaged;
- desired learning outcomes which lead to favouring some presentations of work over others;
- views of mathematics which lead to different aspects being recognized and valued;
- past personal experiences which lead to different inferences being made.

In the next chapter I look in detail at how easy it is for even the most aware and well-meaning of teachers to form judgements which are not fully informed, and how the mechanisms by which this happens are unavoidable.

5 The fallacy of 'getting to know' learners

In this chapter I will illustrate how conscientious, experienced teachers of goodwill, who are disposed to act fairly, can develop judgements of their students which could be strongly challenged. We can misunderstand learners merely by believing that we *can* and *must* understand them. Because we are professionals, we are encouraged to believe our judgements are necessarily professional and therefore fair (Blease 1993, 1995). This is the wrong way round. We ought to earn our professionalism by, among other things, ensuring that the judgements we make as professionals *are* fair, and by informing ourselves about possible alternatives. A truly professional teacher would not say 'this category of child is not capable of learning trigonometry' any more than a professional doctor would say 'this category of patient is not capable of being cured' without considering several alternatives, keeping up to date with new ideas, and so on.

The aim of the study in this chapter is not to throw stones at teachers, but to argue that no teacher can know fully a learner's capabilities and potential. However, the classroom situation makes it likely that teachers can easily imagine they 'know' things about a learner. When asked about the assessments she had made of her new students, one of the teachers I interviewed said, early in the school year: 'Let's put it this way, there will be no surprises now.' By contrast, in response to the same question at the same time of year another said: 'I am now ready for surprises.'

The study

In this chapter I am going to show how a teacher who was more like the latter than the former, open-minded and willing to challenge his judgement, developed views about one learner among 30 during his first term with them. At the same time I was researching alongside him, deliberately collecting data in order to construct my own characterization of the same learner. You will not be surprised to learn that we constructed different views of her, but the findings in this chapter go further than that; they get near the heart of the intractable problem of teacher judgements – that you can *never* know enough about a learner to make high-stakes decisions completely fairly.

Details of the teacher and learner have been heavily disguised, of course, and the learner never knew she was a research subject. This was entirely ethical because we had to learn how such judgements are made in the normal flow of classroom life, and she benefited from the frequent conversations we had about our observations. No judgements were made about her, and other focus learners in the study, without a level of professional discussion and examination of alternative interpretations far beyond what is usual.

I attended one mathematics lesson a week of a Year 7 class at a secondary school, new to the teacher, Alan, at the start of the term. They had mathematics four times a week with the same teacher. The class contained slightly fewer than 30 learners for most lessons and was predominantly white, co-educational, in a school used by a wide cross-section of society in a medium-sized town.

I observed the same six learners in every lesson, keeping observation notes about their behaviour, utterances (public and private, overheard), actions, and looking frequently at their written work, sometimes with their knowledge (Watson 1997; Morgan and Watson 2002). All the learners I observed had English as their first language and a UK home culture. My aim was to see what kinds of evidence were observable by teachers about their students, even if they were not actually observed, and how they developed 'knowledge of the child' from that evidence.

I was introduced as someone who was finding out about mathematics teaching. Learners' ignorance of my observation was essential in order to maintain their normal behaviour as far as possible, although there were a few times when, just as with any visitor to a classroom, I played the role of another adult to talk to about work. I was able to base myself in a position in the classroom which was physically close to my subjects yet was also an obvious and sensible place for any visitor to sit. I used a combination of systematic observation, writing down what was happening every few minutes and staying with extended episodes of action and interaction as they unfolded, resuming systematic observation after each one.

I shared all my information with the teacher, not just for research purposes, but also to ensure that my close study was to the learners' benefit by helping the teacher to know them better. I gave the teacher copies of all my notes. Anything I observed which was particularly interesting would be reported to the teacher straight after the lesson concerned so that appropriate action could be incorporated into the next lesson plan. Additional data about the teacher's views of the learners was collected in conversation at several points throughout the term, and in two informal interviews lasting about 45 minutes each. I had access to all written work done by the focus learners, and in addition the teacher talked to me often about events which had happened during other, unobserved, lessons and added to my knowledge with anecdotes about non-curriculum aspects of their behaviour. I needed to have detailed knowledge of the kinds of signs (words, actions, etc.) which were being generated by learners in this interactive situation in order to think about possible 'teacherly' interpretations.

Although I intended to observe only what was technically observable by Alan, I knew that neither of us could see everything. He typically spent part of the class orchestrating discussion from the front, or working on the chalkboard, and the rest of the lesson going around the room helping, encouraging and challenging pairs, groups or individuals. The focus learners were not in his field of vision for much of the lesson. Also, for most of the exposition parts of lessons, I was closer, or had a better view of some focus learners, than the teacher did. Alan rarely, if ever, stood still and kept an overview of the whole class, and he never did unrelated tasks like marking or administration while I was there. Alan and I therefore saw different events, or saw the same events with two different perspectives. Sometimes these coincided, but in general I saw much more of the behaviour of the focus learners, and in more detail, than he did while I was there. It became clear, as the term progressed, that other factors were also influencing what we saw. It is also important to note that I did not set out to criticize Alan; I set out to find out how he made, built, or accumulated judgements about his students.

The data

Detailed analysis was carried out by extracting all observations, comments and summaries of written work for each learner from the raw data, constructing separate stories for each focus learner. Social behaviour, oral contributions, written work and mathematical actions were observed.

I decided to include as 'behaviour' those actions whose relationship to mathematics could be interpreted ambiguously. For instance, 'hands up' might mean the learner knows the answer or needs help, but might also mean that a learner is merely fitting in with classroom behaviour and might not have anything to say; a learner who frequently erases work might be showing a desire to take a long time on unchallenging or repetitive work, an obsession with neatness rather than content, or careful self-correction; a learner who chooses to copy down everything on the board even when this has not been an instruction could be time-wasting, or avoiding work, or it could mean a determination to correctly record something of value in her own book, or she might be completely stuck about what else to do and copies in order to do something. These kinds of actions were therefore noted as ambiguous, being possibly maths-related, unless subsequent information confirmed that an action had, indeed, been about a mathematical decision in which case it was recategorized as 'a mathematical action'. Behaviour that was clearly negative, such as not working, banging on the window or wandering around the classroom chatting about other matters, was noted in case it was taken to indicate rejection of mathematics; positive behaviour, such as smiling and chatting pleasantly to the teacher, was noted but not seen as related to mathematical learning. Classroom norms had to be taken into account too. One focus learner was often out of his seat and talking to others, but that in itself was not regarded as negative behaviour by the teacher, although in another class it might have been. Therefore, in this class, such wanderings were not in themselves noted but the actions and interactions with others, where I could overhear them, were noted.

In some theoretical frameworks, the distinction I am drawing between social, casual, peripheral behaviour and mathematical actions would be seen as spurious since all learners engage in classrooms as arenas in which they continue the holistic adolescent project of becoming a person. The ambiguous actions described above demonstrate the importance of this view, that learning cannot be separated from other aspects of identity. I shall return to this after describing the data and the comparisons in order to justify my attempt to make such separations.

As oral data I included public contributions to whole-class discussion, question-and-answer sessions and anything I heard between the teacher and learner, or between learner and learner which was about maths, the lesson, the teacher or maths lessons and teaching in general. I did not pay attention to talk which was about other things, nor did I judge social talk as negative, because I have noticed that my own behaviour in sessions, and that of other responsible hard-working adults, includes straying from the topic from time to time.

For written evidence I saw books, tests, and other artefacts on paper, and the occasional contribution to class boardwork.

As 'mathematical actions' I included observable involvement in practical work, and other physical actions which were obviously about learning, such as using rulers to measure or draw necessary straight lines, fetching equipment, changing answers, looking back and forth through written work, looking up information and so on. I also included actions which related to progression through tasks, such as checking work with the teacher or asking for help, as evidence of doing mathematics.

In this classroom there was no use of information and communications technology (ICT) of any kind during my observations but I am aware that if, for instance, learners had been encouraged to use an interactive whiteboard, I may have had to develop this category further or develop others.

ICT has the potential to display thinking which previously could only be expressed through words, static written symbols and arm-waving. Thus, a full picture of the evidence teachers have of learners' thinking would have to include dynamic manipulation of symbols, diagrams and formats, and examination of trickle files which record the way learners go about constructing electronic mathematical objects (Harries 2001). However, my aim in this book is not to produce advice about detailed assessment of individuals but to question the role such detailed work plays in structuring mathematical achievement, so, although there is much research to be done about assessment in an ICT milieu, I can proceed without it.

Alan used a variety of teaching approaches: practical work, discussion, investigation, exposition, practice, bookwork and problem-solving. He attempted to generate questioning and conjecturing in his classrooms through the kind of activities offered and his own teaching interactions. The profile of observations varied from lesson to lesson because there were different things to observe. Sometimes there were many oral incidents and few written ones; at other times there was plenty of action but little clear oral data.

Comparing what we saw

It turned out that for the lessons I attended I generally saw more behavioural features and actions than the teacher did – unsurprisingly, as I was watching the learners centrally for much of the time. In the domain of actions related to doing mathematics I not only saw more than the teacher in the lessons I attended, but also saw more detail. In the oral domain the teacher's and my experiences overlapped but not completely, as I often failed to hear what students said directly to him, and he did not always hear what they said to other students. Only in the written domain did I have the same evidence as the teacher, although I sometimes knew more about what had been achieved but not written down, or what had led to the written work, such as copying, correcting, or writing down first and talking it through with a neighbour afterwards.

In the following comparison I am not saying that one of us, the teacher or I, is correct or incorrect; I am merely showing the possibility of different interpretations arising from the relative dominance of different data.

It was apparent from my discussions with Alan that actions most clearly associated with learning mathematics, such as silent mouthing while thinking through a question, were often the least noticeable and that behaviour which contradicted the classroom norms, such as throwing paper across the room, was often the most noticeable. In many cases, it would not have been surprising for the teacher's view of a learner to be overwhelmingly negative, given the impression the learner was giving physically. One learner, for instance, was frequently involved in arguments, chatting, fiddling with her pencils and other off-task activities. I also observed, but Alan could not, that this same learner (not the focus learner for this chapter) had several ways of getting others to do her work.

The next most frequent observations in the classroom were public and private oral interactions about mathematics and questions about procedural matters such as which question to do next, or which sort of paper to do it on. It was in this domain that many differences of interpretation emerged between the teacher and me. For instance, Alan thought Andrew was articulate, and yet according to my records Andrew hardly ever spoke about maths, and nearly half the times he did do so he was merely reading what was already on the board. Alan thought Janet was 'brighter' than Carol at mathematics, yet in my observations Carol talked more about maths than Janet did. They sat next to each other so I was able to observe Janet and Carol equally. Alan valued two of Janet's comments quite highly and said that they had contributed to his view of Janet as a strong learner: firstly Janet had said that the work they were doing with shapes was 'just like Tetris' (a computer game involving fitting shapes together rapidly), which Alan took to be indicative of her forming relationships within mathematics; secondly, Janet identified two shapes as reflections of each other, a statement which was made by only two other students who had each subsequently proved to be 'very good at maths'. I, on the other hand, had been influenced by the tiny quantity of oral discussion rather than its mathematical quality.

Written work provides an opportunity for a teacher to reflect on learners' work rather than react instantly to it. One learner, in spite of often visibly getting others to do her work and being skilled at presenting it as her own, still produced many errors and misunderstandings in writing. Alan took these to be her misunderstandings, but I knew they could also be those of the others who did the work. The relative strengths of Carol's and Janet's written work did not clearly support the teacher's view that Janet was stronger. At the end of term, Carol demonstrated an ability to handle abstract symbolism and to construct new knowledge while Janet's work appeared to fizzle out. The relationship between written work and Alan's views of learners was not straightforward; his images of them as active class members, or not, appeared to dominate his descriptions.

The last domain of recorded observations contained mathematical-work-related actions. These are the hardest to observe and, of course, I did not see everything that went on. Some work-related actions which I did observe were very slight, such as seeing Carol search back through her book for a formula, or watching Janet's eyes as she scanned a page of shapes for the ones she had to identify, or observing Sandra counting on her fingers under the desk. However, I noted as much as I could, and was able to collect enough evidence to support, for example, my view that one learner engaged in greater mathematical-work-related activity than Alan could observe. Alan described this student as 'always asking for help', and yet my records of her utterances were dominated by true mathematical statements and her actions always appeared to be focused on the board and on her own writing.

Comparing our views of Sandra

Sandra sat at the edge of the front row, next to one of the aisles along which Alan frequently wandered. She was moderately tall for her age, slim and blondish.[1] Within the class her appearance was not outstanding in any way.

By the end of the first term the impression Alan had of Sandra's mathematics had changed from rather low initially to a fairly high estimation of her number skills. In other aspects of mathematics he rated her about average for the group, but believed that she was not very good at working in open-ended situations. How had he come to that view, and how did it compare to mine?

Alan, while being aware that Sandra sometimes altered her arithmetical answers when marking her own work, was not aware of the extent of this practice and had a view that she was mainly good at mental arithmetic, changing written answers very occasionally in order to keep her confidence up. My view was that Sandra *wanted* to appear to be good but was making and hiding errors regularly and frequently. I had noticed that nearly all of her enthusiastic contributions to class (calling out, hand waving energetically in the air) arose from work done at home with her father's help or, very occasionally, from discussions which Alan had already had with her. It was as if she knew that to get approval from the teacher you had to show right answers publicly, but that she was skilled in getting those right answers not from her own head but from her father, or from the teacher (and it is also possible that his gender was important here).

I had evidence which indicated specific weaknesses in number work, such as the use of fingers for subtraction in situations where a competent arithmetician may have known number bonds or have developed some patterning strategies. In one lesson she had generated a collection of 'sums to 34' using a system she had developed, but she did not consistently use patterns and systems in other suitable arithmetical situations. Further evidence of specific arithmetical skill was provided by her use of the 'grid' method of long multiplication in which she had carried out the method, with appar-

---

[1]   I mention the colour of her hair to show that there was nothing particularly outstanding about her appearance. However, Brophy and Good (1974: 20) found that some teachers assumed that students of culturally attractive appearance were more intelligent than average. Neither Alan nor I ever considered this effect.

ent understanding of the size of the subproducts, but had made an error in one which led to an answer of quite the wrong size, which she had not noticed.

I noticed that Alan's estimation of her arithmetic, initially low as a result of a test, had risen to a relatively high level as a result of her oral contributions to class. My estimation was that she lacked useful internalization of arithmetical facts, and had previously relied on performance of algorithms which she failed to remember. She had some understanding of number structure and relative magnitudes. For example, I heard her mutter about dividing a four-digit number with 5 in the units place by 5: 'well it's got to end in 5'. She would not necessarily notice inaccurate answers. She was interested in arithmetic enough to want to look good at it but had to depend on help, asking and cheating to do it. It was as if her social skills had convinced him that she was stronger than the test result showed.

Alan's early comments in our discussions were mainly about Sandra's social and personal traits, some given as straightforward accounts of behaviour, but others as interpretations. He said about half way through the term:

> Sandra was independent at first, happy to sit on her own and lively, though she later asked to be moved to sit next to another girl. She craved reassurance.

> In the use and application of mathematics she is relatively weak, asking for direction and asking me to check her work often. She does not 'see new ways' to do the work.

He seemed to justify his use of the word 'weak' by talking about behaviour which he interpreted as expressing need; does he assume that only those who *cannot* do things ask for such reassurance? Or does he believe that being able to do anything has an affective dimension, and that intellect and emotion have to be in harmony for anything to be done? While his judgement conformed in part to the theories about teachers' expectations by being dominated by personality, he also showed some flexibility and managed to avoid global cognitive judgements, such as those which Ruthven (1987, 1994) highlights as being problematic. But his statement, taken as conscientious and professional, expressed that the distinction between personality and learning which Ruthven went on to explore cannot be made; emotion and learning are entwined.

Later in the term, when through our discussions he knew that she often changed answers in self-marked arithmetic tests, he tried to make more sense of this:

There are some signs of correct working out in her arithmetic work as well as alterations of the answers. There is some kind of smoke-screen she puts up which prevents the teacher knowing exactly what she can do and why she changes answers.

In his interpretations here he was also taking a holistic view of the observations we had both made. This could have been an attempt to retain the view that she was strong in arithmetic, but was more likely to be the recognition that making judgements about her arithmetic was a complex business as much to do with her behaviour, emotions and actions as with her intellect and mathematical capabilities.

Alan was unaware of how much time Sandra spent carrying out mundane parts of activities or not working at all. She had successfully, by her frequent questions, given him the impression that she was a keen worker, if frustrated and in need of support. It was as if he had a neutral view of her until something outstanding happened, in her case enthusiastic contribution to homework feedback sessions or her grabbing him to ask questions as he passed her desk. Her alteration of answers became under-represented in his picture of her and the pattern of her responses was not obvious to him. Meanwhile my interpretation was that she also successfully masked her inactivity by asking him a question nearly every time he walked past her chair, and at other times as well. Each of us wavered, but wavered differently, in our view of whether she was a keen worker or not.

Evidence of a genuine interest in arithmetic was supported by her contributions to class discussions on magic squares, and an exclamation 'Ooooh!' when the teacher had helped her to see that two number patterns generated in different ways were actually the same pattern. I could also interpret this to show that she had some sense of the internal links and connections of mathematics. This contrasted with Alan's view that she was weaker in open-ended work, as I saw at least four instances of spontaneous engagement with reasoning processes, which I shall now describe.

Task 1

Make as many different shapes as you can by joining five squares edge to edge. Can you fit these together to make a rectangle?

I observed Sandra trying to fit these pentominoes (the shapes made from five squares joined edge-to-edge) together to make a rectangle: she calculated an appropriate width and length, 6 and 20, and then used those as constraints within which to work.

Task 2

Construct a 'magic' three-by-three square containing numbers 1 to 9, so that the rows, columns and diagonals all add up to the same total.

Find as many properties as you can, and see how many other arrangements of the digits, with the same row, column and diagonal total, have the same properties.

Construct 'magic' squares which are four-by-four, five-by-five, and so on, exploring each in similar ways.

As a result of a question from the teacher 'how many rows and columns do you have?', Sandra realized that there would be a connection between some previous work she had done, generating sets of four numbers which totalled to 34, and the placement of numbers in a 4×4 magic square: she then talked about her reasoning publicly in a plenary session.

Task 3

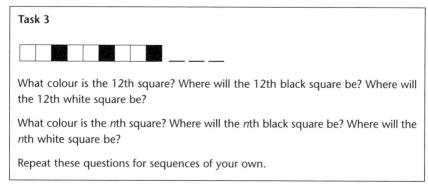

What colour is the 12th square? Where will the 12th black square be? Where will the 12th white square be?

What colour is the nth square? Where will the nth black square be? Where will the nth white square be?

Repeat these questions for sequences of your own.

Sandra had made up her own sequence, and reasoned that white would appear every other even number in one of the patterns and asked 'does this mean it appears every 4th?'

Task 4

Build complicated shapes out of multilink cubes. Draw various views of them on isometric paper.

When you are confident about this, draw on isometric paper only the final edges of overall shapes you have made by joining cubes.

Sandra was erasing lines from an isometric drawing of a complicated shape made of cubes so that the only lines left were the edge-lines of the whole shape: most found this hard but she was relatively successful compared to the rest of the group.

These observations suggest that she was devising strategies, reusing strategies which have been effective in the past, describing patterns and making conjectures resulting from the pattern, and using mental imagery of three-dimensional objects; all these appear in Krutetskii's descriptions of strong mathematical thinking (see Chapter 2). Alan had formed a view that she was weak in the skills of exploring and reasoning with mathematics, and did not 'see new ways' to do things, needing direction and reassurance. The instances above could suggest that his teaching was helping her achieve progress in these areas, or that he underestimated her thinking, since the only times he may have noticed the quality of her thinking were when she asked for help. Perhaps there could be a combination of both; initially he could have been right in his assessment, but she was developing better reasoning skills which he had not yet noticed.

Compared to my observations, Alan seemed to overestimate Sandra's skills in the area of mathematics in which she wanted him to be interested. She used considerable social skills in communicating her arithmetic to him and hence, creating a positive impression. He appeared to underestimate her skills of reasoning, perhaps because she was less confident about them or had less opportunity to articulate them, or perhaps because she asked for help relatively often, hence, creating a negative impression in that respect. Alan recognized this. Towards the end of term he said that it was hard for him to know how good she was because she always checked with him before doing anything.

Also, it is important to notice that Alan was always seeing her work in the context of what the rest of the class did and what his own expectations were, making a judgement which is *comparative* to what she had done before and to the rest of the class. But 'what she had done before' included creating an impression in his mind, therefore, judgements were relative to the picture already formed.

There is another feature of this case, which is that I as observer was able to see a pattern to her oral contributions which the teacher could not see. It was the pattern and circumstances of the contributions, rather than their quantity or nature, which indicated the contrast between her arithmetical abilities and her desire to be good with calculations.

Making a fair judgement about Sandra

Professional judgements depend on what *observable evidence* is available to the teacher, and this depends in part on what the learner can bring to the teacher's attention, and how this is done. Perceived *patterns* of response are important here. Judgements also depend in part on what a teacher takes to be *significant*. Teachers are likely to notice *outstanding attributes* early in their relationship with the learner while they are getting to know them, and to interpret subsequent actions in light of this.

Alan's construction of a view of Sandra's mathematics vividly illustrates:

- teachers seeing only part of the whole story;
- teachers seeing, or failing to see, patterns in responses and behaviour;
- types and patterns of behaviour being over- or underrepresented in the teacher's mental picture;
- teachers being over-influenced by learners' strong or weak social skills;
- teachers comparing work to early impressions and to the whole class;
- teachers interpreting work, where there is doubt, in the light of existing impressions;
- time constraints on the teacher preventing full exploration of mathematics;
- teachers' inability to see and use all the details which occur in class-rooms.

I have shown that Alan was willing and able to alter his initial views of Sandra, but that this was done only by her production of outstanding incidents which provided the framework for future interpretations of her actions, and by the presence of another observer. Stories of other students in the class, and in another class with another teacher similarly observed and researched, showed the same propensity of the teacher to pick up on obvious signs and use them to make future judgements, while showing in conversations with me that they had open minds and were able to maintain an inquiring attitude about their students' learning.

I have attempted to show that different judgements might be reached, quite legitimately, by different professionals who have access to similar, but differently weighted, data.

Even a conscientious teacher like Alan, who was aware of my focus on Sandra, could not avoid making judgements based on partial evidence in order to function in the day-to-day world of his classroom. There is nothing wrong with that when a teacher is questioning and inquiring into his own impression-making, thinking it always possible that he might need to rethink his ideas. Problems arise when such flimsy judgements are not left where they properly belong, as temporary decision-making frameworks which are open to question, but instead become embedded in high-stakes decision-making.

While Alan believed Sandra to be good at arithmetic, she was not getting support for this, and was not being engaged in one-to-one interactions which might help her to develop her thinking further. Instead she was locked into asking for *ad hoc* help and reassurance, and he into providing them, rather than more fruitful and appropriate one-to-one inter-actions. Later in the year, decisions were made about setting learners based partly on test results and partly on teachers' judgements. In this case, due to our sharing of data, Alan knew more about Sandra's strengths and weak-nesses and was able to take a more complete view than a teacher normally could, but without that it would have been perfectly possible to act with good intentions, to believe a judgement was fair, but for Sandra's work to have been under- or overvalued in some way, according to some normative yardstick.

In nearly all the individual learner cases we discussed, Alan's views were based on partial evidence and could be challenged by more detailed obser-vations and by different interpretative readings of the evidence. Yet Alan was a good and caring teacher who was open to self-criticism, self-doubt, constantly reappraising his practice and deeply concerned with equity.

A thought experiment

But let us suppose for a while that this had not been the case, and that Sandra had been in a class with a teacher who was more self-confident than Alan about judgements, had more belief in differentiated provision, in a school in which setting was fully based on previous test results and perhaps with a curriculum in which underlying mathematical habits of mind were not seen as important.

Sandra would have entered a set slightly below the middle, because her test results in Year 6 were in the middle of level 4. Perhaps there would be learners in most sets who had achieved level 4 because this school's intake was skewed towards lower achievement levels. In this case further distinc-tions would have been made but Sandra may have ended up in a middle set. Let us also suppose that Sandra behaves in the same way in this class as she did in Alan's. The work is less open-ended, and there is less exploration, so Sandra asks for reassurance more often. This cannot always be provided, because the nature of the work offered to learners means that more will get stuck and more will need help. At the same time, there is little work set which plays to Sandra's strengths, such as her willingness to get involved in a private exploration, so she spends a lot of time being stuck and not knowing what to do. Perhaps she forms a working pair with someone else who can help her out, and give her reassurance, but their chatting is seen as distracting and they are split up by the teacher from time to time. The test results have shown up her arithmetical weaknesses, so she is getting lots of input to help her with these. She can no longer hide her wrong answers, so some progress is being made, but in relation to the whole cohort the learners in her class are spending more time repeating old stuff and not doing new stuff. She also does the same work at school that she does at home with her father, who still helps her with arithmetic. There is nowhere in her maths lessons where her sense of shape and pattern are of any use, and on the few occasions when she has said to the teacher 'look at this!' there has not been time to discuss her observations. She is only in Year 7, and there are four more years of compulsory mathematics ahead of her, but she is already receiving a limited curriculum based on past test results, and based on the belief that this is the best way to address her learning needs. Because she is getting bored her participation is less energetic, and her behaviour less perfect.

Many teachers in my initial study wanted to have more input into setting decisions made solely by test results at their schools. When setting decisions are made at the end of the year for Sandra, should they be based solely on test results, or should teacher judgements play a part as well? In a centralized assessment regime it is attractive to plead for more autonomy for teachers. But who is best served by such a return? Equity and justice for teachers, and room for them to take proper professional responsibility, are laudable aims but ultimately my greater interest is in equity and justice for learners.

My thought experiment about Sandra is not far-fetched. I could have made it more colourful by having her taught by someone who is not among the best-qualified teachers in the school as she is not one of the 'brightest' students, by punishing her for cheating with her arithmetic answers, by taking her out of mainstream to stop her counting on her fingers, and by sending her to booster classes to improve her short-term performance in tests, in both cases missing out further on the core curriculum. These would have been realistic in terms of the national picture of what happens to learners who are seen to be below average. All these scenarios are possible in schools, and are described in research. In particular, we see this kind of thing happening in a delicate picture drawn by Houssart (2004) of learners becoming gradually alienated and excluded from mathematical activity because their ways of working were not valued by the teacher. I have even wondered if such scenarios are a form of low-level bullying of students who 'don't fit'. The tragedy is that they arise from good intentions and are perfectly acceptable in schools. They are not even 'beneath the radar'.

Tasks in Alan's lessons

Before I finish talking about Alan's classroom, I will revisit some of the tasks he used during the term's work. Each task appeared to have open and closed elements, but this turned out to be rather a crude distinction, because the ways in which his students tackled the tasks seemed to cycle between 'open' and 'closed'. What seems to be more important is not the openness of the questions posed, but the ways in which different learners started the task, how they chose to problematize the situation, and what knowledge and experience they could bring to bear on it.

For example, one task involved fitting different shapes together to make other 'standard' shapes. Some learners played with the shapes to 'see what we can make', others aimed to 'see how many we can make' and others tried to make specific shapes such as squares, parallelograms and so on. This process of task reconstruction created some closed tasks out of open tasks by defining goals. In some cases Alan gave input by challenging them to 'see if you can make an isosceles trapezium', thus, posing a possibility which may not have occurred to them. Another prompt was 'can you make shapes with two axes of symmetry?' so that, by introducing a constraint, the challenge was increased. This led learners to make mathematical distinctions based on properties rather than merely revisiting definitions they had known before. Alan seemed to be pushing them to think in more refined ways through opening up and closing down the task – processes which they could also do for themselves.

The work based on magic squares continued for over 2 weeks, and involved Alan's students in successively more complex investigations during which the knowledge they gained in easy cases was then applied more fluently in harder cases. Starting with a three-by-three square they learnt what a 'magic square' was, saw how numbers could be moved around to create new squares, found relationships between the central number and the row and column sums, and formed conjectures about larger squares. With larger squares they already had some knowledge of what to do and how to do it, and had conjectures to test and new relationships to find. Each learner could sense their own progress as their experience of such squares grew and they were able to say more about them, and with more confidence.

It would be possible to criticize the latter task as not contributing much to progress through the curriculum, but the point I am trying to make is that the whole class, including some students who had very low achievement grades in the previous year, were expected to think mathematically, to work on an extended, continuous piece of work, and to get a sense of the relationships and connections within the situation. In the course of doing this, they need to use more and more sophisticated reasoning skills. The former task is easier to justify, since well-posed questions and prompts could introduce learners to all the significant properties of shapes which they are supposed to learn about in school.

Justice and decision-making in mathematics teaching

Even within a regimen of regular testing and ubiquitous setting practices there is much that could be done to put working structures and habits in place which challenge possible sources of injustice.

A colleague of mine, a head of mathematics in a comprehensive school, has two lists of learners, one male and one female, ordered according to their achievements as reported by feeder schools. She selects the 'top' 15 of each list to be in the top set, and the 'bottom' 10 of each list to be in the bottom set, the rest being in parallel sets. This strategy to avoid gender inequity is certainly not detrimental to the school's results, indeed they do better than comparable schools. This is not the place to discuss whether this strategy could fairly be extended to other well-defined disadvantaged groups, since it could result in a complex quota system for setting which could exclude as many as it might include. At the very least schools could look critically at the results of their decisions in terms of race, class, gender and language difference and ask themselves whether their decision-making procedures managed to do anything other than replicate divisions in society.

> I observed a new teacher in an inner-city comprehensive school teaching a Year 7 class of 30, which consisted of 25 boys and 5 girls. Two of the boys were black; the rest of the learners were white. I thought this an odd collection of adolescents so went for a walk down the corridor, peeping through the glass panels of the class-room doors as I passed, to see what the other maths groups looked like. All other groups seemed to consist of mixtures of genders and racial groups as I would expect, except for a little group of six Asian young women, huddled in their veils around a computer. I had not thought to ask if the class I was observing was a 'top set' and now I did not need to. Somehow this school had managed to separate out a significant number of white middle-class males at age 11 for special treatment and higher expectations – what a colleague has called 'make-up for those already beautiful'. The group of young women was described to me as 'bottom set ... language, really'.

How could the managers of a multi-racial school be blind to the inequity of their setting system when it was so obvious to an outsider? Whatever the method for making these setting decisions, they ought, in my view, to be questioned since what is being 'measured' can only be truly described as 'mathematical achievement' if mathematics is essentially biased for white middle-class boys. There are, indeed, those who would say that it *is*, in which case my story could stop here. Heather Mendick (2006) makes a powerful case for mathematics as being heavily male-gendered and there are aspects of how this comes about which overlap with my perspective, but for the purposes of this book I claim that bias is not in mathematics itself, but in the ways in which judgements are made about learners.

> A learner who was shouting out a lot in class was sent from the room. He had been calling out remarks all lesson, to the teacher's growing annoyance. The teacher had warned him that he would be sent out if he did it again, and sure enough he did it, so he was sent out. As he left the room an eerie silence fell as learners watched him go. The teacher continued to teach and the class was hushed. So far, so good; there had been a public demonstration of what is unacceptable, clear drawing of lines, clarity about what would happen if the line was transgressed – all very normal aspects of textbook advice given to teachers. The result was silence, just as such advice predicts.

The learner in this story had been the only black person in the class. How had the situation developed that he was the one whose behaviour was so disturbing that he was sent out? As an observer I was impelled to ask this question. The teacher, who was sensitive and professional, realized on reflection that, although his treatment of this student was clear and appeared to be fair, what had singled him out for special treatment compared to others who were also calling out was that:

- some of the others were girls and their voices were not so disruptive;
- this student had been sitting to one side of the front row so his voice, which was quite deep, was always straight in the teacher's ear;
- there were established patterns of behaviour between the boy and his teachers which were well known in the school and which this teacher had just unwittingly re-enacted.

The silence with which the class watched his exclusion might not have been due to the realization that they all needed to be quiet, but might also have been discomfort as they saw that he was being sent out yet again. The learner and the teacher were acting out a routine which was familiar for this student and this class, indeed the reason the boy was sitting so close to the teacher was that he was often 'disruptive', but this put him in a location which made his comments more obvious. The teacher was enacting a familiar general teaching routine. If he had not used this routine, but had responded in a different way, normal patterns of behaviour would this time have been disrupted by the teacher, and new patterns might have eventually been created.

These two stories are especially poignant when I recall the publication in 1971 of a small book entitled *How the West Indian Child Is Made Educationally Subnormal in the British School System* (Coard 1971). Why has so little changed? Coard (2005) himself asks this question, pointing out the cumulative effects of unredeemed low self-esteem and low self-belief on subsequent generations.

Whenever we meet new people, it seems that we take some time to form some kind of picture of them which informs our interactions. To a certain extent this is influenced by the norms of the situation in which we meet them. The situation presents us with things to talk about and normal patterns of activity; how the other person functions within these gives us clues about whether we want to continue the interactions outside in other situations. Someone who fits the norms well might be judged to be dependable, while someone who makes a mess of the norms might be thought amusing or gauche. These first impressions tend to linger; indeed, psychologists have found that it is very hard to break first impressions, even when contradictory information comes along. For example, a learner who arrives late for the first lesson with a new teacher can easily become 'the learner who arrives late', and one who answers the first question correctly becomes 'the learner who answers correctly'. Furthermore, it seems that subsequent information about people is rarely used to rethink first impressions radically. It is usually only used to 'tweak' the original view a little bit (Tversky and Kahneman 1982). This universal tendency acts out in classrooms when teachers attach labels to learners and then tend to notice only those events which confirm the labels, interpreting contradictory evidence as aberrations. They proceed to provide learning opportunities which only permit continuation and confirmation of their labelling (McDermott 1993).

There is another side to this analysis, and that is the behaviour of the individual in portraying particular characteristics. This can be seen as playing out a role in a situation (Goffman 1959). Thus the person who does everything which fits the situation is portraying themselves as dependable, but people who break the rules are choosing, consciously or unconsciously, to portray themselves as unconventional. Learning to identify and act out appropriate roles is part of growing up.

This combination of role-playing and impression-forming becomes particularly potent when an adult forms an impression of a less mature roleplayer; the teacher can exercise power over the learner. Indeed, the teacher feels that this is part of the expected role, saying things like 'I have to control the class' while the learner says 'This teacher can/cannot control the class'. The power relationships act to magnify a cycle of behaviour which can become the norm by positioning the teacher and learner in a ghastly dance of negativity such as I have illustrated above.

To make fair judgements about matters which affect life chances, like mathematics achievement, I am led to a number of recommendations:

First, teachers could incorporate systematic self-criticism into their casual judgements, informed by awareness of how they form such judgements. This could go some way to preventing hasty decision-making, or decisions based on a selection of evidence influenced by initial or out-standingly strong impressions. The staffroom talk of one primary school I visited was full of discussion about alternative ways to interpret the actions of various students whose language and cultural knowledge was very new. One way to develop this is to ask 'could I be mistaken?' when reviewing incidents in a lesson, perhaps with a colleague from another school, or a teaching assistant, or someone who teaches the same student for a very different subject. In the Japanese practice of shared, systematic lesson study, teachers are commonly asked to explain their oral, informal, responses to individuals' ideas.

Second, schools could incorporate systematic examination of teachers' judgements, including exploration of other possibilities, into their decision-making. This could enhance the professionalism to include criticism as well as experience. Morgan's (1998) study of different teachers' reactions to the same pieces of written work could provide a model for such exploration.

Third, judgements can be made by more than one person, from more than one source of evidence. For example, students could present work to a panel of teachers and outsiders, or could collate a portfolio of various pieces of work plus video clips of discussions in which they have taken part for assessment.

Fourth, irreversible decisions and actions based on teachers' judge-ments, such as setting, test-level entry, curriculum limitations, could be systemically avoided. This would reduce the long-term effects of flawed decisions and might also generate flexible expectations of learners by teachers, parents and learners themselves. If teachers work as teams, even when teaching segregated groups, they could develop complementary pro-grammes of study between which it is possible to move without disruption. Test-level entries could be decided by students and teachers together, perhaps with the decisions being left to the last possible moment so that levels become outcomes, rather than targets, of learning. One school I know about leaves entry-level decisions until the spring of the GCSE year, mean-while teaching every student at an aspirational level.

Finally, cultures of individualism, judgement, selection and elitism in school mathematics could be replaced with cultures of professional self-doubt and an open-minded approach to the potential achievement of all. Models of teachers as habitual researchers of their own practice, and networking between teachers to provide critical friends, are helpful in supporting this shift here, but will not necessarily challenge orthodoxy.

Moderation as a mechanism for ensuring equity

What could be put in the place of casual judgements? Teachers' judgements and assessments, where these have to be made, could be moderated by systems which:

- are about mathematics rather than character and behaviour;
- use a range of methods of assessment;
- use and interpret criteria about mathematical learning;
- include interpretation of learners' work by more than one person;
- consider a range of work (oral, practical, exploratory, technical);
- examine judgements for bias.

Such developments would enhance the professional life of mathematics teachers, and improve mathematics teaching and learning. In the busy life of schools, where are the places and times for these moderations to take place? I set out with my trusty notebook and high ideals to observe some teachers' meetings which were called 'moderation' meetings.

The discussions in the book so far imply that within-school moderation processes have four overt purposes relating to justice:

- to agree interpretation of mathematical criteria being used for assessment purposes;
- to agree interpretations of the mathematics in a range of learners' work;
- to scrutinize individual teachers' assessments against criteria;
- to examine the effects of teachers' informal judgements to ensure that no one is being further disadvantaged.

Further functions of such meetings could include monitoring overall standards between teachers, identifying teaching and learning weaknesses and strengths within a team of colleagues, and attending to external validity and accountability. The process of coming to agreement could also act as a mechanism for giving confidence to teachers who may feel vulnerable when exposed to inspection by outsiders, through building a community which agrees on the standards it sets and maintains.

At the end of the study reported in earlier chapters I gained access to seven 'moderation' meetings in a range of secondary and primary schools. They turned out to be of a variety of kinds with a variety of stated aims. They were all based on grading learners' written work against national, statutory, standards and all had an element of high stakes. This means that decisions were going to affect a school-leaving award, or the transfer of information about individuals between schools, or the curriculum a learner would be offered in future. All the meetings focused on one common written task. Although the meetings yielded an immense amount of interesting data, some of it quite worrying, I will focus on the role of teachers' individual judgements in the process to see if indeed these meetings provided a forum for moderating them in terms of justice.

I tried to use an observation pro-forma which related to the findings of previous chapters so I could see how teachers used their evidence for judgements in such meetings. This schedule proved completely inappropriate; none of the methods teachers had reported using to form their judgements were brought to the table for discussion during such meetings. Instead I made notes about topics discussed and also recorded occasional verbatim remarks. Copies of the notes were returned to each school within a few days of the meeting, and one school asked me to summarize their discussion and comment on its comparability to other meetings I had visited. Apart from the latter school, which had used me explicitly as a monitor, all the schools agreed that the notes, though terse and requiring some elaboration from me, were a fair record of the proceedings.

On examining the notes it was obvious that there was little evidence to analyse. Factors contributing to teachers' informal judgements had not been systematically professionally and critically examined in any of the meetings. However, teachers' judgements *did* play a role in the meetings, but it was a very different one.

Interpretation of criteria

This purpose dominated all of the meetings. The primary schools were reaching understandings of what was meant by externally produced criteria, while the secondary schools were trying to fit their own constructions of mathematical knowledge and processes to the given criteria, not without criticism. Both of these approaches attend to the criteria for equity and fairness I have discussed above in that teachers were reaching agreement about common usage of criteria.

Interpretation of the mathematics in a range of learners' work

Discussion in all the meetings focused on specific pieces of written work, rather than a range of work. This gave teachers a common experience to talk about, and much of the discussion was about general issues which had arisen through their consideration of particular work. All schools were ready to give credit for any mathematics which was contained in the learners' work, whether it was intended in setting the task or not, so long as they were sure it represented the learner's own level of understanding.

In general, these meetings attempted to validate interpretations of work, but most were limited to written work produced in particular circumstances, namely special assessment tasks. There were no instances of moderation of the kinds of observational evidence which teachers use for the informal judgements and which were sometimes used to support what was said. For instance, in one of the secondary schools it was suggested that one learner had 'got the formula from a friend' but no one asked for evidence of that; the onus seemed to be on some, but not all, learners to convince the teachers it was their own work. For example, teachers expected to see signs of how a formula had been derived, possibly from a difference pattern, which shows 'insight into the general principle'.

Scrutiny of individual teachers' assessments against criteria

None of the meetings scrutinized individual teachers' assessments in any systematic way; where this had been done it had taken place before the meeting as paired marking of written work, or through discussions. During some meetings individual teachers asked for advice about particular difficulties they had encountered in reaching decisions. There was usually a clear expectation that teachers would scrutinize their own assessments afresh in the light of the discussions at the meeting.

Examining the effects of teachers' informal judgements

There was no examination of the effects of teachers' informal judgements in any of the meetings, but there were several ways in which they influenced the meetings.

In one school it was agreed that a rather uncommunicative learner had probably made a deliberate decision to work in a particular way, thus, revealing himself to be a systematic thinker. One teacher remarked 'you'll think differently about him in future', and the learner's teacher replied 'definitely I will'. So learners' work during assessment tasks does have the potential to inform a teacher's views of their mathematics in general.

In one secondary school a teacher commented that she had used her own previous judgements to inform a decision. Another secondary teacher, in another school, said that her previous knowledge of a learner gave her a 'quick way into the meaning' of a piece of written work. Another teacher spoke of 'gut reaction' and assessing the 'overall feel' of a portfolio of work. It was worrying that none of these statements was questioned or challenged, particularly the last which is about high-stakes assessment. One teacher wanted to know 'what my best mathematicians can do' in order to monitor the rest of her assessments, and another said 'this must be a grade A, it's my top student'.

In one school the meeting agreed that no learners in a particular class could be 'expected to achieve anything on level 3 or above at Key Stage 3'. In another school it was also said of a group that 'they weren't going to get anything on a 3 or above because they were a special needs group'. In both of these cases, the best work was awarded a 3 and no discussion of a possible 4 took place.

Explanations of individual results included 'he works slowly' and 'she doesn't do well in tests' and 'he's one of my brighter ones'. In one school it was agreed that it was important to know what previous teachers had said, and also to know what the expectations of previous teachers and schools had been, in order to assign a level.

Far from being a place where individual judgements would be critically examined, these meetings were places where individual judgements placed ceilings or floors on the range of possible levels assigned to learners' work.

Several of the above instances relate to explanations of low achievement by comparing them to low expectations. Again it was worrying that this kind of input was not questioned or challenged. Perhaps the interpretations of the criteria were not clear, or agreements about what constitutes evidence of achievement are not clear, or the idea that mathematical achievement can be reduced to a list of hierarchical criteria is itself flawed. Teachers trying to make sense of a flawed system seem to be prepared to accept non-criteria-related evidence through shared professional understandings with colleagues. Teachers' judgements had the status of undisputed evidence in such meetings, rather than of testable evidence, and this generates double jeopardy since they have already limited the levels of achievement available to certain learners. The multiplier effect of making positive and negative distinctions between people, which lead to more positive and negative distinctions being made, is not challenged.

Changes in assessment regimes can edit this kind of decision-making out of the process, but it still shows that teachers can confuse targets and expectations with actual achievement in a regime of 'levelization'. After the formal study I found a school in which levels were awarded by starting at the highest available and working downwards, explaining at each stage why the student did not yet meet the description. After the group had rested at a particular level, discussion would follow about what would have to be done to achieve a level higher, and whether there were any signs of this or not. Unfortunately this is a time-consuming process and more often teachers construct encapsulated, workable meanings of what is meant by a level. These derive from an implicit dialogue between statements, experience and exemplification.

Telling the difference between social and mathematical behaviour

I said earlier that I would return to the question of separating mathematics learning and mathematics-related actions from other aspects of identity and behaviour and why it was important to try to do that. At the time I did this research I wanted to know, among other things, why teachers describe individuals as characters when asked about their mathematics. I claimed in Chapter 2 that this is significantly due to a lack of language for describing mathematical learning, and separating mathematical actions from other behaviour helped to reveal this gap in our knowledge.

But more is involved. Imagine a child whose first response to being asked to work on a task on his own is to go and sharpen a pencil. Lay this image alongside tasks you perform yourself when it is time to do work on your own. Perhaps this is work avoidance; perhaps it is preparation of appropriate tools; perhaps it is mental preparation, a buffer between one arena for action and another; perhaps it has elements of all these and is now a ritual. A distinction between social behaviour and mental action becomes impossible to make; all an observer can do is describe the behaviour but not imbue it with purpose and meaning (as I have tried to do when telling stories and describing events in this book). Perhaps the child cannot imbue it with purpose either, except to say 'this is how I start work'. To say 'I need to sharpen my pencil before I start work' would be dangerous because an adult could then ask 'why?' – and there may be no answer. Is this action social, cognitive, affective, intuitive or what? None and all of these, yet it is by trying to make these distinctions while seeking for multiple interpretations that I learnt how impossible it has to be. Rather than chastising teachers for using social signals to decide who is 'good' or 'weak' at mathematics we could see, instead, unhelpful behaviour as an expression of cognitive confusion or disaffection. But it is a short step from there to putting all the least motivated, worst-behaving learners in the 'lowest' sets – a decision which helps neither them, nor other low-achieving learners, nor teachers.

All the time teachers spend on making distinctions between learners for external purposes would be useful if, at the same time, it was informing their teaching. In the next chapter I shall show how learners in a 'bottom set', being taught by a well-intentioned teacher, were able to show themselves capable of much more sophisticated mathematical thought than was being nurtured in their lessons. The process of deciding these students should be in a bottom set did not simultaneously provide information about their full capabilities.

6 Thinking mathematically in low-attaining groups[1]

In Chapter 2 I showed that, although learners' personal traits dominated teachers' descriptions of learners, it is possible for teachers to recognize and value some mathematically specific ways of thinking. I described in Chapter 3 how teachers form views of learners, and developed this idea critically in Chapter 4 to show how significant differences in the way teachers do this can lead to very different treatments of learners. This was all quite general, so in Chapter 5 I described the process in more detail, showing how even a caring, fair-minded and self-critical teacher could, nevertheless, construct questionable judgements about learners which might lead to inequitable treatment. In this chapter I will offer a more accessible and functional language about doing mathematics, and show that learners in a very disadvantaged group were all able to demonstrate mathematical ways of thinking. This contrasts with 'normal' practices in which low-attaining learners are taught simplified mathematics. I argue for a new mindset based on proficiencies of thinking rather than deficiencies of knowledge; thinking abilities ought to be nurtured, rather than left to atrophy while focusing on mundane content. Nurturing mathematical thinking is a job requiring skills and techniques which come from a structural understanding of mathematics.

'These learners' cannot ...

It is common to hear teachers saying in staffrooms that 'these learners cannot think for themselves' and 'these learners have short memories' or 'these learners cannot concentrate'.

With some exceptions, namely those who have neurophysiological problems, these statements are unlikely to be true, since many can

---

[1] An earlier version of some of the material in this chapter appeared in Watson (2002c).

remember copious facts which relate to interests such as football or pop music, and can indeed concentrate for long periods on computer games or the plots of soap operas. It occurred to me that learners may not be being offered opportunities to think, remember and concentrate so get out of the habit of doing so in mathematics lessons, indeed they may not know *how* to do these things in mathematics lessons. There is also huge social pressure and support for remembering football facts or focusing on a computer screen, and much less social pressure or support for focusing in mathematics lessons.

'Boring' lessons

Observation of many mathematics lessons aimed at low-achieving learners, together with the research done by Boaler *et al.* (2000), among others, confirms that many such lessons frequently deal with simplified mathematics, broken down into step-by-step processes, offered in short chunks, or packed with practical features such as colouring in, cutting out, tidying up and so on. Typical arguments for this approach are persuasive and commonplace. For example, it is said that learners who cannot concentrate for long periods need frequent changes of task; they grow bored if you do not change the topic every lesson; they need activity which uses their energy because many are so-called 'kinaesthetic' learners; they need the quick success which comes from getting things right easily; and so on. The irony of these arguments is that if you follow these guidelines low attainment is the inevitable *result*, as well as the reason. It is simply impossible to learn mathematics if one is constantly changing topic, or task, or doing related but irrelevant tasks, or only doing the easy bits, or being praised for trivial performance.

A problem with a fragmented, mechanistic approach to teaching mathematics is that learners who find mathematics hard are thus often taught in ways which make it hardest for them to learn it. Simultaneously, students who get stuck at the lower levels of the National Curriculum in secondary school have to churn through content requiring a high level of accuracy and technical recall, while peers are doing work which is much more interesting and in which technical inaccuracies such as minor algebraic mistakes, dropped negative signs, and forgotten multiples are tolerated as less important than overall conceptual understanding.

When I am trying to do something which is hard for me and someone then changes the task, or comes and helps me do it, or makes me stop and listen to their advice, I am quite likely to give up trying. In my own work I can arrange things so I am not interrupted – redirect the phone, close the door, ask someone to go away and so on. I can also repeatedly return to a task which has proved too hard for me at first, having developed new approaches in the interim. I can make a mess of things and sort them out later. Although in mathematics I am not a 'low attainer' I still think my own experience is informative. In some areas of intellectual life, notably learning other languages, I am very unskilled and lack confidence. I have indeed failed to concentrate, but when I am in other countries I begin to get more confident and articulate. I claim to know something, therefore, about low attainment and failure to learn. More than this, as I said in Chapter 1, if I am guided by the claim that people are much more the same than they are different, then what I observe about myself is a starting point for understanding others.

What I observe about myself tells me that lessons with features like those described above can indeed be trivial, boring and a waste of time. It is no surprise that learners often describe them as such (Cooper and McIntyre 1996; Boaler 1997) and often set up counter-cultures within the classroom in order to make them more interesting (Houssart 2004) or become passive, submissive and helpless in order to cope (Peterson *et al.* 1993). Maybe calling such lessons 'boring' is not a fault of the adolescent who is saying so, but an accurate description.

'Helping' learners by simplifying mathematics

Teaching mathematics to low-attaining learners in secondary school is often done by simplifying the mathematics until it becomes a sequence of small smooth steps which can be easily traversed. Even in exploratory situations, little is expected beyond generating data. Frequently the teacher will 'take the learner through the chain of reasoning' and the learner merely fills in the gaps with arithmetical answers, or low-level recall of facts and so on (Pimm 1987: 53; Watson 2002d). Achievement in such situations is identified as getting to the end of the work, completing something successfully, filling in the required partial answers and maintaining some degree of concentration throughout. But none of these definitions of success necessarily indicates that anything new has been learnt. All they signal is engagement with expected classroom behaviour and observable completion of clerical work. Learning, at best, might be characterized by the reproduction of algorithms, so long as the learner knows what algorithm to apply.

A colleague reports asking three students in a 'bottom set' what they were doing. On probing a little, he found they could anticipate the tiny variations in subject matter which would be dealt with on the next four pages of the textbook. They did not appear to be interested in this, saying that 'We have to work slowly'.

This kind of path-smoothing is unlikely to lead to learning on its own, since it deliberately reduces a problem to what the learner can do already in terms the learner already recognizes. No cognitive processing is required. Learning for higher-attaining learners includes deciding what to do and ring the steps together – but for lower-attaining learners a teacher has already made these decisions! Furthermore, the learner is re- ɪ the view that if she sits there doing nothing for long enough, the ːhe teacher will provide the appropriate task transformations which ͵ task to something straightforward (Holt 1964; Bauersfeld 1988).

is an example of such a task transformation. It took place in a ͵eous Year 7 class in which learners were using fractions and percentages of quantities interchangeably to experience shifting between equivalent representations. At one table there were four students working with a classroom assistant because they were seen to need special support. His strategy for helping them find 75 per cent of 16 was to say to them: 'Can you see that 25 per cent is 4 and then what you have to do is times 3 by 4, so what is 3 times 4? Three lots of four? That's four add four ... add four?' A learner replied 'Eleven, no twelve', and was praised for completing the work. In this case the overall task was transformed into a multiplication task, which was further transformed into adding. The result of this was that an 11-year-old was praised for adding $4 + 4 + 4$. I am not saying that he was or was not capable of more, but that he was not given the opportunity to engage in more interesting mathematics. In fact, this incident, far from allowing the learner to take part in the lesson, effectively excluded him from the work the others were doing, which was thinking about relationships between some common fractions and percentages.

The assistant's claim was that this was all this student could do, and his aim was to help him feel he had achieved something by getting a correct answer. But students can also become incapable of doing more with that kind of help. When adolescents look around themselves, as they are wont to do, to see how they measure up against other people they are not easily going to be convinced that they have achieved anything by performing the simplest addition. This second claim would provide some sort of argument for separating learners so that they do not know how little they are achieving compared to others – but low-attaining learners are not fools. One such learner said plaintively to researchers: 'We've still got to learn' (Boaler and Wiliam 2001). In a school near my work, students were so aware of the different opportunities to learn they would have in different sets that one who had been 'demoted' wrote to her teacher, accompanied by a beautiful cartoon of two girls crying: 'I am very upset that you have chose [sic] B and K over me and my friend. I would like a letter to say sorry and you to move me and my friend back into your class.'

If learners have not realized just how far down the pecking order they have been positioned, they can find out by looking at their predicted GCSE results. As if to rub salt in the wound, one foundation-level textbook asks this question:

> St Aidan's School is ordering Key Maths GCSE books. They order Foundation, Intermediate and Higher levels in the ratio 4 : 5 : 2. They order 176 books altogether. How may of each type of book do they order? (Key Maths 1998: 336)

In contrast, I recall an incident in my own teaching which brought me face to face with the idea of diverse proficiency.

> I was teaching a Year 9 (13-year-olds) all-attainment class a few weeks into their first term in the school. They had been working on this task:
>
> > On a coordinate grid you are only allowed to move to the right or upwards. You can do this in any order you like. How many routes are there from the origin to the point (1,1)? How many routes to the points (1,2), (2,1), (1,3), and so on?
>
> After about 10 minutes I gathered all the students around the board and asked them what they had found so far. Silently at the back of the group sat Paul, who had been described to me as having special needs. When he had entered school aged five he did not talk, and still at 13 he could neither read nor write. After several students had described how they had counted routes systematically, and deduced a sort of symmetry emerging, I challenged them to find a method which allowed them to work out how many routes there would be to get to any point, for example (6,7). Paul said immediately: 'If I knew how many it would take to get to (5,7) and (6,6), I could add them to get (6,7).' This reply would have been a pleasant surprise from any student, but from Paul it was doubly so because it was his first utterance in such a group. This was a turning point for me as a teacher, and for him as a learner. My expectations of his mathematics had been biased by what I had been told, yet he was able to grasp spatial situations with an abnormally skilful level of generality and structure. I would have to work on my expectations and Paul would have to work on mathematics through spatial representations.

But I need more than criticism and personal experience to back up my discomfort with normal practice. Is my argument based on anything more than a desire for equality, which might be misplaced?

Mel Ainscow and David Tweddle, who have extensive experience of working with low-attaining youngsters, wrote a book in 1979 which seems to support the step-by-step, path-smoothing model. They advocated the use of detailed learning objectives to structure the teaching, learning and assessment of low-attaining students (Ainscow and Tweddle 1979). By 1988, however, they realized that such detailed approaches could have unintended consequences of narrowing the curriculum, segregating students and increasing learner passivity (Ainscow and Tweddle 1988: 29). They replaced narrow objectives with a more flexible, positive, proficiency-based approach which encouraged holistic tasks and more open-minded assessment. But mathematics, seen as hierarchical and abstract, might not fit their transformed views. The first book gives examples of carefully defined mathematical objectives; the second book gives no mathematical advice. Do low-attaining learners *really* have any useful proficiencies in mathematics? Or is it kinder to smooth the path and provide them with less challenging tasks?

Proficiency in what?

I decided to find out more about the nature of the thinking some typical 14-year-old 'bottom set' learners were able to do in their normal lessons – could they think at a level higher than recall and reproduction during their ordinary classroom mathematics activities? I contacted a school to see if I could observe and participate in mathematics lessons.

Analysis of classroom interactive episodes revealed many instances of mathematical thinking of a kind which was not normally exploited, required or expected in their classes. I shall describe five episodes, comparing the learners' thinking to that usually described as 'advanced'.

Before going into the school classroom to look for something more than repetition, recall and practice of routines, I needed to develop some clear ideas of what I might be looking for. I was not expecting to find examples of higher-level knowledge. Instead, I was interested in signs of the kinds of mental activity which could, if harnessed and developed, aid learning mathematics. At the time I thought of this as 'mathematical thinking', as if there are identifiable ways of thinking which can be called 'mathematical'. There are some useful descriptions of such thinking. Some of them concentrate on problem-solving heuristics (Pólya 1962; Schoenfeld 1985; Romberg 1993). Other descriptions of 'mathematical thinking' relate more directly to the development of conceptual understanding in mathematics (Krutetskii 1976; Tall 1991) such as being able to grasp structures, being mentally flexible, having an inclination to generalize, a memory for the characteristics of members of classes, and the ability to create valid shortcuts. Others describe overarching features of mathematical engagement such as exemplifying, generalizing, conjecturing, justifying (Mason *et al.* 1982).

One might think it is irrelevant to refer to these skills in a book about low attainment, since they all relate to advanced mathematicians, but most of these are also ordinary ways of thinking and problem-solving which happen to play a specially important part in mathematics. For instance, it is common to exemplify in order to illustrate complex descriptions; it is common to switch from one representation to another, such as when one draws a map to accompany verbal directions; it is common to generalize, such as when one uses words to describe classes of objects. Thus, it is plausible that we could expect to find the roots of this explicitly mathematical behaviour in most human beings, even those labelled and classified as low-attaining learners. Consequently, I felt I could look for evidence of these powers being employed in work on elementary mathematics, rather than purely on advanced concepts. I therefore set out to look for evidence that low-attaining learners could:

- identify and use patterns to generalize;
- recognize abstract features through reflecting on processes;
- exemplify and counter-exemplify in ways which do more than imitate what a teacher has offered, since this implies some level of generalization;
- develop and use images of concepts;
- change and manipulate representations;
- perhaps work with abstractions and relations, which is generally a feature of advanced study.

(By the way, cutting to the chase, this list turns out to be very useful in designing tasks for all learners. Most school learners can do all these things, given the opportunity.)

A study to find proficiency

The school I used for this study had an intake skewed towards below-average attainment levels. They had recently been concerned about their underachievement compared to national standards. They restructured the curriculum to raise standards through providing more advanced content to all learners, and had paid no special attention to teaching style or meta-cognitive factors such as self-assessment. Most of the teaching was of a traditional, text-based type. I was permitted to work in a non-intervention-ist way with a Year 9 low-attaining group, because I 'wouldn't do any harm' to the school's attempts to raise standards.

Their usual teacher, called Jane in this book, was a 'learning needs' specialist who was assigned to the class because she knew the learners well through her general support and pastoral work. As well as having low achievement in mathematics, the learners had a mixture of patchy school histories, behaviour problems, personal difficulties outside school, low self-esteem and disaffection. They were normally taught through a mixture of practical activities, repetitive exercises and practice of number skills. Oral tests were regularly used to monitor the accumulation of skills, facts and their application in simple contexts. Jane talked of 'settling' learners at the beginnings of lessons, offering step-by-step approaches to answer routine questions, giving them 'something to do', and 'keeping it simple'. Even with the school's shift to more demanding curriculum content, these learners were given very elementary mathematics. During the lessons there were very few class discussions; learners sat at some distance from each other so that they could not disrupt each other's work; there were two support assistants in the room; a calm and quiet tone was the norm; learners were usually compliant and were treated kindly if they were disturbed or disturbing. Jane cared passionately for her students, providing them with human warmth, safety, and generous attention. Lessons and teaching style seemed to be selected in the belief that such learners should not handle anything challenging or complex, cognitively or socially.

I intended to observe lessons, record learners' responses and comments in field notes, discuss mathematics with the learners in the naturalistic setting of their classroom and normal tasks and write notes, verbatim where possible, of what they said. It was possible in every lesson to arrange individual interactions with some learners and keep systematic records of these so that I interacted with everyone more or less equally. In addition, Jane sometimes let me teach the whole class and keep records of what happened. The prompts I used, both during one-to-one interaction and whole-class teaching, were about seeing and generalizing from patterns, using and generating examples, communicating a sense of mathematical concepts and describing underlying structures. In other words, I was prompting them to do the things in the list above. These prompts had been developed previously from observations and experiences in a wide variety of teaching contexts (Watson and Mason 1998; Bills *et al.* 2004). I would ask:

- 'What is the same or different about … ?' (encouraging learners to give attention to pattern and classification).
- 'Describe what happens in general' (nudging learners through generalization towards abstraction).
- 'Can you give me an example from your own experience?' or 'Give me an example which fulfils certain conditions' (prompting exemplification).
- 'Can you show me one which wouldn't work?' (prompting counter-exemplification).
- 'Show me …' or 'tell me …' (eliciting information about images and other aspects of their understanding).
- 'Can you show me this using a diagram/letters/numbers/graphs?' (prompting flexible use of representations).
- 'If this is an answer, what might the question be?' (shifting the focus onto structures rather than answers).

My approach was usually to focus on interactions in the teaching context which already existed in the research classroom, giving extra prompts where possible and relevant. I wanted to see if these learners *could* act in a cognitively sophisticated way with mathematics. If they could, then it would make sense to question the use of teaching styles which avoid the use of such thinking with similar learners.

I analysed my notes to identify any learners' remarks which might show the features of mathematical thinking in which I was interested. I tried to analyse carefully; I wanted so strongly to find evidence of good thinking that I had to impose a very rigorous watch on my interpretations. But at the same time I was aware that in the teaching profession we usually interpret the actions of those labelled 'high attainers' as positively as we can, and those of 'low attainers' negatively. There is a balance here which needs to be redressed. As far as possible I tried to focus on episodes in which I found it impossible to find alternative interpretations. For instance, if a learner gave me an example of something, it is tautological to say that the learner was able to exemplify in that situation. If a learner made a general state-ment, then I assumed that some generalizing *had* taken place, even if I did not know *how* it had taken place or what had prompted it. In fact, the only focus of observation not directly connected to something one could see or hear incontrovertibly was the idea of developing and using images. It is pos-sible to develop and use images without expressing these, but explicating one's images through diagrams or speech, or even arm-waving, cannot be done unless there is an image to be so expressed. In other words, there were episodes which revealed the existence of images to me, but as with any observational research, there may have been other images for which I never saw evidence.

As a result of analysis of episodes after each lesson, I planned prompts to use in the next lesson, and decided on whom to focus these. For example, after one lesson I found that every learner except one had given an example, either prompted or unprompted, during the lesson. Exemplification being a characteristic of mathematical thinking, I decided to ask the 'missing' learner directly to give an example, when appropriate, in the next lesson. In this way I systematically explored evidence of the types of response iden-tified above, in the context of their normal tasks.

I chose the following five episodes to illustrate important aspects of mathematical thinking.

1   *Pattern; creating shortcuts; generalization; understanding structure; exemplification.* Learners had been given a sheet of questions about the seven times table, having been given similar ones for other times tables before.[2] There were four columns of calculations to do. They were supposed to fill in the answers. Here is a part of it:

---

[2]   This is where I first began to think about some of the ideas presented in Chapter 2.

$5 \times 7 =$	$7 \times 5 =$	$35/5 =$	$35/7 =$
$6 \times 7 =$	$7 \times 6 =$	$42/6 =$	$42/7 =$
$7 \times 7 =$		$49/7 =$	
$8 \times 7 =$	$7 \times 8 =$	$56/8 =$	$56/7 =$

In response to 'show me' requests it became clear that learners soon realized, if they had not known before, that answers to the first and second columns could be obtained by the shortcut of adding 7 to vertical sequences. Answers to the third were all 7, and answers to the last were the natural numbers in order. That is, learners had 'spotted' and used vertical patterns which enabled them to complete the worksheet. When I asked 'what happens in general?' they generalized from their experience of similar mathematical tasks and reported that this was how they had filled in similar sheets before. To draw their attention to the structure which I saw in the horizontal patterns, I gave them '$23 \times 7 = 161$' as the start of a row and asked them to finish the rest. All could do this after some thought, although their previous patterns working down the page did not help them in this case. I prompted two learners to make up their own examples of other rows to illustrate the structure further, and they managed to do this. They were able to shift to observing less obvious, structural patterns, and to exemplify and use them. All that had been needed was the indication that more could be found by looking 'across the grain' of the way they naturally worked (Watson 2000).

2   *Finding and explaining structure; generalizing; abstraction; shifting representations.* June was drawing a square in the normal orientation on a coordinate grid and noting the coordinates. I do not know if she would have reflected on the coordinates if she had not been prompted to do so, but once prompted to say what was the same and what different about the coordinates she was able immediately to say which ordinates were equal. I asked her if this pattern of matching coordinates would always be true for a square ('what would happen in general?') and she replied 'yes'. She then explained without prompting why it worked, so I asked if she could say it using algebra. Although the expressions she developed depended on specified coordinates at one vertex they were in other respects generalizations of such squares, that is families of squares sharing a vertex. So she said 'if this is (2,3) then this vertex will be 2 plus *a* and this one 3 plus *a*', where someone else might have said 'if this is (*a*, *b*) then this one will be *a* plus *c* and this one *b* plus *c*'.

She had been able to make a transition, on the basis of one example and application of knowledge of squares, from a specific case to a more general symbolic representation, and to justify this. In this situation, for this student, expressing a generalization in algebra seemed easy and obvious, and, what is more, the generalization was made on the basis of one example and knowledge of structure, as mathematicians do, rather than on a collection of examples as is often encouraged in schools. This episode suggested to me that the practice of getting learners to generate lots of numerical examples to generalize is not necessarily helpful, and might stifle the more insightful use of individual cases, as shown by June.

3   *Using pattern; classification; creating a new concept; working with relations; recognizing and using new entities.* Learners had been given a printed blank coordinate grid and a long sequence of coordinate pairs which they had to plot. They would then have to join the points they had plotted to make a shape. I think the final picture was going to be an ostrich or something similar – not at all appropriate for this age group! All learners except Almira were plotting points in the order given. She had restructured the task by picking out all adjacent coordinate pairs which would give the same vectors when joined. She knew nothing about vectors and had effectively invented the concept for herself. When questioned, she pointed out that if the first number went up and the other down by one, she would draw:

If both numbers went up by one she would draw:

She could predict other vectors similarly.

Almira had created a more complex task by using pattern, similarity, and classification. This led me to suppose that others in the room would also be able to work in this way but may not have thought to do so. By asking a few other students to look at similarities in the lines joining adjacent points, they came to look at the task as a different sequence of actions: classifying patterns in the coordinate pairs, selecting and drawing the similar vectors corresponding to the classifications. This done, they were able to reverse the process and predict generalities about coordinate pairs which would arise from similar lines on the grid. For example, to get a line which slanted downwards with a particular slope (these learners did not know about gradients) they could show that the x coordinate (not using this language) of the second pair had to be one more than that of the first pair, and the y coordinate had to be two less, or three less etc. Some could write this as (a, b), $(a + 1, b - 2)$ when given a and b as a starting-place. Inspired by Almira's insight, I had ratcheted the aims of the task up from mundane completion to classifying and expressing general features of the classes, and the learners with whom I had done this were well able to respond.

4   *Exemplification; working with relations; working with structure.* Learners had been using flow diagrams to calculate outputs of compound functions involving the four basic operations. For example:

They were asked to make up some hard examples of their own for the whole class to do. Most learners' idea of complexity was to use either more operations or bigger numbers, which is a common response. Then Boris suggested constructing one in which the operations and output are known and the input has to be found. Andrew then gave one in which input and output were given but the last operation was missing. These two learners seemed to be working with the relations rather than the numbers and operations. They saw the 'givens' of the structure as something they could vary, rather than following the template of teacher-given questions.

5   *Giving examples and counter-examples; having a concept image.* Elvira had been asked to round 83 to the nearest 10. She replied, without further prompting: '80, but if you had asked me about 87 I would have said 90'. In this case, the learner seemed to have had an image of what it means to round numbers and had used the image to generate a counter-example in order to indicate to the teacher that she knew more than had been asked.

These learners, even in the extant climate of procedural, prescriptive and unchallenging mathematics, were able to demonstrate collectively several characteristics normally associated with successful mathematics learners *without being taught explicitly to do so*. Indeed, the only extra factor in their lessons had been the presence of an extra adult who posed certain kinds of question, and sometimes passed their ideas around the classroom.

Proficiencies in mathematical thinking

The examples above collectively illustrate nearly all the features of mathematical thinking for which I was searching, and in some cases go further, because the learners were able to justify their ideas. They also illustrate strategies for adapting the task to prompt deeper thought: looking 'across the grain'; conjecturing a generalization from one example; classifying tasks; varying givens and structures.

Exemplification

Another feature which arose frequently in this classroom was the use of examples to explain and explore the mathematical topic. In episodes 1, 3 and 4 learners demonstrated their willingness to generate and use special examples. Since exemplification requires a sense of structure, domain or generality, the teacher can help learners shift to more complex cognitive levels by asking for examples. In episode 5 a counter-example, or an alternative example, was given voluntarily.

Symbolization

Also worth noting is that, in episodes 2 and 3, learners who articulated the relationships found it easy to write them algebraically. This is not a new claim (Chazan 1996), but it is important to see it at work when a teacher makes encouraging noises at the right moment. Indeed, all the learners in this study showed that they were able to make mathematical sense from mathematical experience. All were able to participate in learning interactions which were not based on simplification, step-by-step approaches, learnt procedures, but which expected conjecture, exemplification, generalization, reflection on pattern and other aspects of advanced mathematical activity.

Structure

When I do mathematics it seems to be the case that, to learn about underlying structure, I have to reorganize my initial approach to a concept by reflecting from another point of view, such as looking at several examples at once, or thinking about the procedures I am using as a general algorithm which can be expressed algebraically. Confident mathematicians do this for themselves; they see generalities and grasp them in several examples; they see global similarities in locally produced examples; they see possible generalities even in single examples. The common experience in episodes 1 and 3 above is that learners were comfortably generating answers through a repetitive activity which took no account of the whole task. In episode 1 the method of generating answers had little relationship to multiplication, which was the intended mathematical context! I have called this kind of low-level generative activity 'going with the grain'; it is easy, obvious, can lead to rapid completion – and splinters! Once learners' attention is directed *across* the grain, so that they observe a cross-section of their work, using the generating strands of activity as raw material for contemplation, they have the opportunity to see structure and hence transform or reorganize their view of the concept. It is harder to cut, less obvious, but stronger. I realized that many learners can make this shift, but that the presence of a teacher who recognizes its power is vital. It is not enough to be encouraging learners to look for patterns, using them to generate more examples, or expressing them in general terms, because this can lead to giving praise for fairly trivial mathematics. The mathematical quality of the generalization is important.

Changing from deficiency to proficiency

Because of these findings I was led to claim that some potentially powerful mathematical talents of these learners were unrecognized and unused in the teaching of mathematics. This classroom was not unusual in the way mathematics was normally taught, so it was likely that similar findings would arise elsewhere if observers and teachers are attuned to noticing and prompting features of mathematical thinking during ordinary tasks.

But the simplicity of the mathematical contexts also needs to be considered. Can it really be said that these learners were doing mathematical thinking, when the contexts were so simple? Can it be deduced that they might be able to do harder mathematics just because they can work in sophisticated ways on simple mathematics?

And what about the teacher, who was so caring and well intentioned? How could features of her good practice, which enabled learners to feel calm, comfortable and unthreatened, be reconciled with the challenges, risks and uncertainties which are associated with mathematical conjecture, attempts at abstraction, and exploration which sometimes inevitably leads to frustration and, possibly, more failure?

It is unlikely that a *deficiency* agenda which focuses on remediation and repetition will provide insight into the questions just posed. Yet this is common practice with low-achieving learners everywhere. The provision of low-level activities accompanied by low-level expectations can only limit learners and might lead to disaffection, disruption and disability.

It is inevitable that we have to work against a language and discourse of deficiency since we identify 'low attainment' according to some expected average norm which other learners have in common. Yet dwelling on general lack can draw attention away from individual capabilities. The effect is to label the *learner* negatively as one who has a complex range of deficiencies, rather than merely labelling the *behaviour*. Skills-focused approaches to directing teaching rarely describe the competent or incompetent mathematical *thinking* which might accompany such skills. In some well-intentioned approaches, low attainment in comparison to others is expected even within the raised attainment of all, so special programmes are set up which, while providing the knowledge, fluency and skills to pass certain high-stakes tests, trap the lowest attaining students into imitative and procedural patterns of response.

An exception to this is provided by the Cognitive Acceleration in Mathematics Education project, and interestingly their evaluations suggest that organizing learners into sets deprives those in lower sets of the full benefits of their approach since such classes contain very few learners who quickly respond to the challenge of cognitively focused tasks (Adhami *et al.* 1998). My experiences with the group above suggest that patience and appropriate tasks are what is required, but perhaps the classroom management issues which arise in underchallenged groups where low expectations have been the norm make the turnaround more complex to handle.

An alternative *proficiency* agenda need not dwell only on the positive aspects of behaviour, motivation or attitude, although those would play a part. It could also recognize and emphasize the thinking skills which learners exhibit and offer opportunities for these to be used to learn mainstream curriculum mathematical concepts. The low-attaining learners in this study were already able to think in ways normally attributed to successful mathematicians; they responded to opportunities and encouragement to use their existing abilities in mathematical ways. These ways included the ability to exemplify, to generalize, to develop and use images, to abstract from experience through reflection on processes, to work with structure, either voluntarily or when helped to do so, to participate in mathematical discussion, to work in complex situations. They did not need training in thinking skills; they needed appropriate tasks and opportunities, and they needed to know *how* to use their skills in mathematics lessons. I was surprised and pleased at how the use of a fairly limited collection of little prompts could so easily unlock learners' insights into their work, even fairly mundane work. But I was in a special position, being able to work one-to-one with learners and not having responsibility for their behaviour as well. Is it possible to transform whole classes of low-attaining learners, with the inevitable social and management problems? This question will be the focus of the final chapters.

7 Approaches to reconstruction: test cramming versus developing proficiency

It is in the inherently conservative nature of systems that the onus is often on those who want things to be different to produce the evidence that the current ways do not work, unless those requiring change have government support. Glenda Lappan, when she was president of the US National Council of Teachers of Mathematics, described rote memorization as a long-running educational experiment which has never worked (Senk and Thompson 2003: 16) and this in itself provides enough justification for trying something new. The onus is seldom on those supporting current methods to show that they *do* work.

In England, about 50 per cent of students fail to achieve the treasured grade C at GCSE, so clearly something is wrong with the prevailing teaching and assessment methods, whatever they may be (Smith 2004). To know what they are in practice, rather than what they are supposed to be in official guidance, we have Ofsted reports. These have to be treated with caution since they compare everything to a standard kind of practice which needs to be questioned. Nevertheless, the Ofsted report on mathematics in secondary schools in 2003–4 says that, in too many schools:

> Teaching and learning styles in post-14 mathematics lessons are often too limited to motivate and engage pupils ... Inflexible setting arrangements in Key Stage 4 lead many pupils to believe that their GCSE goals in mathematics are limited in nature and ambition ... For pupils who achieve lower than average levels at the end of Key Stage 3, subsequent provision or support is not sufficiently tailored to their needs; this then reinforces their fears and fails to rebuild their self belief or self esteem.
>
> (Ofsted 2005: 5)

In Jo Boaler's (1997) book, a teacher she called Jim Cresswell used methods which led to better GCSE results for his students than those in a comparable school, but his teaching was unusual and hard for casual visitors to decipher. Students would be working on extended exploratory projects, consulting with each other and with the teacher in an *ad hoc* manner, and the atmosphere and behaviour in the room were informal and often noisy. His headteacher decided that this kind of teaching would not survive an inspection and eventually Jim left the profession. Despite this, his teaching, or what people deduce about it through Jo's book, has inspired teachers all over the world.

What is the role of this counter-example to the expected 'normal' methods of teaching? As a mathematician I know that the existence of a counter-example means I have to be wary about making the generalization which this counters. Jim Cresswell's case tells me that I cannot say there is a 'best' way to teach – for him, his way was effective. This upsets some people who wish to be more conservative; one mathematician has told me that in this case a counter-example has no value. Far worse, some academics in the USA accused Jo of inventing the data on which her study was based, as if the UK academic standards were so low that she would be awarded a PhD and a thesis prize for fictitious data (Boaler 2002). It is sad that the existence of a teacher in a UK school who had unconventional ways of teaching, and who made a demonstrable difference to his students' achievements, provoked such disbelief and academic hostility.

More commonly, teachers who achieve significantly better results than are seen as normal can be dismissed by others as so special that their methods would not work in other classrooms. The phrases 'that wouldn't work for my kids' or 'you can't do that with these kids' are common enough. Another way to avoid the challenges of change is to evoke curriculum pressure, so that 'there isn't time' to use methods which are not directly focused in content because more topics have to be 'covered'. In particular, learners' lack of progress is often taken as evidence that they need extra teaching to pass tests. A significant part of their school experience is then taken up in cramming for tests so that they pass them at a level which is supposed to show that they are ready for the next stage of the curriculum.

In this chapter, I report briefly on a study about the effects of some test-cramming lessons which were government-funded and then, by contrast, look at some very different approaches to raising achievement.

The 'booster' study[1]

Does teaching designed to improve test performance help students become ready for the next stage of the curriculum? Much attention has been given to the fact that learners transferring from primary to secondary typically make negative progress, in measurable curriculum terms, during the first

---

[1]   Results of this study were first published in Watson (2001a).

few months at their new school. Transfer between schools involves much more than discontinuity of curriculum; it involves social and emotional factors, new peer groups, teachers and environments. It seems reasonable to ask what can be done about this regression, so I decided to look at what happens in a middle school where these factors *do not* affect learners between Years 6 and 7. When problems of transfer between schools do not exist, what can be learnt about attempts to 'boost' achievement of learners who are failing to achieve government targets at the end of Year 6 so that they reach the desired levels to embark on Year 7 work? Public money had been provided for 'booster' classes to try and get 'level 3s' up to 'level 4' (the political target grade). This way of describing learners according to the levels of mathematics they are assumed to have achieved is ubiquitous.

I decided to select learners who had attended booster classes and test them again, 9 months after the original test for which they had received special extra teaching, with the same test paper. After all, if a test result is being used as a measure of 'readiness', their newly acquired knowledge ought to be hanging around for use later. I compared the two versions of their test papers, the official one and the unofficial retest, to see how their achievement had changed, and whether aspects of their mathematical knowledge which might be expected to provide a sound basis for secondary work had, indeed, been retained.

The school I chose had earlier been judged to need improvement and was rigorously following the guidelines and materials produced by the relevant authorities in order to claw its way back to a level of reasonable official achievement. It had been recently reinspected and found to be teaching and organizing its curriculum according to government expectations. Mathematics classes, which had been described as 'good' in the recent inspection, were based on materials provided nationally through official channels of support. The focus was on arithmetic. The teacher was an honours mathematics graduate who had been trained in an institution which is highly placed in initial teacher training league tables and whose lessons had consistently been considered good by inspectors. I mention all this to emphasize that this school was thus operating in full accordance with the official view of 'best' teaching at every level. Over the 2 years which bridged this study the school raised its mathematics achievement level at the end of Year 6 from 34 per cent to 45 per cent and then to 58 per cent at level 4 and above. This, given that teachers and schools quite rightly vary in their practice, was the closest I could get to a situation in which an outsider cannot say 'maybe the teaching was bad' or 'maybe the curriculum did not match the test'. This teacher was under constant intense scrutiny and doing everything he was supposed to do to match teaching style, lesson content, curriculum and test requirements to each other in the prescribed fashion. Shortly after this study, the school was judged to have improved sufficiently to relax this level of scrutiny.

Nine learners who had attended special classes were still available the following February to be tested again. I selected the 'no-calculator' paper because the focus of the original extra lessons was on arithmetic, but in the analysis which follows I am not going to make the simplistic assumption that arithmetical skills are either necessary or sufficient for preparedness for secondary mathematics.

Test results

Each learner's new script was marked according to the original marking scheme. Old and new marks were compared. Levels were calculated on the basis of what a new level would be if the nature of the changes was extrapolated over all three papers. Since there were only nine cases (made anonymous) all this data is presented here in Table 7.1.

Table 7.1: Results of retaking Key Stage 2 SATs

Name	Old marks	New marks	Change of marks	Old level equivalent	New level equivalent	Change of level
Tyrone	33	34	+1	5	5	0
Nyree	24	20	−4	4	3	−1
Dean	21	14	−7	4	3	−1
Mairead	21	18	−3	4	3	−1
Yolande	20	14	−6	4	3	−1
Tamsin	19	18	−1	3	3	0
Wendy	15	17	+2	3	3	0
Karen	14	14	0	3	3	0
Sam	13	15	+2	3	3	0

It can be seen that one learner, Tyrone, probably had not needed to attend these extra classes which were designed to help those on level 3 achieve level 4. Of the four who achieved level 3, two had improved since the test. All those who achieved level 4 had regressed since then to level 3. It is this group which causes most concern. Clearly achievement of level 4 has not been robust and sustainable for these learners at this school when it has been achieved with the help of extra classes. Additionally, none of these learners has progressed significantly since the original tests.

However, this raw information on its own does not offer explanation, and it would be possible to argue that not enough is known about what went on in the extra classes, nor what has been taught since, which might explain the changes in marks and the lack of progress. After all, as I said earlier, the onus is on me as the dissenter to criticize this process rather than on supporters of current orthodoxy to justify it! One expectation might be that some of what was learnt in Year 6 had been forgotten and replaced with what has been learnt in Year 7, some of which has not yet been understood to a sufficient level to answer test questions. What is more robust is that these results illustrate the findings of John Anderson and others (Anderson and Schunn 2000) whose quantitative, psychological, large-scale research approach to learning suggests that teaching to the test is less effective in the medium term than providing repeated experiences over time. Rather than providing 'quick-fix' and 'cure-all' lessons, the focus should be on developing the underlying connections which support learning. The recent provision of 'intervention' lessons which target particularly problematic key ideas in an attempt to get failing learners back on track, much in the way described by Ann Dowker (2005) in her arithmetic recovery programmes, seems to have more potential.

More importantly, perhaps, we need to know whether the learners have a grounding which prepares them for secondary work, and whether it is robust. After all, the attainment of level 4 is only of real value to learners and teachers if it does indeed describe an appropriate starting level for secondary work. In other words, do the marks subsequently lost matter in terms of their preparedness? In order to find out about this, I analysed answers on the old and new tests in detail, and brought to bear knowledge of mathematics and the curriculum to decide what constitutes such grounding. If the testing system and teaching methods are well chosen, regression would only take place in areas which are not crucial to progression at the next stage.

I will use three questions to illustrate the results of this analysis.

Place value

The first is about place value, because, without this knowledge, learners are calculator-dependent for calculating and, more importantly, for estimating, verifying and evaluating answers. In the question learners had to choose, from a given list, two numbers which could be added to make 0.12. Adding decimal numbers involves an understanding of place value on which further arithmetic, including estimation and awareness of the reasonableness of answers, will depend. There was no request to show working, and none of the learners did anything except circle numbers on the printed list.

This was relatively easy to analyse. Tyrone correctly selected 0.07 and 0.05 each time. Tamsin (whose marks went down overall) progressed from choosing 0.7 and 0.5 to choosing 0.07 and 0.05. All other students chose 0.7 and 0.5 on the new test, although three of them had chosen 0.07 and 0.05 correctly the first time. Among those who had achieved level 4, two were wrong both times and two changed from right to wrong.

The apparent understanding of place value and/or addition of decimals, which three had exhibited in the first test, was not robust. Four learners who had achieved the target test level did not have a robust knowledge of place value. Does this matter? It depends very much on what levels of understanding the original three correct answers were based. If they were based solely on a remembered algorithm given by the teacher in order to 'pass' the test, then passing is not a measure of preparedness for further work, since memory can fail. If they were based on insecure understanding then more work may be needed with other representations and mathematical contexts before understanding and memory become secure. This suggests that learning is non-linear. There may be an ebb and flow of competence during the learning process. A test might act like a flypaper, catching hold of passing tentativity rather than collating a picture of static, permanent achievement.

Reading scales

The second question I analysed was a familiar type using a thermometer to represent positive and negative numbers. The two parts of the question involved reading the thermometers, comparing temperatures in two different places and dealing with negative numbers as temperatures fell and rose. The abilities to read scales correctly and to calculate with negative numbers are crucial to secondary mathematics, and reading scales is a skill required outside school, hence I regarded this question as important. Three learners, including two of the higher-achieving learners, were totally wrong on this question, apparently misusing the well-known instruction that 'two negatives make a positive' in order to add when they should have subtracted. Either that, or they could have added two numbers merely in order to do something rather than nothing. Two of the stronger learners did these questions correctly. The rest seemed to use counting methods on the thermometer diagrams rather than attempting to deal with negative numbers, and were mainly correct the first time and incorrect on the new test. Their incorrect answers could be explained by counting the lines marking the scale rather than using the gaps between the lines – in other words, by counting discrete points on the scale rather than using it continuously. An analogy would be finding the length of a fence by counting fence posts rather than by counting unit lengths. One learner progressed from this miscounting to correct counting.

Summarizing, two higher-achieving learners ended up getting these questions right, the other two were unable to deal with negative numbers or to resort to correct counting methods. The latter is a particular worry when the use of a number line is seen to be central for arithmetic, and the thermometer is traditionally seen as a very good way of using this image to extend number knowledge. This image use was not robust for three learners. Overall performance was erratic and the fact that no generalization can be made of it indicates the ill-definition of testing outcomes. It clearly cannot be said of learners achieving the supposed level of preparedness that they *can* read scales and deal with simple cases involving negative numbers and/or artificial thermometers. A model of learning which copes well with this finding is that learners need several experiences of mathematical concepts before they can produce consistent performance in a variety of contexts, such as tests and questions about thermometers. Occasional failure is not as important as whether they are constructing some understanding from a range of experiences.

Application of maths to shopping

The final question I chose provided the most complex analytical task and the most varied and inconclusive results. The question asked learners first to calculate the cost to each of two people jointly of buying a pack of four batteries at £1.48, then to calculate the difference in cost of buying two packs of two batteries at 85p per pack and one pack of four batteries.

Four learners provided correct answers in both tests, and none of these used standard vertical written methods both times: two learners had changed from *ad hoc*[2] to standard methods; one learner had changed from standard to *ad hoc* methods; and one used *ad hoc* methods for both tests. One learner changed from standard methods incorrectly done to *ad hoc* methods correctly done. Three learners were correct in the first test but not in the second, of whom two had changed from standard to *ad hoc* and one had changed from *ad hoc* to standard. One learner was wrong both times with a persistent error, subtracting small digits from large digits in a vertical layout.

Among those who attempted to use formal methods, two had tried to deal with '148 ÷ 2' in an idiosyncratic vertical format and one of them had been successful somehow, though it was not clear how:

$$
\begin{array}{r}
148 \\
\div \quad 2 \\
\hline
74
\end{array}
$$

This made me wonder whether vertical formats were being used to calculate or merely as the way to present mentally worked-out answers because learners thought that was required. It was not clear that vertically set-out calculations had been *used*.

Of the four who had achieved level 4, one used *ad hoc* methods successfully, one changed from standard to *ad hoc* and was unsuccessful the second time, one did the reverse and was also unsuccessful the second time. The other changed from *ad hoc* to standard and was successful both times, but with an unusable vertical layout!

---

[2] I use *ad hoc* to refer to methods which may have been specially chosen to answer this particular question, such as repeated addition, doubling and halving, estimating and adjusting (all of which could have been formally taught) or, more commonly, mixed fiddling around.

There is no clear sense of progression or regression here, only of difficulties surrounding the interface between formal and informal methods, which methods might have been emphasized by teachers, and learners' choices about which methods to use in a test situation. Julia Anghileri (2006) shows that such choices can also be gendered. Good mathematicians and expert arithmeticians choose methods according to the numbers with which they have to work, not according to the imagined preferences of the working context. The implication in much curriculum material is that progression between informal and formal methods is one-way and natural. Teachers are more or less directed to believe that formal methods are, in the end, better and more advanced than informal ones. This view is also promulgated in the comments which will inevitably affect teachers' pre-test instructions to learners. For example, teachers are told that formal methods are a more efficient way to calculate 3.5 × 60p than *ad hoc* methods (QCA 2001) – a view which denies the importance of mathematical flexibility and pragmatism and certainly does not reflect the way I would calculate it! Teachers might therefore try to teach formal methods without taking care to enable learners to see how they relate to their own informal, mental or *ad hoc* choices. Apart from this, the question shows that the capability to work with simple money calculations in test situations at this level is not robust and is not clearly related to the use of formal methods. Maybe such questions should not be used to draw distinctions between those who can do maths to an acceptable level and those who cannot.

Summary of question analyses

A sample of nine is too small from which to do more than raise questions, and we do not know what happened to those who achieved similar levels at Key Stage 2, without attending 'booster' classes. To have asked to test them too would have been too much of an intrusion. But this study gives enough information to point to possible areas of concern such as the following:

- standard test levels may not provide robust or useful measures of preparedness for the next stage;
- moves between formal and informal methods may create confusion and cannot be regarded as a one-way progression;
- growth of understanding is neither linear nor uniform;
- provision of memory-aids or booster classes for 'passing' tests may not have a lasting effects in terms of understanding.

Of these, the main one for me is that the analysis gives the lie to the model of linear progress in mathematics which underlies testing, standards regimes and levelization. Once again, as with so many of the characteristics of mathematics teaching described in this book, it is the weakest who suffer. The testing regimes are unfair, and trap them into patterns of underachievement and low expectations. The targets are mathematically meaningless but politically manipulable. The teaching methods are short-term and confusing. It is not surprising that underachievement is gradually exacerbated as students grow older to the state where 50 per cent fail to achieve the nationally valued levels at 16.

None of this will come as a surprise to teachers, mathematics educators and researchers. A theoretical approach to critiquing the effectiveness of booster classes, calling on constructivist theories and recursive models of mathematical learning, would have achieved the same results. It has been well known for some time that learning mathematics is not a uniform, linear process (Denvir and Brown 1986) and that the interplay of formal and informal methods is messy (Thompson 1999; Anghileri 2000). Teachers have always known that it is possible to teach to the test in mathematics without supporting sustainable understanding. Nevertheless, I saw it as important to examine this issue within its own terms, taking a superficial view of mathematics knowledge, testability and progress. Test results on a national scale, and even on a whole-school scale, tend to present a smooth picture which masks the actualities of the mathematical experience of individual learners.

Recognizing proficiency

The approach to maths shown in these tests, and the valuation given to levels achieved, are in stark contrast to the proficiencies shown by learners in the previous chapter. I set out to do better and to find teachers who were working, or would work, with secondary low-attaining learners in ways which focused on the development of thinking, on their long-term development of confidence and mathematical skills, rather than on short-term test results – an approach which is based on a belief in proficiency. I wanted to know about ways to work with such learners, ways which value and use their proficiencies, rather than using a discourse of deficiency in which learners are seen as lacking things, or being unable to do things, or presenting nothing but problems, needs and difficulties (Watson 2001b, 2002c). I was aware that my target learners would already have been labelled as 'failures', and would usually be found together in teaching groups consisting of others in similar circumstances.

Research shows that low-attaining learners can and do think in ways which are similar to those described as mathematical (Ahmed 1987; Ahmed and Williams 1992; Harries 2001). Indeed, I reported this from my own findings in the previous chapter. For example, some have shown an ability to use examples and counter-examples, to generalize, to develop efficient methods of working, to identify abstract structures in contextual examples. Research associated with the development of thinking skills in mathematics shows that achievement *can* be improved through explicit use of thinking skills and cognitively well-structured lessons (Feuerstein 1980; Adhami 2001). There is also a growing body of research evidence that learners from educationally, socially and economically disadvantaged backgrounds can benefit from mathematics teaching which allows them to exercise and develop their thinking, and that they also do better in standard tests as a result (Tanner and Jones 1995; Silver and Stein 1996; Boaler 1997; Senk and Thompson 2003). There are several paragraphs in this book which start with 'research shows …' and end with the thought 'so why do education systems act differently?' This is one of them.

How can such studies be ignored? The published studies tend to have at least one of three characteristics: intervention with methods and materials; intervention with professional development activities; and high levels of teacher commitment. In studies which involve innovation, results which purport to be about particular methods may say more about the commitment of teachers and the professional development benefits of research than they do about the materials and methods. Boaler's study is a rare example in which there is no imposed intervention from outside in the more successful of two schools, nor is the commitment of some of the teachers particularly high. But the unusual way they teach seems to benefit learners more than methods used in the more traditional school. They use consistently an approach based on offering learners in heterogeneous groups situations to explore, sometimes purely mathematical, sometimes 'realistic'. There is much in her study of the more successful school which can lead to rejection: the casual nature of classroom discipline, the lack of attention to coverage of the examination syllabus, the apparent 'off-task-ness' of some learners – all these cause problems for readers who cannot grasp why examination results from these classrooms were better than those from a school in which lessons and students were orderly and the full syllabus was rigorously covered. It is hard to let go of the established traditional belief that orderliness of classrooms and crisp curriculum management are key factors of attainment, instead of the development of learners' engagement, effort and ways of thinking.

In the Improving Attainment in Mathematics Project (IAMP) study which I am about to report the only common features among the teachers were their high commitment, their belief that all can learn mathematics, and the inevitable professional development effect of being in a project. There were no imposed innovative methods or materials, and little in common among the teachers' observable practices. There is nothing for doubters to reject except the commitment of the teachers, and it is always true that teachers without commitment will not teach as well as those with commitment, whatever the methods. In the study we learnt about how high commitment can translate into action, and can transform teachers' and learners' abilities to incorporate thoughtful activity into *every* lesson, of whatever type.

Defining mathematical thinking

The IAMP study asked teachers what they felt they could do, within their current practice, to develop mathematical thinking. All the teachers could agree on *some* aspects of mathematical thinking, such as the importance of generalization, but there was much early discussion and little initial agreement about its full meaning throughout school mathematics. For example, is 'ordinary thinking in the domain of mathematics' a more useful activity on which to focus? Can choice of operation in a word problem be described as mathematical thinking? Discussions around these issues were rich but inconclusive (Pitt 2002). We chose to take an empirical approach and compare the practices of teachers who had deliberately taken the decision to work with the target learners in ways which included specific attention to development of mathematical thinking, *whatever meaning a teacher attached to that phrase*. In addition, these teachers did not stick to the current official guidance, which was described as enabling 'catch-up' and consisted mainly of revisiting previous topics in ways which were already familiar to learners.

Data from classroom observations, teachers' notes, interviews with teachers and group discussions led to the creation of descriptions of the types of learning activity that the teachers in the group identified as evidence of mathematical thought (Watson *et al.* 2003a). These are categorized in Table 7.2 into two types, those which were specifically prompted and those which occurred unprompted in classroom settings. It can be seen that some learners eventually take their own responsibility for acting in ways which were initially prompted by the teachers.

The list is similar to the descriptions of the mathematical behaviour of high-achieving mathematical learners generated by Krutetskii (1976) yet arises solely from the data of this project with low-achieving learners. Rather than expecting this kind of behaviour spontaneously, as one might from stronger learners, the teachers deliberately framed and organized the classroom environment to make it more likely that learners would behave in these ways – and were rewarded by seeing learners who were thought to be 'less able' in mathematics spontaneously behaving in these ways. In the book so far, therefore, we have moved from a few teachers being able to articulate specific mathematical abilities which Krutetskii found to be characteristic of gifted mathematics learners, through finding that learners in groups labelled as 'low attaining' can exhibit these abilities when prompted, to observing some teachers who work explicitly on developing these abilities and are rewarded by seeing their low-attaining learners take these mathematical actions without prompting.

Table 7.2: Observable actions indicating mathematical thought

Prompted	Unprompted
Choosing appropriate techniques	Choosing appropriate techniques
Contributing examples	Contributing examples
Describing connections with prior knowledge	Describing connections with prior knowledge
Finding similarities or differences beyond superficial appearance	Finding similarities or differences beyond superficial appearance
Generalizing structure from diagrams or examples	Generalizing structure from diagrams or examples
Identifying what can be changed	Identifying what can be changed
Making something more difficult	Making something more difficult
Making comparisons	Making extra kinds of comparison
Posing own questions	Generating own enquiry
Predicting problems	Predicting problems
Working on extended tasks over time	Changing their mind with new experiences
Dealing with unfamiliar problems	Creating own methods and shortcuts
	Initiating a mathematical idea
	Using prior knowledge

How did the teachers teach? The answer to this question is very complex, for each teacher taught in ways which seemed sensible to them, and which developed from their own thinking and reflection. What the researchers found were common principles which are seen by the teachers to be central to higher achievement of the target learners, but which were enacted in very different ways.

Principles of reconstructive teaching

From our analysis of teachers' practices and beliefs the following features turned out to be the dominant common intentions and principles behind their planning and teaching:[3]

---

[3]   See Watson *et al.* (2003b) for more detail on these.

- guiding learners into mathematical cultural practices;
- making connections;
- preparing to 'go with the flow';
- allowing thinking time;
- varying task types;
- extending duration of tasks and developing concentration;
- prompting learners to create their own examples;
- respecting learners.

Guiding learners into mathematical practices

Teachers saw their task in terms of structuring teaching to enable learners to make contact with mathematics using their own powers of thought. They recognized the learners' entitlement to access mathematics as an established cultural artefact and did not offer watered-down, concrete, procedural versions of mathematics, nor versions constrained by the learners' current context. They did not simplify mathematics to make it more accessible. Rather they chose access points to complex mathematics based on what learners already knew, such as asking them what they knew about percentages and building lessons on that knowledge, rather than starting from scratch in some other place. Teachers focused also on adapting the habits both of the learners and the classroom so that the learners could be gradually enculturated into the world of mathematics. Here are some examples:

- They offered situations in which there are dimensions of choice so that learners learnt how to choose appropriately, such as discussing the best choice of method for a multiplication, or the best way to express a newly constructed definition.
- They asked for examples in order for exemplification to become a habit, such as 'give me an example of something we did last lesson'.
- They found playful ways to elicit responses which became more mathematically sophisticated, such as asking 'we know more about numbers than whether they are odd or even – what else do we know now?'

This approach depended on trusting learners to respond appropriately, and by and large they did, slowly, gradually, and with wobbly but growing confidence.

Making connections

All the teachers wanted learners to view mathematics as connected rather than as separate topics, using structural links between topics to design tasks. Some teachers were explicit with learners about making links within and across topics. Sara organized her scheme of work so that links were obvious; Anthony explicitly encouraged learners to express any connections they saw with previous work, with other mathematics or with other contexts. Algebraic representations cropped up in geometry lessons; methods last used a month ago suddenly became the precise tool needed for today's lesson.

Preparing to go with the flow

Teachers deliberately planned to 'go with the flow' of learner response, not to move on rapidly when problems, tentative chains of reasoning, or alternative ideas were offered.[4] This sometimes entailed planning a range of approaches to anticipate flexibility so that practical, spatial and numerical approaches were possible. The teachers decided during their lessons which approach was appropriate and when to move between them. They also responded to learners' moods, such as excitement, frustration, boredom, using them constructively to mould the progress of lessons rather than battling against them.

Allowing thinking time

All teachers found they were giving learners a longer time to think, including long wait times with whole-class questions, and in general throughout their work and interactions. Giving more time, creating space rather than imposing pace, came to be seen as having positive emotional, behavioural and cognitive effects. Teachers balanced carefully the length of time they spent on a topic with the externally perceived need to 'cover' topics. One teacher spent 2 weeks on 'difference' (as subtraction) because it provided a context for discussion, for creating their own examples and questions, and for establishing images of number and ways of working, and because it would have been pointless to move to another topic until something as basic as subtraction was fully understood by all. Class discussion, with space given for individual thought, was used more and more but not without difficulty.

Varying task type

All teachers found themselves, either deliberately or incidentally, using fewer worksheets and textbooks and more home-grown activities, developments from starter tasks and learners' own questions, presented through

---

4   As with most strategies, there are teachers who do not follow up every problem but still get good results; see the description of Susan's practice in Chapter 9.

discussion and shared stimuli rather than on paper. This meant that the learning environment was likely to be more collaborative from the start of each task, and teachers used more visual, active and dynamic forms of presentation than the static images used on printed material. The researchers on the project provided some sources of appropriate ideas, but most of these offered methods for constructing tasks rather than ready-made activities.

Extending duration of tasks and developing concentration

There was in general a shift towards longer tasks in the project, if for no other reason than the fact that teachers are building more thinking time into their expectations and allowing more lines of inquiry to develop. However, for a few teachers this was a deliberate, major move in order to create an atmosphere in which learners are embedded in a mathematical situation for several lessons. Sara provided each learner with a plastic wallet which, on opening it at the start of each lesson, immediately took the learner back to the mental state in which they last worked with the contents. This goes completely against the normal belief that such learners 'cannot concentrate' and need to be offered task variety, or 'cannot remember' and have to start each lesson with a recap from the teacher. Some project teachers focused on developing ongoing questions and inquiries. This was particularly well developed in Becky's case. For example, she gave learners straws to make and discuss angles and their relationships by intersecting the straws. Learners managed to find all the usual angle rules for intersecting lines, triangles and parallel lines over a period of 2 weeks. This method allowed them to generalize because it offered them unlimited possible angles and the space to make conjectures, experiment and think things through. In contrast, some other teachers introduced shorter, high-concentration tasks to enable learners to learn that they *could* concentrate, so that they could build on this new behaviour later with more extended tasks.

Prompting learners to create their own examples

All the teachers used 'create your own example' tasks as part of their everyday lesson structure (Watson and Mason 2005). For example, Andrea deliberately included some blank places in an otherwise teacher-driven activity so that learners could create their own examples with which to work. Several teachers use 'if this is the answer, what is the question?' tasks. One learner said: 'Making my own examples makes me think. I think about half the time in class now.' This was said with some pride, so we took it to be indicating improvement!

Respecting learners

Overwhelmingly, the teachers respected learners as learners and did not use the kind of language which can often be heard in staffrooms: 'waste of space', 'dimwit' and so on. One teacher said of one child: 'Some have called her slow, but she isn't slow. When she learns, she learns just as quickly as anyone else; it is just that there is a longer run-up, it doesn't happen so often.'

Teachers did not try to guess where the learners were in their mathematical development. They asked and listened. The teachers provided scaffolding; the learners constructed meaning. The curriculum did not dictate progress, the learning did. Even the few teachers who imposed very disciplined, traditional, behaviour did this out of respect, seeing that adolescents may need to be reminded of how hard they are capable of working and how much can be gained through concentration.

Differences among IAMP teachers

We learnt that, contrary to the expectation that there might be 'best' ways to teach, it is possible for two teachers to make apparently contradictory decisions about classroom norms, but to have and achieve similar aims. What seems to be important here is not the decision that is made, but the *purpose* of the decision. For example, all teachers thought it was important for learners to discuss mathematics with their peers, be it in pairs, in groups, or whole-class discussions, where the whole-class discussion provides models for how to discuss mathematics. They also believed that everything said in class was valuable and everyone should hear it. But for one teacher this led to the practice of repeating everything which is said by learners (ensuring everyone hears); for another this led to the practice of repeating nothing and orchestrating discussion around what each learner says (ensuring everyone listens).

All the teachers recognized a link between thinking and writing about mathematics. For one teacher, the act of writing was seen as forcing thinking because it has to be expressed in a linear form, using logical connectives like 'and, but, if, then, because, so, ...'. The effort required to communicate forces clarity – speech demands transformation of thinking into what makes sense to others. Others believed that writing gives you something of your own to look back at; a way to remind yourself what it is that you know. One teacher, however, saw writing as a serious *distraction* from thought. She saw mental visualization, and struggling to visualize, as acts which make future access to mathematical facts and methods easier because the memory has been activated by the effortful creation of an image. For all the teachers the purpose was to promote thought, but different decisions about writing arose as a result.

It was immensely liberating to find that different decisions could lead to the same kinds of progress. This does not, however, mean that 'anything goes' – the persistent, sustained aims of teachers and the consistency of their teaching were important in establishing new habits.

Difficulties of working with 'bottom sets'

Of course, persuading the target learners to adapt to these ways of working is not easy. Many 'bottom set' students had developed powerful habits of rejecting the curriculum, understandably given their past failure and, sadly, sometimes their past treatment. Project teachers did not give up attempting to turn rejection into engagement, but the response could be frustratingly slow and temporary. We found out from Sara that in one term the proportion of responsive learners had changed from one-third to two-thirds, but her feelings about the class were dominated by the intransigence of the remaining ones and she could not see this change as important progress. Siobhán created a boardroom arrangement of desks in some lessons so that learners could discuss more easily, but they had been used to being seated separately, all facing front, and it took time for them to cope with new expectations. Another teacher excluded two learners who quietly refused to work and kept those who were noisy and disruptive but took part in the mathematics; this went completely against the grain of what most teachers did, which was to exclude disruptive students and tolerate quiet refusal, and hence brought the issue of effort to the fore in the classroom. An important part of the study was the recognition of the realities of working with segregated groups of 'failing' learners in secondary school, and that the processes involved are of re-enculturation, reconstruction, rescue and even retraining.

Andrea used an imaginative problem-solving approach to retraining learners to act appropriately. She reasoned that she would have to take a behaviourist approach to developing work habits in order to get a starting place for their attention. She gave learners the task of taking a piece of paper to and fro from home and persisted in this training until everyone could manage to organize themselves to do this. Once they had this to-and-fro habit she gave them a homework task of writing something of their choice about mathematics on the paper. The training does not relate easily to beliefs about how learners learn mathematics, and how rewards might be intrinsic, but enabled the class to get to a place from which they could work more creatively. Through training behaviour she had provided the bedrock from which other habits could develop.

Learning more mathematics

Teachers were naturally worried that their students might not learn enough if they did not cover enough topics, but eventually the group settled to the view that 'enough' was more to do with learning and understanding than with covering topics without understanding or remembering them. Some groups which had been taught by the project teachers took national tests and teachers were able to provide comparison results from other similar classes in their own schools. They chose their own comparison groups and provided us with the data. We did not have this kind of data for every teaching group. Some teachers refused to use national tests for their students because it would be too daunting to see questions on mathematics they had not been taught. They did not want learners' hard-won confidence to be shattered.

For those we did have, the results were encouraging. The project learners did at least as well as other groups in most kinds of question, even where other groups had covered more of the syllabus than the project groups. In questions which involved more than performance of techniques, or remembered facts, but expected some transformation or adaptation of knowledge to fit an unfamiliar question, the project learners did better in relation to their overall results, whereas the comparison learners generally did less well on this type. These results were calculated as rigorously as possible, given the paucity of data and the different kinds of comparison group which were used, but they are more rigorous than the usual raw comparisons used to compare teachers and schools. Each teacher also had other school-specific data from which to draw her own conclusions about success, and as a result they all felt that the classes were doing better, and learning better, through being taught with these broader foci.

This result is not isolated (Watson and De Geest 2005). In Boaler's (1997) study, previously low-attaining learners who had not been taught the whole syllabus, but had been enabled to explore and create understandings for themselves, did significantly better than comparable learners in another school where the focus had been on coverage. Indeed, they did significantly better than groups who were deemed to be in the 'top half' of the other school. In Senk and Thompson's (2003) compendium of results from the USA reform curriculum, similar results are found. In no such comparative studies, within countries, has it been shown that learners who have been taught in ways which focus on thinking and understanding do worse than comparable learners focusing on coverage.

So, while in comparison to some other countries UK mathematics performance in national tests is not good, within the UK and USA it has been shown that emphasizing mathematical thinking benefits lower-attaining learners compared to teaching which focuses on topic coverage. However, in Chapter 9 I will show some examples of reconstruction practices which offer more insight into this result.

Deep progress in mathematics

How do teachers evaluate improvement in their own classrooms? This question has to be asked because we already know that teachers find it hard to use the results of research, however rigorous it has been, unless they are convinced of its value. The most significant outcome of the IAMP study for many of those involved was the notion of 'deep progress in mathematics'. This concept allowed teachers to work on several levels, without expecting progress to be steady and uniform in all three. We defined deep progress in mathematics as:

- learning more mathematics;
- becoming better at learning mathematics;
- feeling better about learning mathematics.

In this trio we recognized the importance of rescuing disheartened adolescent learners through cognition, habits of learning, self-esteem and development of identity. This trio resonated with teachers because it matched what they instinctively felt about their students, providing a key framework for planning, teaching and assessment.

What did the teachers do?

After the results of this project had been published, many people asked for more details of what the teachers did. This misses the point. What these teachers did was to identify problems, to develop their own solutions to classroom behaviour and learning problems, while responding to learners' ideas and understandings. We gave them very few resources to support this process: a book about mathematical questioning (Watson and Mason 1998), a book of tasks which could trigger mathematical activity (Ollerton 2002), a book about creating interesting tasks from textbook exercises (Prestage and Perks 2001), and some advice on developing tasks around particular topics. However, none of the teachers used these in great detail; it was more important that they shared ideas and felt supported when teaching, as one of them said, 'off piste'.

For example, one teacher used a task from Mike Ollerton's book (2002) which involved finding how to arrange four congruent squares so that they are all touching but have a minimum or maximum perimeter. In her class, this became the starting point for extended exploration in which she focused on:

- the fact that with fixed areas a wide variety of perimeters could be made (indeed, the same perimeter could relate to various areas and *vice versa*);

- helping learners to express arguments which justified their answers;
- their increased ability to deal with abstraction as they used more and more squares;
- the motivational effects of continuing their own lines of inquiry.

The task itself does not automatically lead to these outcomes; it is the combination of teacher, learners and task which leads to learning. The same task could be presented as a chance to practise very simple area and perimeter 'counting'; a chance to fill in and make inferences from a table of values; an opportunity to create a coloured wall display; and many other outcomes of even less mathematical merit.

Similarly, several teachers used 'if this is the answer, what was the question?' but some of them used this as a quick way to generate mental arithmetic exercises while others used it to explore how much variation there could be in certain question types. The task on its own did not turn itself into lessons. However, some tasks seem to promote good teaching more than others, but a good teacher can transform tasks to create good mathematical activity. During the project we all learnt that the injection of very few prompts, such as those in Table 7.3, could make a significant difference to the kind of thinking learners expected to do. Some of these prompts were similar to those I had used in the previous study, some had been found in books provided for the project (in particular, Watson and Mason 1998),[5] and some were established practices of individual teachers which became shared through the project.

Compare	Organize	Classify
Exemplify	Give more than one example	Counter-exemplify
Say if something is always, sometimes or never true	Describe relationships	Generalize
Change representations	Vary a feature of the problem	See how far something can be varied
Look 'across the grain'	Make up new questions	Apply ideas generated recently in similar cases

---

[5]   See also Bills *et al.* (2004) and Swan (2005).

Most lessons involved discussion, either between pairs or among the whole class. Most lessons involved visual, practical and/or physical activity of some kind as well as symbolic and numerical work. Most lessons allowed learners time to think, and elicited their ideas with respect. All teachers were persistent in their expectations that students could and would participate positively. Learners were expected to develop ideas and give reasons for them.

It is easy to say what the teaching was *not* like. Because the focus was on development of thinking, there were very few lessons which involved only imitating algorithms, or copious amounts of bookwork, or quick changes between topics. Very few lessons depended on reading textbooks, or deciphering detailed written instructions of any kind. No one was ridiculed for wrong answers, indeed wrong answers were often welcomed as an opportunity to think about how to put them right. Students were not expected to rehearse complicated methods without the support of developing their own descriptions, explanations, ways to remember them, and commentaries. Only rarely were they offered 'tricks'.

In the next chapter I will show more about how the different emphases of different teachers are revealed in learners' work, and conclude that it is the teacher and teaching which matter more than the task.

8   Identifying deep progress[1]

I have shown throughout this book that it is difficult to say exactly what is meant by 'being better at mathematics'. If we only refer to high-stakes tests we exclude all kinds of subtle arguments and untestable achievements. If we look at mathematical work more holistically, we have to accept that different learners, teachers and examiners use different interpretations. This affects lower-attaining learners disproportionately because they are more likely to have difficulties in expressing themselves in ways others can interpret, and less likely to interpret others' mathematics in conventional ways. Nevertheless, in order to make some convincing claims about the effectiveness of teachers and teaching when test results are not an appropriate measure, such as for the target learners in the IAMP research described in the previous chapter, some kind of comparative device is required – we cannot convince others by merely using a personal feel-good factor.

It may be erroneous to claim improvement individually just because we feel better about teaching. Research into the implementation of national mathematics strategies showed that both teachers and learners enjoyed lessons more as a result of using its ideas, but this did not mean more was being learnt (Brown *et al.* 2003; Ofsted 2004). But a 'feel-good' factor counts for something, because it makes it less likely that teachers will leave the profession, more likely that learners will enjoy mathematics, and more likely that teaching and learning will eventually improve. Ann Brown (1992), in a seminal paper, makes it very clear that feeling positive about what you are doing makes it far more likely to lead to improvements because you will *want* it to work, rather than unwillingly applying new tactics without commitment. A major problem with improving mathematics learning is that there are so many ways in which 'want it to work' can be interpreted that, where teachers might use 'increased enjoyment' as a yardstick, parents and authorities may use 'test results' (which may rise, Ofsted 2002), researchers

---

[1]   The work reported in this chapter was carried out with Els De Geest and Steph Prestage with the support of grants from the Esmee Fairbairn Foundation, 01–1415 and 02–1424.

might use absolute standards over time (which may not rise, Brown *et al.* 2003; Tymms 2004), and universities might use numbers choosing to study further (which may fall, Smith 2004).

In this chapter I describe how we decided that learners had made deep progress in mathematics. This serves two purposes: first, to demonstrate that it is possible to 'measure' deep progress; and second, to show that these low-achieving learners were able to become better mathematical thinkers during a year of teaching which challenged them intellectually and socially, sometimes fundamentally attacking how they saw themselves as mathematics learners. Many who saw themselves as invisible, silent and passive became visible, active and proactive participators. Some who saw themselves as knowing nothing became able to contribute ideas, to volunteer to take certain roles, to be confident about what they knew.

'Measuring' progress

We took the view that, in the end, what is wanted for all learners is that they could act mathematically in a situation which is, to them, non-routine. In other words, testing with standard test-type questions may not tell me about anything other than whether they have been effectively drilled to do test questions. However, as soon as you look at non-routine questions many more confounding variables come into play. If the question involves too many words, language can confuse; if it is about a real-life context, learners from certain social groups can be confused (Cooper and Dunne 1998, 2000). For learners who achieve low levels there are likely to be other potential problems which we might not be able to identify.

We decided to use the same task as both pre- and post-test at the start and finish of a school year in five of the project classes, even though it would be more familiar second time around. We used a task from Ollerton (2002). He does not claim originality. His version of the task is as follows:

---

21 can be made by the addition of consecutive numbers in the following ways:

$1 + 2 + 3 + 4 + 5 + 6$ $6 + 7 + 8$ $10 + 11$

Explore other numbers and their consecutive sums. Which numbers do not have a consecutive sum?

We could fully justify the decision to use the same task twice. First, variables inherent in mathematical tasks which could affect performance are controlled for each learner, so that for each learner both tests can be compared legitimately, even if some of them felt the task was more or less accessible than others for linguistic or other reasons. We intended to look at changes in the way each learner pursued the task, not to compare actual performance of learners and classes. Second, since the task was done with 9 months between, we thought that learners might not recognize it. Third, if they did recognize it, and this made it easier, then this demonstrated one of the characteristics Krutetskii (1976) found of gifted mathematicians: that they have a good memory for mathematical structure. To do anything of interest with the task you have to engage with structure, not with remembered algorithms, and even remembering number bonds is not of much help. Thus, memory for this structure and any relevant results would be an indication of mathematical capability.

This particular task was selected because, while being non-routine (and initially unfamiliar), it addresses the central curriculum idea of multiplicative number structure. It would also be accessible to all learners, because it only assumes an ability to add fairly small numbers – though this may have made it look a bit childish for some learners whose first response was to dismiss it as 'boring'. It has no contextual matter, apart from mathematics itself, so the chances of being distracted away from the mathematical content are reduced.

Each teacher was free to choose how to present the task, and they told us how they did this. The meaning of 'consecutive' had to be discussed in most classes, for example. In general, teachers gave less input the second time than the first time, though some gave no input at all except the written task for both events. We compared individual learners' performances, taking into account how the teachers had varied their presentation and whether they had given learners any specific training in heuristics for doing that kind of task during the year. We only used five classes for analysis (although all classes did the tasks) because there were problems getting enough comparative data. Attendance was always erratic in these low sets, and we also had internal communication problems in the project which meant that some data went missing![2] I am quite happy to be open about this because everyone who works in education works under stress, and often priorities clash so that holes appear between what is intended and what is achieved in research. My own priorities are not to research for the sake of research; the messiness of researching in natural settings is an essential part of all my work.

In this case, the five classes used for analysis were not specially chosen except that they just happened to be those for which we had enough data. In the post-test no learner commented that they had seen the task before.

---

[2]   I cannot make any claims about teachers being more or less committed based on their fulfilment of the research requirements. Quite rightly, their priorities were elsewhere and one of the least organized teachers, from a research point of view, was one of the most committed from a practice point of view – indeed, he went on to institute radical changes in his school which entirely altered the focus of their early secondary mathematics.

They seemed to treat the end-of-year task as unfamiliar, and the perform-ance on it in most cases bore very little relation to what they had done at the start of the year. Nearly all learners used completely different approaches the second time around. We also learnt that teachers gave much less help and structure the second time, which means that any improve-ments in performance are not confused with the effects of teacher input during the testing itself.

How we analysed their work

The learners' work was assessed using criteria for mathematical exploration developed by the ATM (SEG 1988). These criteria expressed constructs devel-oped by a team of practising teachers in a manner similar to that described by Wiliam (1994). He writes about people working as a team developing shared understandings of what they value through creating practices which express those values, rather than through defining them at the start. In the ATM work, teachers jointly explored what was of value to them in their teaching and in their students' mathematics, and fashioned descriptions of desirable outcomes which would be met if learners benefited from their teaching in the ways they hoped. The team met at least three times a year to discuss learners' portfolios of work and their own teaching methods. Over time the criteria were developed and agreed as an outcome of the edu-cational progress of the teachers involved, who were overtly learning critically from each other both about mathematics and about practice. Agreement was reached and the assessment system ran as a nationally recognized option for 6 years, awarding recognized high-stakes grades which met national stan-dards.

Using these criteria in our study was justified in three ways: they gave details about what it means to work mathematically; they had been devel-oped in similar ways of working to those of this project; they had been developed to meet national standards.

From the ATM criteria, taking the nature of the task and the age group into account, the following were selected as an appropriate frame for assess-ment for a one-off task:

Implementation
- Select and use mathematical strategies.
- Sustain a chosen study.
- Use information, make initial conjectures, simplify, plan, formulate extensions, be accurate, classify, specialize, generalize, test, justify, experiment.

Improvement can be indicated by: use of more, or more sophisticated, strategies; staying with the task for longer; making more conjectures; needing less help deciding what to do; generating more examples.

Interpretation
- Draw conclusions.
- Make inferences.
- Make valid observations.
- Relate results to each other.

Improvement is indicated by doing more of these.

Mathematical attitude and autonomy
- Look for and recognize structures.
- Take responsibility.
- Make decisions.

Improvement can be indicated by recognition of more, or more complex, structures and evidence of more, or more robust, choices in direction of work.

Before I say more about the analysis, it is worth spending some time playing with the task to get a sense of what is possible. Learners might start by checking the given sums and seeing if there are any more. They might then generate some of their own, either haphazardly or in some order. It is highly likely that some learners will choose big numbers because they look harder, or even their friends' birthdates, favourite numbers and so on if they have not grasped the power of systematic variation. There are a range of possible orders: one could try all those which begin with 1, or all which arise from triples, or all which add up to certain totals which could be randomly or systematically chosen. We were hoping that some learners would notice patterns and consistencies in their results, not just look for the numbers which could not be achieved. Choices could be deliberate, arising from what has already been noticed; for example, if someone notices that all triple sums are multiples of 3 they might then try adjacent pairs or quadruple sums. Learners who are comfortable with algebra might not test particular sums at all but pursue the whole task symbolically – but we were not expecting any learners to do this.

Analysis was restricted to what could be gleaned from the written work, which was sparse for most learners, without overinterpretation. The comparison between a learner's pre- and post-test work was made by crudely counting what was countable (numbers of inferences, concluding statements, strategies used, examples used, and so on), combined with mathematical judgment about the quality, correctness and usefulness of what was done. For example, generating lots of unsystematic examples was not seen to be as good as generating systematic examples, unless the unsystematic ones were special cases to provide insight, or for testing. In contrast, generalizing from one example was only seen as useful if it was a structural generalization which showed mathematical insight, such as showing that $6 + 7 + 8$ had been treated as $(7 - 1) + 7 + (7 + 1)$ and hence, offered a general way to add consecutive triples. Thus, merely following exploratory methods, such as example generation, was of value in showing engagement and willingness to work, but not of mathematical value unless accompanied by evidence of mathematical insight. The comparison of work, and identification of improvement, was therefore not amenable to rigorous quantitative techniques, but was more akin to marking coursework with the instruction to 'give credit wherever possible, but don't overinterpret'.

All learners recorded their work on paper, with many including rough work. Some of this was separate from neatly written lists of sums; some was integral so that playing with numbers and usable results appeared in sequence, complete with crossings-out and dead-ends; sometimes all the written work was what one might call 'rough' and was hard to follow. When they wrote conjectures about what they found, we could not always deduce how they had arrived at, or tested, their conjectures. Sometimes we could ascertain this from written records, but communication skills were generally so weak that we could not assume that a lack of written evidence implied a lack of thoughtfulness. If a learner had interpreted the task as 'do as much as you can' instead of 'find out as much as you can' (and it seemed some of them did this) they may have underperformed. For all these reasons the analysis is likely to underestimate the level of thinking which went on; it could be seen as a 'worst case' analysis. A further limitation on the analysis was the fluid nature of the sample due to high levels of absence and social dysfunction, so that the proportion of learners for whom we had both pre- and post-tests was as low as 50 per cent for some classes.

Improvements between pre- and post-test

By qualitatively recording, for each learner, features of the pre- and post-test which matched the above criteria, it was found that all but two learners appeared to do very much better the second time than the first, even though there had been less teacher input and guidance during the task itself. As might be expected, there were differences between the teaching groups, so I shall summarize results for five of the groups to show the kinds of improvements which were made.

In Sara's class the first time, most of the 15 learners analysed generated strings of numbers which added up to 21, with a few random consecutive sums and no conjectures. The second time, eight learners recorded systematic explorations, compared to none the first time. A different eight of the 15 learners wrote well-founded conjectures the second time, compared to one learner the first time. Some conjectures were evidenced through written examples; others appeared to be the result of unrecorded experiments. Two explained in writing how the structure of exploration related to their conjectures. This was achieved in less time because Sara's plans were constrained by other considerations, so we also have evidence of engagement through increased intensity of work in a shorter time.

Kevin's group showed similar characteristics to Sara's, and also showed more sustained motivation and interest the second time than the first, choosing to continue the work in a second lesson. There were marked improvements in effort, engagement and achievement evident in the work. The first time, most learners produced unsystematic examples; the second time over half were working in obviously systematic ways, and nearly half wrote down valid conjectures. In one case a conjecture was made, followed by use of a counter-example to raise doubts about it.

Linda's students mostly worked in a more sophisticated manner in the second test, choosing their own systems and generating more examples with less input from the teacher. They were much more systematic in the second test, their avenues of exploration being clear from their choice of examples. There were two main systems being used: looking for existence of sums for each number in turn, or generating systematic lists of consecutive numbers and seeing what their total is. Some who had been satisfied with finding one sum in the first test found several versions in the second, thus showing more determination. A few changed their method of exploration autonomously during the second test. Three students wrote conjectures and observations in the second test, compared to one in the first.

Only three of Siobhán's students made conjectures the first time; these were about even, odd and 'double' sums. The second time everyone made conjectures, some about parity but mostly about multiplicative patterns, resulting in attempts to find formulae to match subsets of their results. Half the learners found correct formulae, expressed as flow diagrams rather than with letters, for one or more 'lengths' of sums. One correctly predicted what would happen for sums of six consecutive numbers. Learners worked on the task for three lessons and asked for more time, but could not be given it. The first time, everyone had used the method of finding sums for each integer in turn, where possible, but rejected the task after a very short time. The second time a generative method was used, which I describe later.

Claire's students sustained the task for two lessons the second time, compared to one earlier, and produced more writing. In this group there was little systematic work either time, but most learners tried many more examples the second time, and there was more variety in the size of numbers used. Several used some three-digit numbers as well as smaller ones, and two-thirds of them wrote valid conjectures about relationships between odd and even numbers and sums. In the pre-test most learners had merely written some sums to 21, as given in the task, and nothing much more.

Thus, over all the groups analysed, learners' willingness to engage with mathematics that had not been taught to them had undoubtedly improved, as had their resilience to stay with the task over an extended period of time in four of the classes. Furthermore, they took the initiative when it came to exploring, devising their own systems for doing so. The second time around the task was largely pursued in a more complex way, either using bigger numbers, more systematic approaches, more variations and/or with reflective comments. Some learners laid out their work in ways which suggested certain conjectures, because certain patterns emerged spatially, but we could not tell for sure that this had happened. There were many conjectures made about the results of the sums, distinguishing odd and even inputs and results, with a few learners recognizing multiples, indicating an understanding of mathematics as arising from patterns, and the value of reflecting on results. This was more than just spotting patterns; they were also using them to make inferences.

All learners produced much more written work the second time, suggesting an increased willingness to engage in effortful work and writing. Learners needed little input from the teacher the second time to interpret the task and choose what to do, suggesting they were more able to be precise in the interpretation and more willing to engage in tasks with more than one constraint. Thus, we saw that learners had become more willing to work, but also that all of those for whom we had scripts (except two) knew more about how to work on unfamiliar mathematics.

What do these improvements tell us?

In the project we had set out to show that low-attaining secondary students whose teachers focus on the development of mathematical thinking, even while working within a heavily prescribed national curriculum reinforced by national testing and inspection, could make meaningful progress in mathematics. Standard test results showed that these learners' achievements are at least as good as those of comparable groups, and in some aspects of mathematics are better. The pre- and post-tasks showed that they also improved significantly in willingness, engagement, and capability to work with novel mathematical situations. Thus, the project learners improved in standard and non-standard mathematical situations, and in other aspects of behaviour (Watson *et al.* 2003b).

We had no comparison groups for this particular task, and could therefore be accused of lacking rigour. But what we wanted to show was that it *is* possible for low-achieving learners to become better mathematical thinkers and learners in general, and to become more interested and motivated to work on mathematics which is not being 'sold' as closely linked to future exam performance. This would contrast with the growing disaffection that learners who are struggling sometimes have with school mathematics, and their teachers with them! Either the progress is due to the teaching, or is something which happens anyway due to maturation and the improved reasoning skills which are reputed by some to come with adolescence. The latter is doubtful, since going from 25 per cent failing to achieve the expected level at 11 to 50 per cent similarly failing at 16, as happens currently as I write, does not sound as if progress can be due to maturation. This study provides more data for the role of teaching as the factor which makes a difference.

How do teachers make a difference?

I shall show how teachers make a *specific* difference by comparing features of learners' work on the final task between the five classes. In doing this, I am thinking about what aspects of this task, and the way the learners tackled it, were truly 'non-routine' for these different groups of learners. While analysing learners' work, it became clear that each class exhibited some distinctive habits in their mathematical work, and in some cases we had audio-tape evidence that these reflected their teacher's priorities. The teacher's imprint can be discerned on the learners' work. Hence, what is routine in terms of approach to this kind of task for one class may be non-routine for another, because the one class may have that kind of activity embedded in its practice, where another class has different kinds of activity embedded.

I want to draw a distinction here between the task, which is the words and numbers as stated at the top of this chapter, and activity, which is what each learner makes of it. (This distinction is not mine, it derives from the work of Leont'ev and has been interpreted mathematically by Christiansen and Walther 1986.) Each learner has a different history of experience and knowledge on which to draw, a personally organized set of images and meanings, slightly different access to the ways in which the teacher and others see mathematics, and a personal history of what has worked, and not worked, in the past. Thus each learner will respond differently to a task. These different responses will be strongly influenced by what the teacher and others value, the norms of the classroom, the kinds of mathematical behaviour encouraged and discouraged. They will also be influenced by the language used in the presentation of the task and by the way language has been used in the past to structure activity and thought. So although we expect differences in individual response, we expect similarities within classes, unless natural maturation is the sole cause of improvement in reasoning.

There were no 'better' or 'worse' teachers in our study. Instead I learnt something about the robustness of the enculturation process which took place during the year and was manifested through the learners' work. Furthermore, I want to focus closely on the mathematical differences in the sense described in the assessment criteria.

Routinizing of non-routine tasks

Linda's students shifted from needing support to making up their own minds; from being mainly unsystematic to mainly choosing and using their own systems. We assume that some expectations and conjectures were probably formed which led to the choice of system, but few were written down. Kevin's made the same shift, but in addition made many justifiable written conjectures (some of which were explicitly justified) about what emerged in terms of odd or even sums, which numbers could not be made, which numbers could be made several ways and so on. However, the conjectures often did not arise in an obvious way from the written examples, making me wonder if there was also a classroom culture of sharing conjectures. Sara's students made a similar shift towards being systematic and making many more written conjectures and observations, in some cases giving justifications for these. In her class, conjectures arose obviously from the written examples. In Claire's class nearly everyone made observations, usually in speech bubbles, and these were nearly all about odd and even numbers. As in Kevin's group, these did not necessarily arise clearly from the examples. In addition, several wrote final statements of this kind: 'if I had more time I would look for more patterns'. Choice of examples was fairly random, and over the whole group it was clear that learners wanted to show their confidence with large numbers – several focused on three-digit numbers. Although large numbers were used in other classes, there was not the extended use which appeared in Claire's class.

These four cases seem to suggest that a shift from being unsystematic to systematic is not necessarily due to maturation, nor closely connected with the ability to make valid conjectures. All classes show evidence of emphasis on being systematic, but this happens in different ways. Linda's students chose their own systems, and mainly focused on how they could generate particular answers. Claire's students chose methods and focused on odds and evens. Methods arose from learners, not from the teacher, but these differences must have been influenced by the focus of the teaching.

The approaches to systematization and conjecture varied between classes. Some teachers may emphasize being systematic more than others; some may ask 'what do you notice?' more than others. Particularly interesting is the appearance of valid conjectures which do not arise from written examples, but must come either from unrecorded calculations, discussion with peers, or from appreciation of mathematical structures. This contrasts with the written wish of many learners in Claire's class to 'find more patterns' but their failure to generate systematic data from which patterns might be spotted. Clearly they understood that finding patterns is a desirable practice in mathematics, but do not yet connect this with decisions about data generation. Others in Claire's group, and many in Kevin's, made successful conjectures arising from deductive rather than inductive reasoning. In Kevin's class valid conjectures were usually not associated with systematic generation of examples, but were sometimes accompanied with deductive justifications. Yet the impression given by most students was that an empirical approach had been encouraged because their written work emphasized lists of examples.

In Siobhán's class a strong story emerged about how generalization arises empirically. In the pre-test, all learners without exception wrote numbers from 1 to about 20 and tried to find consecutive sums for each in response to the original problem statement from the book. Remember that they also rejected the task quite early on in the pre-test and she had to abandon spending much time on it.

During the early stages of the post-test the following exchange was observed while Siobhán presented the task:

SIOBHÁN: What happens when you add two consecutive numbers?

LEARNERS (after some exploration):
The answer will always be odd.

SIOBHÁN: How can you be more confident?

LEARNERS: By being systematic.

SIOBHÁN: What might my next question be?

LEARNERS: Adding three consecutive numbers

SIOBHÁN (after further discussion)
We can use ICT if you can suggest a way to use it.

LEARNERS: Spreadsheets.

SIOBHÁN: What would a suitable spreadsheet look like? What would the formula be?

This exchange demonstrates that learners had become enculturated into:

- a conviction of the value of being systematic;
- a way to develop mathematical questions;
- use of spreadsheets;
- an empirical approach to exploration;
- an understanding that the calculations are merely to provide data for future thought.

Siobhán's written responses on their work between lessons showed clearly that she wanted them to call on previous experiences. For example, on one sheet she wrote: 'Where are your comments? Please write them next time.' On another: 'Don't focus on odds and evens only – we have a lot more ways of describing numbers.' Nearly all her class recognized the role of multiples in the sums, most of them producing flow diagrams for sums produced by 2, 3, 4 consecutive numbers. During the year her students had, according to our reading of the data, been deliberately enculturated into thinking about multiples, rather than just parity, when looking at empirical numerical data.

Was this task really non-routine for any of these learners? It is non-routine in the sense that it is not a performance of a standard mathematical technique, but there is a sense in which these teachers had familiarized, or routinized, their students' approaches to such tasks. The emphases with which they did this varied, and that helped us to see that what had gone on during the year was more than age-related maturation. In all classes learners made conjectures, and all classes showed some increased systematization, but some were more mathematically complex than others. Some were making deductive conjectures from structure, while most were acting empirically with calculation data, an approach encouraged by most teachers. Some were encouraged to look for multiplicative structures. Those who chose the system of finding what sequences sum to 3, 4, 5 and so on were less likely to sense the structure of the calculations than those who generated the sequences first, and then observed the results. It matters *how* a learner focuses on what varies in the calculation and the outcome, not just *whether* they focus (Mason 2002; Marton *et al.* 2004). It matters whether students focus on 'finding and expressing patterns' of any kind or 'finding and expressing mathematically complex patterns'. To describe 'complexity' solely in terms of enculturation into practices of exploration masks the inherent mathematical complexity of some structures when compared to others, although the mathematical processes of finding, conjecturing and expressing each are similar. Siobhán's students knew, from their experiences in her classroom, that multiplicative patterns are seen as more desirable mathematically than those based on parity.

Teaching ordinary mathematics harder

This idea of gradually shifting learners to appreciate and adopt more powerful methods is illustrated further in an example from another area of mathematics. Suppose that the topic is percentages, and the teacher has taken the usual line of getting her students to construct percentages based on 50 per cent, 10 per cent, 5 per cent and so on. This approach is often used for all learners, but particularly for low-attaining students, perhaps because it is assumed they will be unable to remember how to calculate percentages directly. How can such learners be encouraged to go beyond this building-up method, which can become tedious and error-prone in practice? Rather than expect learners to be willing to grasp the more direct method immediately, it might make more sense to develop the idea of having pre-calculated tools to hand by asking: 'Suppose we have to calculate 86 per cent. What percentages would it be useful to know to help us do this?' or 'What can we make if we already know 17 per cent?' Some will enjoy suggesting various combinations of simpler percentages, particularly if they have calculators to use. Other target percentages can be offered, and they can invent some of their own, until eventually percentages which have to be constructed from 1 per cent are in the frame. At this stage someone, maybe the teacher, might point out that all percentages can be made from 1 per cent and perhaps this is the most powerful toolkit.

The point being made in this example is that no one gives up an easy method or approach unless they can see a reason for needing a more universal method. If all linear equations have small integer solutions, they can be solved quickly by trial and error so no one needs a function-based or balance-based method. If all multiplications can be done by repeated addition, why would anyone need other knowledge? A similar problem is encountered when creating methods of enlarging shapes. If the shapes on offer are all rectilinear, tidily presented on squared paper, learners will be able to find many ways to enlarge them. If they are then gradually led to shapes with more and more awkwardness, not on squared paper, they are more likely to accept a method of constructing from a centre of enlargement than if they are just offered it as *the* method. In fact, it is worth thinking about every standard method as a special method which gives power in problematic cases, and learners need help to see why they need it instead of methods with which they may feel more comfortable.

But Siobhán brought something more than this to her teaching, she brought her own mathematical sensitivities to bear. I once saw a teacher getting a class to debate whether $0.\dot{9}$ was less than or equal to 1. The class was an all-attainment group in lower secondary, and contained several people whose English was not very strong. Nevertheless she got them involved and forced them to take sides. She knew that this is an important idea in mathematics, and that it is hard to understand. They had been working on ideas which were nearby – recurring decimals – so she decided to take them to a well-known place of potential disagreement. The debate did not reach a conclusion, but her aim had not been to resolve the matter. This kind of attention to the integrity of mathematics, rather than pretending that it can be simple, and that anything which works is as good as anything else, is, in my experience, a hallmark of the practice of teachers who make a difference to otherwise disadvantaged students. It is as if they teach ordinary mathematics harder, so that more thinking has to go on and the outcome is richer understanding.

I am confirming here that 'teaching matters' – not a very surprising outcome – and this analysis adds some specific knowledge about *how* it makes a difference. Subtle differences in practice can result in mathematically significant differences in the way learners routinize unfamiliar tasks. These teachers did not use common tasks in their teaching, nor common lesson structures, nor common teaching methods, but all their students made deep progress in mathematics, contrary to normal expectations for such groups. Their teaching principles are described in the previous chapter. In this chapter, I have shown that their students made progress by their willingness and resourcefulness in tackling unfamiliar tasks. Further, this happens partly through using routines learnt through their usual teaching, but the nature of these routines makes a difference to the mathematical outcomes of their work. Most knew that they could generate examples and look for patterns, and try to make general statements. Only some knew that to find patterns you might need and use *systematic* examples, and that general statements might be explained, or counter-examples found, using examples. Some knew that deduction from individual, structural examples is possible, but nevertheless still generated examples. Some knew that some types of pattern are more interesting and powerful than others. Some knew that the choice of system they made would lead to different possible patterns.

Differences between groups suggested that, within the overall improved achievement of all the target learners, some teachers were focusing more on mathematical structure than mathematical process. This interested me, because the prevailing view nationally is that process is important, and that mathematical thinking processes are valuable in themselves. Thus learners are all encouraged to look for patterns, to generalize, and to use other problem-solving heuristics – these are stated curriculum aims. The differences in these groups highlight that this thinking can be more useful or less useful, depending on the nature of the mathematical structures being explored and how they are perceived.

What is particularly powerful about these results is that the learners in these classes are those who are traditionally described as 'low ability', 'cannot concentrate', 'cannot think for themselves', 'need more structure', and so on. What we have shown is that, given time and appropriate teaching, they have shown that they can concentrate, think, 'structure' their work once they know some ways to structure it, and display complex mathematical thinking once they know what is possible.

Siobhán was particularly good at making this a focus of her teaching, while other teachers had different strengths such as focusing on mental arithmetic (developing mental representations of number structure) or participation (incorporating learners' ideas into the way the lesson proceeded).

How to teach ordinary mathematics harder

For me, this whole body of work has revealed two weaknesses in the community of practice of mathematics teaching: a lack of language to describe mathematical activity and, related to this, a lack of knowledge about how to harness mathematical thinking to learn curriculum mathematics. This leaves mathematics teachers in significant limbo: they want to help learners make deep progress, but they have to 'cover' the curriculum for the next test and see themselves as not having time to use exploratory methods; they are urged to develop learners' thinking skills, but the generic skills on offer do not address curriculum mathematics; they are torn between wanting everyone to succeed and having to segregate learners in order to manage their version of the curriculum.

Wherever students are segregated according to some notion of ability some learners are being constructed as deficient. Yet when the phrase 'less able' is used one might ask what exactly it is that these students are less able to do. Often what is seen as lacking is a skill or behaviour which, as we have seen in this and the previous chapter, *can* be taught, learnt, or encouraged, or which the student has already displayed in some other arena but has not used in mathematics. Opportunities to learn new behaviour, or to use what one already knows in other contexts, can open up opportunities to learn mathematics. In most classrooms, particularly those of low-attaining learners, opportunity to learn is limited by a narrow construction of mathematics and of mathematics discourse, and a limited view of learners, reduced to 'learner types'.

By watching teachers like those in the project over many years, I have been able to become significantly more articulate about the techniques of 'teaching ordinary mathematics harder'. Throughout this book I have written about question types which can use learners' proficiencies to promote harder engagement with school mathematics. Most of these relate to a particular view of mathematics and how to engage with it (Watson and Mason 1998). Conventional mathematics consists of a collection of different kinds of nouns which can become the objects of learning. In no particular order, they include:

definitions	facts	properties
theorems	examples	counter-examples
techniques	instructions	conjectures
problems	representations	notations
symbolization	explanations	justifications
proofs	reasoning	links
relationships	connections	...

These can, of course, be offered in a low-level way as objects to be memorized and reproduced. However, mathematics can also be described as a collection of actions, the things mathematicians do, which can be acts of engagement, of seeking understanding, of constructing meaning, or of creation:

exemplifying	specializing	completing
deleting	correcting	comparing
sorting	organizing	changing
reversing	varying	generalizing
conjecturing	explaining	justifying
verifying	convincing	refuting ...

All of these, to a greater or lesser extent, are natural ways for humans to behave which can be harnessed and enhanced in mathematics lessons.

Learning mathematics can then be seen as a dynamic process of organizing, enriching, extending and elaborating experiences of these activities. Thus, any mathematics question or problem triggers a personal collection of examples of past experience, and these examples are organized and interconnected in certain ways to form a clump – a 'personal example space' (Watson and Mason 2005). Teaching ordinary mathematics harder involves recognizing that each learner has a different clump, and that learning involves adding to and reorganizing example spaces so that, next time they are triggered, they may be richer. In any situation, the examples which come to mind are influenced by past and recent experience and associations; the words, images, social and affective circumstances of the environment; the learner's expectations of the situation and interpretation of the expectations of others; and the way in which the learner has structured and elaborated past mathematical experience.

For instance, in an introductory lesson on coordinates some learners may respond to the visual stimulus of a diagram by thinking of graphs they have seen, or 'joining dots' puzzles, or of other grids which are ordered from the top left corner, or of map references, or of the squared paper in their exercise books. The practice of bringing prior experience to bear on the current situation is universal, but what is brought is individual. Then learning about coordinates can be seen as extending the space of potential responses to seeing square grids and the relationships which come to mind when individual points are marked on it. A teacher might decide to incorporate the notion of relating x and y coordinates, so that the purpose of conventional numbering and ordering is clear from the start. To focus on relationships, she would probably reject $x = y$ as a starting place, since it is too special, but might choose something like $x = 2$ to counteract the tendency for learners to believe there is only ever one 'answer', follow this up with $y = 3$, and then ask 'where is the point (2,3)?'

In the final chapter, I describe the practices of some teachers who are making a significant difference to the mathematical progress of previously low-attaining learners, and offer some examples of ways in which mathematical thinking, curriculum mathematics and self-perception can be combined to rescue learners.

9 Construction, reconstruction and renewal

All of the differences in practice described earlier in the book are important, but it is the *belief* that learners *can* change which seems to make a significant difference to teachers in the last two chapters. Hart *et al.* (2004) call this 'transformability', a word which helps to focus teaching on the transformation of individuals through engagement with a subject.

In this chapter I describe the practices of some mathematics teachers who make significant differences to their students' learning. In doing this, I shall try to return to the distinction between habits which are solely mathematical and those which are more generic, such as those which aim at developing kind classrooms in which self-esteem can flourish and succour is freely sought and given. There may be classrooms in which a form of low-level bullying based on punishment, fear and strict disciplinary measures unrelated to learning produces better test results in the short term, but I am not interested in these. Sometimes, as in the incident I now describe, this kind of bullying is unintentionally institutionalized.

> While covering for the absent teacher of a Year 9 'bottom set' I intended to spend some time in the lesson working with Mark, whom I had previously observed to have a possible problem with short-term memory. I was not recognized by the school as a teacher, so another member of staff had been timetabled to 'run' the lesson within which I would teach. This teacher came in shortly after I had started talking to the students and proceeded to shout at them about how he wanted them to behave while being taught by a visiting teacher. He threatened them with detentions if they misbehaved, and then sent Mark, who was quietly gazing out of the window, to work elsewhere, saying 'We'd better not have you in here today'. Having established an atmosphere of tension and silence, not what I had wanted at all, he then said to me: 'Now then, you can get on'. This was one of those scenes which come back to haunt me every now and then – what could I have said? What could I have done? It had all been so quick that I just gaped open-mouthed at what
>
> *cont.*

was going on. I realized later that I had actually been more sensitive about challenging his status in the school than about challenging the students' status in the classroom. I had allowed the teacher to keep face while allowing Mark to lose what little dignity he may have had. I never had another chance to spend time with Mark and his mathematics.

Rather than support this kind of disciplinary approach to achieving an orderly classroom, I am concerned with the kinds of integrated practices described by Ollerton in various books (Ollerton and Watson 2001, Ollerton 2003) and by Hart *et al.* (2004). Hart *et al.* describe a mathematics teacher who has exceptional qualities of kindness and nurturing which he has developed from an underlying philosophy of equity and a developmental approach to the notion of 'ability'. This is reported in generic terms, and gives only a little insight into the way he teaches mathematics, the kinds of tasks he uses, the mathematical habits of mind he encourages his students to adopt. How can we be sure that a kind approach to teaching mathematics is possible while urging learners to do more than trail calmly through relatively comfortable exercises?

I am offering real, but disguised, stories of one school, and two teachers at other schools, whose mathematical decisions, within their institutional constraints, are making a real difference to students' achievements and hence to their life chances.

Data on which these descriptions are based is of various kinds – mainly observations and documents, supported and elaborated by interviews and long conversations in which I elicited teachers' reports of practice and underlying beliefs, philosophies and intentions. It is not possible to match all the details, and I could be criticized for lack of rigour in this respect, but I am not setting out to provide comparative cases here, rather I am trying to offer authentic descriptions of what I *know* to be true from observations and documents and what I *believe* to be true from my informed interpretations. The descriptions which follow have all been read and edited by the teachers involved. They can be treated as stories to hang in the air as you come to the end of the book, rather than as blueprints to be followed or examples of generalizable practice.

Adam Bede School

My information about this school comes from conversations with management, Ofsted reports, exam results, observations of lessons and informal discussions with several teachers. I shall call the school Adam Bede School. It is an inner-city school of about 1000 students of whom about 70 per cent have English as an additional language, over half are entitled to free school meals and about 20 per cent are registered as having special educational needs. Far more than 70 per cent come from ethnic groups which are usually disadvantaged in, and by, the UK educational and social systems. In common with similar schools most students had, in the past, very low expectations of themselves. For the last few years there has been a policy of senior management imposing high expectations, a top-down approach, and then providing support for staff to achieve these. At the time of writing, the top set for mathematics in Year 9 has just taken SATs, and also GCSE which is normally taken in Year 11, and has started to study the A-level syllabus in pure mathematics which is normally started in Year 12. I observed a lesson in which students were being 'talked through' the solution to:

$$2^{x^2 + x} = \frac{1}{4^{x + 1}}$$

Just in case you think this is a misprint I shall say it again: the Year 9 top set have just taken both SATs (in which half the class achieved the highest possible level) and GCSE at higher level and have started on the A-level syllabus, normally taken in Year 12, and were working through this question in class. The philosophy is that students are immersed in complex and challenging mathematics because in the course of solving this equation they see how various rules of indices, rearranging equations, and solving quadratics can contribute to something very grown up, yet each separate stage is within their grasp. This may not be true for all students in the class, but they understand that they are not expected to do this for themselves just yet (although some of them can) but are being given a glimpse of what is possible. The class contained about 30 students, a quarter of the cohort. The teaching style was interactive, and recognized that different students would have different methods. For example, the teacher said: 'what is the simplest way of solving a quadratic?' and then went on to say, in response to one student: 'So you prefer the formula? I have to admit that when I see a quadratic I always reach for the formula, but if you spot a factorization then that would be easier – if you spot it.' The interaction was a mixture of talk among equals and students being inducted into making mathematical choices. However, there was an overarching sense of a demonstration of mathematics which was going to be completed, regardless of students' comprehension, rather than a shared development of common understanding. What *was* common were the practices of approaching a new bit of 'hard' mathematics through identifying what is recognizable and what might be useful.

This method of immersion clearly works in terms of empowering students with excellent results in mathematics, and provides a substantial challenge to the prevailing philosophy that teaching should depend on assessment of students' current understanding. Let me elaborate a little, lest the reader thinks that I am advocating ignoring students' problems. If teaching depends on the teacher knowing what every student understands then it depends on, first, the misguided belief that it is possible for a teacher to know this and, second, on beliefs about a fixed order of the development of mathematical knowledge. Both of these, enacted too carefully and conscientiously, would limit students' progress to one pathway and would also require them to express all they know. On the other hand, if the teacher is 'ploughing on' and paying no attention at all to how many students are making sense of what is offered, then few are likely to make any progress at all. Students can, however, learn by experiencing how complex, half-understood mathematics which is hard to express can suddenly 'fall into place' when seen for a third or fourth time. This mimics the ways in which we learn in most contexts other than school, that is, by sorting out complex situations and gradually becoming more and more knowledgeable within these contexts. This way of learning is omitted in teaching which is too dependent on assessing each progressive step, and supported by teaching which immerses learners in complexity. Furthermore, I would argue that complex, hard-to-reach situations give learners a more honest experience of what it means to do mathematics.

The reason why I have talked about the top set, when this book is about lower-achieving students, is that it exemplifies the ethos of the mathematics department. This culture of immersion and exposure, described to me by one teacher as 'the forced curriculum', is carried through all mathematics classes. The 'lower' sets are prepared for GCSE at intermediate level not for foundation level.[1] While observing a lesson I overheard a student ask a teacher if he was going to be entered for foundation level. The teacher replied: 'We don't do foundation level at this school.' In conversation afterwards the teacher suggested that the student had heard about 'foundation' from friends at other schools. In the end some students *are* entered for foundation level, while it exists, but this is used as a safety net and not a target.

The belief is that this is a 'mixed ability' school and, like research into the effects of heterogeneous classes, students who achieve lower results benefit from being taught in more challenging environments than they might be able to reach themselves. In this school this belief does not extend to groupings for teaching. There is a top set, which is mixed gender, and then parallel middle and bottom sets which have recently (at the time of writing) been separated by gender. I do not intend here to say much about the gender split because it has only recently been introduced, and such divisions have been researched more thoroughly by others (Mendick 2006). The

---

[1] This way of measuring success will become obsolete when there are only two tiers of entry, and when different mathematical pathways for 14–19 are introduced. I am using it to demonstrate the significant difference Adam Bede makes to achievement in terms which have social currency. In a different system, there would be other measures of effectiveness.

improvements in achievement I am reporting in this chapter have been mainly due to earlier decisions about curriculum and expectations.

One possible reason for the school's success in creating an ethos of high expectations may be that most of the mathematics department are overseas teachers in their first UK posts, and come from countries in which mathematics teaching groups are not differentiated. Hence, they do not have the differentiated expectations which are endemic in the UK. One teacher, Andy Rivers, comes from Alberta. In 1999, Alberta became the highest-achieving non-Asian English-speaking area in the world in school mathematics and it continues to maintain its high position in international comparisons. His experience was of teaching heterogeneous groups within which students might be identified as needing extra, well-focused help. For this they receive extra teaching designed to help them re-enter mainstream classes. The philosophy is of 'rescue, recovery and return' rather than consigning students to a 'lower' group. He was uncomfortable with the setting philosophy at Adam Bede and felt that students were too affected by the comparative status of different sets. He talked to me in some detail about how he had had to take one lower group back to the basics of multiplication and division, adding decimals and even in some cases subtraction, but he would rather have had a few with these difficulties and worked with them in his own time than a whole class. However, he had not allowed them to get stuck going over and over work they had met several times in the past. The curriculum freedom he experienced at Adam Bede had led him to discover that they loved algebra. It appeared that doing algebra was new to them, and they enjoyed the 'fresh start' of doing some new mathematics which had a higher status than they had been used to doing. They had no preconceptions about whether they would or would not be able to do it, so they and Andy jointly found ways to do it successfully.

At the higher end of the full range of achievement, students' performance bears no similarity to the school's normal results a few years ago, when only a few would have taken higher-level GCSE. Overall, achievements at 14 are way beyond national predictions based on entry levels and other statistical comparisons. In the lowest-achieving groups, changes have not been so dramatic but still show significant improvement. The proportion of students failing to achieve government target levels at 14 is currently 24 per cent, lower than the 29 per cent who entered the school below target level. Among the students who entered the school at level 3 or below there are some significant success stories, such as two students who achieved level 6 at Key Stage 3 but were considered so weak in English and science that they did not have to take the tests, another student who achieved level 8, and eight students who achieved level 5. There is no downward spiral of low achievement during the first few years at the school. In particular, students for whom English is not the first language make significant progress during their first few years at the school.

The more important story about the lower end of achievement is when students are older and take GCSE. Around 2001 over 70 per cent of the students would take the lowest possible level of entry; now only about 20 per cent do. The school is restless about improving results further, since 46 per cent now get grade C or higher while the national average is about 50 per cent. This percentage rises every year and it is fair to say that, at the time of writing, the cohorts who will have been most affected by higher expectations have not yet reached this final hurdle.

This, then, has been a story about how a school can change expectations and make a difference to students' life expectations. But it says little about teaching methods. Indeed, the school sees teachers as professionals who can be given freedom to make professional decisions about how to meet the school's expectations. Beliefs and expectations are clearly an important part of any story about improved achievement, but teaching methods can make a difference too. This is recognized in an imaginative way, in that the strengths of individual teachers are used at times in the students' career when different emphases might be most beneficial. For example, those who are good at 'teaching to the test' are put with crucial test classes, while those who are good at developing mathematical thinking are used during the more reflective years.

In the rest of this chapter I describe the practices of two teachers, not at Adam Bede, who both make a significant difference to students' achievements, Molly and Susan.

Molly

My information about Molly comes from several interviews, lesson observations, Ofsted reports and the local authority advisory team.

Molly is a young teacher of 5 years' experience. She has a mathematics degree from a well-established UK university and trained to teach on one of the highest-ranked PGCE courses. For a year between graduating and PGCE she worked successfully for a bank, but her intention was always to teach. At the time of the observation and interview she was teaching in a coeducational comprehensive school of about 1800 students. It serves a fairly affluent urban area, but there are two council estates nearby also feeding the school. About 10 per cent of students have English as an additional language, 6 per cent are on the special needs register and 4.5 per cent are registered for free school meals. Seventy-five per cent achieve level 5 or better at Key Stage 3, and GCSE results show that roughly 70 per cent get C or above in mathematics, well above the national average. She says that 'these results follow the social intake'. Compared to Adam Bede's students most of hers are privileged, but, as in most comprehensive schools, the lower sets consist mainly of those from less privileged backgrounds, and in this respect some of Molly's groups are similar to those at Adam Bede.

Molly has been chosen for this book because her classes often overtake higher sets in their test outcomes. In a recent set of GCSE results, students who were in a relatively low set achieved an average of 2.3 grades higher than were predicted in standard statistical packages, and she had only taught them for two terms. This success included a decision to enter them for a higher level of examination than the one they were expected, by normal predictions, to take. This level of surpassing expectations is typical of her.

She is generous in her comments about colleagues, claiming that there are many ways to teach mathematics well, and some of her colleagues get very good results with very different methods. The school is somewhat unusual in that teachers are given individual professional responsibility for how they teach – as in Adam Bede, no one is expected to conform to norms such as three-part lessons, always stating lesson objectives in advance, covering topics in a given time and a given order, and so on. Furthermore, students are tested diagnostically in 'basic' numeracy and given specialist teaching, outside maths time, to target particular areas of weakness along-side pursuing mainstream mathematics lessons. In this way the school allows students to 'recover' in ways advocated by Dowker (2005) and sug-gested by Andy Rivers at Adam Bede, rather than keeping them in low sets because of number problems. Nevertheless, unlike the students Andy had experienced in Canada, students are organized into five mainstream set levels, with a very few extremely low-attaining students forming a small set 6 which is taught by the special needs department.

I asked Molly about how she teaches a typical set 5, and she said that she teaches them in the same way as she teaches all her groups; she does not imagine there are limits to what they can do. She has developed a 'normal' structure to her lessons, focusing on conceptual understanding. A lesson has four parts: starter, interactive exploration, whiteboard work, and consolidation. A starter task might be used to revise previous work on related, or unrelated, topics. These serve as mental warm-ups and reminders that 'this is a maths lesson', with all the expectations and opportunities which Molly has established over time with her groups. The main teaching always relates to prior learning and she informs them about what they might meet in the future, in their studies or their future lives, which con-nects to the current work. Thus students are never wondering 'why are we doing this?' since mathematics unfolds lesson after lesson, and they are fully included in the unfolding. Use of personal mini-whiteboards is integral to this process.

I asked her if she had plenary sessions, in the sense of whole-class segments in which learning is reviewed (at the time of writing, school inspectors look for these segments as part of their assessment schedule).

She said that most of her lessons are whole-class experiences, working jointly on understanding the concepts. Students consolidate their understanding through individual exercises which provide practice and other questions which allow them to think things through again for themselves, or argue them through with each other. Typically these are offered at the end of a lesson for only about 10 minutes. This ensures that students who cannot maintain effort on their own are not expected to do so for long periods. Instead, they are expected to maintain public effort in the group for most of the lesson. She achieves this even with classes containing significant numbers of students with attention disorders and behavioural problems such as Tourette syndrome, autism and others. She comments that it is hard for other teachers to take over her classes because students become very noisy if expected to work on their own. She asks them to work on their own very seldom; even when doing exercises they are expected to discuss, argue, and throw suggestions around the room.

How does she motivate her students? She feels that many teachers talk often about 'needing this for exams' but she avoids this, preferring instead to teach for understanding for most of the time, and then to provide separate preparation for doing written tests, which she prefaces by announcements such as: 'Now we have to spend a couple of weeks learning some skills which are not going to be of any use to you except to do well in maths tests.' In these periods the focus is on the language and expectations of maths tests. She points out that maths exams are 'poshly written' and most students have to learn how to decode the 'posh' language and work out what to do. In these lessons they are not working on their knowledge, but on how to apply their knowledge to answer typical test questions. Most of this is done in whole-class interactions, so that when they practise questions on their own they can engage effortfully with the maths content, because they have already become expert at the reading, presentation and interpretation which they have to do in tests.

Motivation does not usually come from distant future promises of grades; instead it seems to come from the shared atmosphere of the group working with Molly to achieve mathematical progress through effort and learning. In doing this she is exploiting her belief that all students want to learn, and enjoy the feeling of having learnt. She claims frequently to students that mathematics is hard to learn, but that she is alongside them, helping them, in the endeavour. They have to play their part in this shared project of learning a hard subject. She says that she has been told that telling students 'maths is hard' will put them off; she asked me what I thought. I replied: 'From your experience, does it put them off?' and she laughed and said 'no'.

She described a typical lesson in general terms, and then with some content, so I shall retell it using the content and pointing out her reasons at each stage in ways which show her underlying thinking about learning mathematics. The specific lesson was about 'substitution'. She wrote the word on the board and asked them to say it, and then to say what they understood by the word, such as its use in football or in 'substitute teacher'. She constructed a spider diagram of their ideas and asked 'what do you think it might mean in maths?', getting the answer 'replacing something by something else'. She then wrote: '$x + 5$' and asked them what it was. Several said 'expression' and she asked why they said that. So far, they had worked on the vocabulary they needed to accompany algebraic understanding, which helped them relate everyday knowledge to what was going to come next. Then she asked them to 'take the risk of suggesting' what might be substituted in the expression and they said several versions of 'substitute a number for x' offering various suggestions (including -1, which gained special praise).

During these kinds of discussion she uses a 'hands-up' approach to getting responses. She never picks students out by name if they do not appear to want to contribute as she does not like to put them 'on the spot'. Instead, she notices that more and more students take part over time, and she might have private targets with some of the less forthcoming ones to offer one answer in every lesson. She praises good contributions and new contributors. Wrong answers might be greeted with: 'Thank you so much, Wayne, for saying that, otherwise I might not have known that it could be seen that way. Let's back up and have another look at this.' And then 'see how being brave and saying what you think actually helps the lesson for everyone'.

After this kind of joint exploration of new ideas, she begins the extensive use of mini-whiteboards. In this lesson she wrote: '$2x + 3$' and '$x = 5$'. Students worked this out on whiteboards and held them up. All answers were written on the board. These included:

$$25 + 3 \qquad 16 \qquad 13 \qquad 2 \times 5 + 3$$

She asked them to check that their answer was there. She then told them which answers were correct and asked for volunteers to explain the right answers. She often says: 'We don't need to know who got the right answers; it is a personal thing, I know and you know and that is all we need.' In this case she asked 'why isn't 16 correct?' and another student explained this. She then asked 'what would this student have to do further to get a right answer?' and students gave more input. After she told me this she said that she had once been told not to put wrong answers on the board as this is what they would remember. Again I asked her 'Is this true in your experience?' and she said 'no'. The discussions of wrong methods are vigorous and emotional. She often asks students to explain to each other, such as 'Jenny, please tell Stan why it isn't 25'.

When looking at the class set of displayed whiteboard answers, she is looking for the full range of responses on which to base her future teaching, and she also looks for the way they lay the workings out. For example, in the question above it is important that they know *how* they got 13, rather than simply its correctness. 'Otherwise when they are faced with something vaguely similar like $2x^2 + 3$ they may not stop and think what to do.' Several examples are worked through in this way, chosen to expose possible problems.

The details of the way she thinks through how flesh-and-blood learners might learn mathematics, and how to harness their emotions and energy to achieve that learning, are astonishingly complex. A casual observer might think that her lessons are merely a noisy, messy, version of exposition and imitation, but in reality they are rooted in her understanding of what might be going on for each student. Her use of exercises for written work illustrates this well. When they start doing questions on their own there are no examples to follow on the board. All the work has been done on their whiteboards and has therefore been erased. Students *have* to think things through afresh for themselves. Sometimes she even gives them the same questions which have been worked on in the whole group so that they reconstruct the answers and arguments for themselves. Thus, the option to use worked examples as templates is avoided and the support for the work is all around them, among their colleagues and from her, because of the extensive discussion which has preceded it.

She says she has no idea why her teaching is so successful, but that students often say that they understand her ways of explaining things. She says that her ways of explaining depend on what students already know and what they say. She also works on maths in front of them when something unanticipated occurs; she says to new teachers 'they need to see you working on maths' as without this they have no models about what it really involves.

It is also true that her students work very hard for most of the lesson. The moment when they start doing written work is near the end of the lesson and is the first break in imposed effort. Until that point there is no opportunity to do anything mindless, but she often has to remind them that they are not working. Her understanding of adolescents is that they are often not aware of what they are, or are not, doing and she constantly reminds them that they ought to be working. Often this is expressed in personal terms, because she has developed bargains with individuals, and only has to say 'what do you need to be doing now?' to get them back on track. There are also whole-class targets in place such as 'I want everyone to have done question 3'.

She never gives detentions. Her reasons for this are about personal sanity and her need to have proper rest periods during the day. Discipline is based on positive work-related relationships with students, close contact with parents, conscientious use of whole-school procedures, and her insistence that students should tell her what they have done wrong, how they are going to put things right and when they will do this by. She reports positive incidents as well as negative incidents to senior staff and expects them, the senior staff, to follow these up with praise. In particular, she makes a big deal of students who have pulled themselves around from some negative habits. She does not see her job as about simplifying mathematics and behaviour, but about keeping students very busy on some hard thinking. 'What is the point', she asks, 'in giving them things they can already do?'

Her students are very fond of her and appreciate her efforts on their behalf. She has good relationships with parents, many of whom tell her of their appreciation of her efforts, and she is respected in the school. She has made a significant difference to the life chances of many of her students. For example, many students have achieved the coveted grade C at GCSE against all expectations and, thus, have had new horizons opened for them. At the upper end of the scale of achievement the numbers getting A* at GCSE and 100 per cent in A-level modules are also substantially higher than the statistical predictions. Unfortunately, the pressure of maintaining high-quality interactive teaching has exhausted her and Molly has now left teaching in order to find a more balanced life.

You may wonder why I have included her story in this chapter. My aim in this book is not only to show that it is possible for students to attain much higher results than are usually expected, but to show how this can be achieved. This necessarily includes the costs to teachers who are faced, day after day, with students whose behaviour is demanding and difficult but who do not give up on them. If governments seriously wish that all students will achieve as much as they can, they must also understand that the costs of such achievement are high and not be surprised when teachers choose either to leave the profession or to ration their energy and input in ways which might be less than optimal for individual students.

Susan

Information about Susan comes from Ofsted reports, interviews, lesson observations by two people, a diploma dissertation and department management documents.

Susan is, at the time of writing, a new head of mathematics in a large semi-rural comprehensive school in a small town which is hardly bigger than a village. Many students are bused to the school from nearby villages, and a considerable number come from the socially mixed fringes of a large city nearby. People commute to work in the city, or in London, and the school neighbourhood is surrounded by farmland. Until recently, some middle-class city families would bus their children to the school to avoid a three-tier system operating in the city, but the whole area is now only two-tiered, so the perceived advantages of this system do not have such a strong effect on intake. As measures of social disadvantage, 7 per cent of students are entitled to free school meals, and 18 per cent are identified as having special learning needs. Recent overall grades at 16+ are slightly above the national average. In national assessments, the school does as well as or slightly better than comparable schools. In terms of predictions about achievements, based on conservative notions of norms, the school does well. Susan, like Molly, aims well beyond such predictions.

Susan has been teaching for 11 years, having come into teaching after some years working in industry. Her first degree was in mathematics with computing, and in her first year there she studied some psychology, and sees this as making a significant contribution to her current practice. She also has a master's degree in computation from Oxford and a PGCE from a high-ranking institution. She describes her background as working class.

The phrase 'working class' crops up a lot when Susan talks about teaching her lowest-attaining sets. She describes typical 'working class' students as having a 'very sharp' sense of humour; they are loyal, streetwise and non-conformist except among themselves. She says: 'I like them, I laugh with them'. Because they are streetwise they have to know why they are expected to act in ways which do not come naturally. For example, one student who would not write anything down because he already 'had' an answer poses the problem for Susan: how would writing down the working be constructive for this student? The answer she constructs depends on how the student might achieve more in maths, not on how he might fit into the normal demands for classroom behaviour.

Interestingly, her somewhat stereotyped view of these students, based on how they are as a group, rather than how they differ from what a teacher might like them to be, seems to be beneficial for Susan's students because the stereotype is positive and contradicts more common views which see them as deviant. Their non-conformity does not mean they do not want to succeed; she assumes that they do, but they express it in ways which are different to those of more conforming students. She told me about how she had lost a night's sleep worrying about one student who had been very negative and disruptive in a lesson, but a few days later was the first to volunteer for extra maths lessons. This was told as an example of how a desire to learn can be masked by other inappropriate emotions.

While some would claim that definitions of social class have shifted during and after the Thatcher years, I am still happy to use 'working class' to encompass those most socially and economically disadvantaged. Used for describing secondary students it might include those from poor families or families with high unemployment or only casual work; those who are less able to engage in dialogue with the school; those who cannot exercise choices which depend on money; those who cannot or do not engage with culture and activity beyond what is immediately available through their community or mass media. Thus, I use it to describe those students who, for whatever reason, are unable to meet the expectations of the education system in terms of choice, participation, activity and support without struggle. Such a broad definition includes poor families who, nevertheless, make education a supported priority as well as those who have disposable income but do not value and support education, among others. In practice, most of these students end up being placed in lower sets in schools, so if the phrase 'working class' proves a barrier for the reader, you can think about lower sets instead. However, 'lower set' implies some cognitive problems with mathematics, whereas a 'class' categorization reminds us that the problems might be social rather than cognitive.

Susan sees her mission in teaching as helping all students to succeed, whoever they are and whatever their backgrounds. While she is not *only* interested in helping working-class students, her approach to them is significantly different from usual practices and leads to her inclusion in this book. She takes seriously the mantra which is used to support the use of setting in mathematics – that different students have different needs and this justifies teaching them in different groups. She identifies learning needs of different groups and teaches them accordingly in ways designed to compensate for, rather than emphasize, confirm or exacerbate, their differences. This does not mean that she is attempting to level students down or up, but rather that weaknesses in their learning are identified and dealt with so that they do not act as barriers to future learning.

For example, some students who did not know enough to do well in a forthcoming exam were given more teaching time. This sounds so simple, but to do this Susan put on extra classes during a Bank Holiday Monday, when the school was normally closed, and invited students to come. In spite of the usual assumption that students from lower sets would not choose to do mathematics during public holidays, Susan assumed that they *would* choose to come – and they did.

Another barrier is ignorance about the full implications of exams. For example, students are fully involved in decisions about which tier of entry to take at GCSE; she says 'they are nearly old enough to marry so I will treat them as decision-makers'. Discussion might include factors such as, when discussing mock exam scripts, 'you lost a mark with this mistake – is that a mistake you will still be making in June?' She discusses the risk factors with them, saying 'I will support you whatever your decision', and shows how this is a risk for her too, as an accountable professional, and therefore a shared risk – they are not alone. Her preference is for students to avoid the tiers of entry which lead to lowest grades as, in her view, these tests are not about mathematics. She prefers them to choose tiers of entry which invite engagement with structure, laws and understanding rather than those which require techniques and answers. For her this is about entitlement to a rich curriculum which treats the big ideas of maths, otherwise it is not maths. It is also, in her view, easier to take an exam which does not depend strongly on remembered techniques and facts but depends instead on understanding mathematics. Knowledge of the key ideas of maths will make it easier for students to do exams, not harder, since they have something to think about, and think with, in an exam setting.

The barriers Susan tries to prevent, and break down, are not only barriers to understanding, but also barriers to self-belief, barriers of expectation and barriers created by institutional norms. As well as actions like the extra lessons, the provision of support at break and lunchtime, the frequent use of deserved praise, and other well-known generic strategies for improving attainment, Susan has ways of working which are more specific to mathematics. These are rooted in commitments to pure mathematics and to the achievement of good results, using the assessment systems as they are. Thus, she is not very bothered about finding relevant contexts to motivate interest in mathematics; she prefers, like Ollerton (2002), to interest students in doing maths directly. She foregrounds the aim of good results, seeing their achievement as a shared task for her and the class, imposed on them by outside structures. Her students never ask 'why are we doing this?' because her attitude is 'learning this is the job we have to do; now how can we do it together?' She does not present maths as if it is something she herself is making them do; it is something they just have to do together to meet society's demands. Mathematics is not seen as a closed world for which she controls entry, 'it's something we are all looking at'.

Of course, establishing new ways of working with often disaffected secondary school students takes time. She uses games to engender a friendly ethos, respecting refusal to join in and not pushing everyone to do so, but encouraging them gradually by asking 'what do *you* think?' and not making an issue of answers like 'dunno'. Similarly, she does not make a big issue of errors: 'there are so many of them around you would never get anywhere'. She just waits until students join into the exposition usefully and correctly and then showers them with praise – but she does anticipate common misunderstandings and takes these into account in her teaching.

I have discussed mathematics teaching with her over several years and have never heard her speak negatively of students' capacity to learn. Comments about learning are always framed in language which provides possible ways forward for her teaching. For example, their needs, as she expresses them, are for a teacher who is always presenting them with something new, and working alongside them on it. They do not develop structures and links which help them synthesize knowledge for themselves, unlike students in higher sets, so her job in the shared task of their learning is to provide ways to see those structures and links. 'They need me to be interested in doing that.' One of the ways she does this is to offer a range of different representations as different ways of looking at mathematics.

Thus, a particular representation is not seen as a distinct topic (as in 'today we are going to do graphs') but as a viewpoint on maths which will shed light on things which are already familiar.

I will give two examples of this approach, one relating to adding fractions and one relating to algebraic representation of linear relationships. In each case, the mathematical focus remains abstract but is brought into the perceptual world through representations which are familiar and can be manipulated. In each case they start with something familiar: Susan asks 'why start with something they don't know?'

A lesson about adding fractions

The familiar starting place she uses for adding fractions is the colouring-in of strips of squares. This was a shock to me, as I had always thought that asking lower set students to 'colour in' leads to too much time being spent on calm, settled activity of little educational value, or too much time and effort spent dissuading students from doing neat and finished colouring. In contrast, Susan has coloured pencils always to hand and gives them out liberally. Her reasoning is that colouring is a familiar starting place, and is of mathematical use for making distinctions. Where her practice differs from mine is that she is successful in getting students away from careful colouring and into the more slapdash approach of quick and easy 'labelling'. Crucial to this is the understanding she has built up with teaching assistants, so that they too scurry round the room maintaining a 'quick and dirty' attitude to colouring. Indeed, giving assistants full information about her aims is very important, since it avoids their tendency to smooth the path for students to get 'the right answer' when what Susan requires is that they mentally struggle, ask questions, offer suggestions and generate their own ways of seeing mathematics.

The use of strips of varying numbers of squares, coloured in to represent fractions, happens not just in one or two lessons but (either actually or mentally) in every instance where fractions are mentioned. She sees representations which can be used as 'workplaces for meaning' as belonging among the regular tools of mathematics, along with pens, paper, rulers, symbols, numbers and so on. Her choice of representation is made very carefully, because to be a useful tool it must lend itself to varied and extensive use. Thus, the strip of squares is much more useful than a circle representation because you can make longer or shorter strips to vary the overall value, and it is easy to represent multiples of the denominator by slicing horizontally to make twice, three times, the number of parts of the strip. If the horizontal approach to splitting is used, there are some similarities with how one might use rectangles to think about multiplying and dividing fractions. Visually, translation between equivalent fractions is achieved merely by inserting or ignoring lines, or by finding ways to 'see' the line differently.

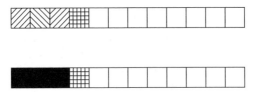

Different ways to write about these emerge through discussion:

$$\frac{3}{12} + \frac{1}{12} = \frac{4}{12}$$

$$\frac{1}{4} + \frac{1}{12} = \frac{1}{3}$$

These two outcomes show different understandings within the group, but are shown through the diagram to be equivalent. There is no pressure, but she makes it clear that the second is the one which mathematicians would write. Moving between the two is just a matter of putting lines in or taking lines out. One could say that this is the way most people teach fractions, but the context of regular use, some might say overuse, of the diagrams and the positive ethos, together with plenty of opportunity to play with their own examples, and the lack of pressure to conform to certain ways of seeing, make this a different pedagogic experience for the teacher, assistants and learners. The strip approach becomes one of 'the regular things we do in maths lessons' rather than a rare occurrence which has to be recalled alongside lots of other rare mathematical experiences.

She offers several things at once: shapes, words, symbols, and different ways of seeing, since she has confidence that this is what helps brains to work and that multiple experiences make it more likely that something, not necessarily the whole thing, will be remembered. The argument that multiple presentations might confuse lower-attaining students is meaningless for her, since it may lead to limited teaching of an over-simplistic kind which contributed to their lack of knowledge in the first place. With these visual tools, used alongside symbolic and numerical representations and words, students can either display fractions and additions which they have been given, or invent fraction sums to display and calculate, or colour the strips first and then represent their sums in a conventional form. This latter approach is the most unusual: using the representation to create examples and learn the concepts and then learning to write these in conventional notation as an enculturation process. She is explicit with her students about the fact that in exams they are more likely to be given the question the other way round, being asked to add two fractions. This kind of question then becomes a challenge for imagination: 'what fraction strips would I have if this is the sum I would write?' rather than the memorizing and application of an algorithm.

Algebraic representation of linear relationships

The approach to algebra I will describe has been published (Fairchild 2001) and is also described further in a book to which Susan contributed some ideas (Mason *et al.* 2005). It stems from an understanding of conservation of area. Throughout their early experiences of formal linear algebra her students work with rectangular models such as, for $3x$ and $3x + 2$:

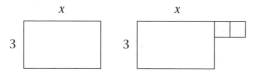

These provide representations of multiplicative algebraic objects, such as might appear in equations and expressions. Students become very familiar with drawing rough diagrams when they are faced with an algebraic task, and the diagrams are drawn roughly, without rulers, on plain paper, so that any idea that lengths have to be neat and accurate is dropped. Diagrams drawn neatly on squared paper do not work, because the lengths would always have a particular value.

In one lesson I observed, Susan started with a diagram, using easy numbers so that she could be sure they would see what was going on and could focus on the use of the diagram to express it:

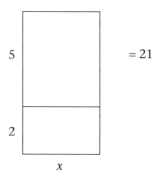

This approach uses familiarity with numbers as the starting point – not a deep understanding of area calculations. Indeed, knowledge of rectangular area can be a by-product of this approach rather than a pre-requisite. There was some discussion with the whole class about what it meant and what other things could be written. The focus was on the relationship between 'what you know and what you don't know'. Next, students made up examples and some of these were written on the board. Some students wanted to write on the board but did not quite know what to write, so Susan quietly helped them – constantly reinforcing the diagram and verbal ways to use it. Eventually, having 'found x' a few times, she chose one of the diagrams and developed, with the students, three ways to write the related calculation, using coloured pens to emphasize the multiplier 3.

$$3 \times 2 + 3 \times 5 = 3 \times 7 = 3 \times (2 + 5)$$

Use of coloured pens is, like many of Susan's strategies, a deliberate act to draw attention to particular features in mathematical notation. In this case, she uses colour to force learners' attention onto the role of 3, and where it appears in the notation. She also uses it to distinguish between unknowns and givens in equations, variables and constants in functions.

She recognizes that her own classes are deeply enculturated into using diagrams for all their work, so she cannot evaluate 'helpfulness' on current classes, since they know nothing other than this and it would be hard to extricate it from other aspects of her teaching. When she first devised it she ran an evaluation in which teachers and classes in one part of a school used this approach and were compared to parallel classes in another part which had used more conventional approaches. The students who had used this approach did significantly better than others. To some extent these multi-use diagrammatic approaches, which start from easy understandings and build complex ideas upon them, are an integral part of well-founded teaching which enables access for all to abstract ideas. Yet it also seems as if other teachers who do not necessarily share the underlying drive towards social equity can also use them effectively.

However, it is always possible for teachers without this drive to reduce tasks to simplistic activity. One example Susan gives is the ubiquitous use of personal data to provide a dataset for learning about means, medians, ranges and so on. Students measure bits of themselves and enter height, circumference of head, shoe size, length of arms, hand span and so on into a spreadsheet. This measuring takes all of one lesson and students often do it in Years 5, 6, 7 and 8 without letting on to their teachers that they have done it before. Susan's view is that this is not maths, so her students do not spend mathematics lesson time on this. The maths is the *nature of the focus* on the data, not the data itself, and for that you need 'instant' data such as 'how many siblings have you got?' or 'how long does it take you to get to school?' These questions give instant data for which a frequency table emerges straight away as an efficient display, with all the attendant potential confusions such as 'number of siblings' with 'number of people with that number of siblings'. Since only one set of data is used at a time, this confusion can be worked on again and again in the lesson – a sharp focus on data and what you can do with it rather than on data collection. For thinking about correlation she could use numbers of aunts and uncles, or, by contrast, shoe size – again instantly available data. The data retains the personal engagement which makes it meaningful, but the lesson does not deteriorate into repetition of low-level tasks. It would be against her principles to waste the time of students who need to do as much maths as possible on essentially non-mathematical tasks, however much they might enjoy them.

Is Susan successful? Her successes shine through in several ways. Firstly, her classes engage in real mathematics and students ask interesting questions about what they are doing. Students choose to study maths in their own time. They therefore make 'deep progress' in mathematics. Secondly, her test results often confound the hierarchies of setting; for example, in one year the mean coursework scores for both her 'low attaining' Year 11 groups were higher than the group 'above'. Thirdly, her groups outperform parallel groups in external exams. Finally, the crucial high-stakes GCSE results achieved by her students are always well above expectations. For example, a whole class of students who had been expected to enter the lowest tier, for which the maximum grade is D, were entered for the intermediate level and many then achieved the watershed grade of C. In this respect, like Molly and like the Adam Bede school, Susan makes a real difference to the future pathways open to her students. She is now looking for ways to extend these effects across the school.

Finally

Adam Bede school makes a difference by imposing high expectations on everyone and teaching harder mathematics, a lot harder than anyone imagined possible, thus raising achievement for previously low achieving students. Susan and Molly find that they can make an astonishing difference to students from socially disadvantaged backgrounds and past lower achievement by providing robust, intense mathematics lessons interwoven with emotional and social awareness. All three schools allow teachers to decide for themselves how to teach; none impose lesson structures or curriculum coverage. None of them pretend that learning mathematics is simple, or can be simplified. None of them expect all students to fully understand before they move on to harder work, but Susan and Molly both have deep philosophies about how students learn, and their philosophies imbue everything they do. Constructing ways into real, complicated, mathematics which make sense to learners is central to their work; the examples they use, the representations, the tools, the words, the activities, the practice questions are all carefully planned.

Molly and Susan do not teach at schools with the same kind of overall intake as Adam Bede School, and it would be tempting to claim that they had an advantage by working in generally more successful schools. I would argue the reverse, that the students they had in the lowest sets were often additionally alienated by their difference from the majority of students at the school. Moreover, their students were often vilified by the system and could adopt extreme behaviour in immature attempts to create a visible identity for themselves, or indeed to become invisible and self-annihilistic. Molly, in particular, describes constant battles between her own positive view of such students and the negative views of colleagues. In order to teach one group of students quadratic equations she had to disobey the instructions of her line manager which were 'not to bother'. I have also heard stories of students being excluded from school but a particularly life-enhancing mathematics teacher negotiating their willing return for maths lessons. In one case this was covert, the student entering and leaving the school by a side entrance! At Adam Bede School, Molly and Susan would be more in tune with the attitudes of colleagues and management.

I have been tempted, as I am sure you have, to imagine the effect of teachers like Molly and Susan at schools like Adam Bede. What would be the effect of having excellent enhancing mathematics teaching like theirs at a school which also imposed higher expectations from above? But this is too simplistic a question. I have not described teaching at Adam Bede in detailed terms because I have not analysed it to such an extent. There is wide variety there, so the still-unanswered question is: are higher expectations effective on their own, or does teaching matter? Having seen many teachers in action during my career, I certainly believe that teaching *does* matter and that it is the way teachers combine love for adolescents with love of mathematics which makes a major difference, rather than lesson structures, textbook choices, class organization and all the other things described in guidelines of good practice. There is nothing new about this finding (Brophy and Good 1974) but it seems as if each successive generation of teachers and teaching needs to be reminded of it as it gets lost beneath the weight of current policies and systems.

Raising expectations and teaching harder mathematics clearly has an effect as well. Adam Bede's curriculum policy seemed, at first look, not so dramatically effective for the lowest-attaining groups, and not so dramatically effective as Molly and Susan's teaching of such groups. We could be tempted to say that their bottom sets could do better if they had teachers like Molly or Susan. Yet, looking at entry levels and measures of disadvantage, I can see that nearly half the school's students are comparable to those in bottom sets at Molly and Susan's schools in terms of social background and previous attainment. In other words, Adam Bede is making the same kinds of difference to the same kinds of students at the whole-school level as Molly and Susan are at their class level.

On what note should I end this book, then? Obviously I want to applaud good teaching, and what I have chosen to describe as 'good' throughout the book depends on a deep understanding of mathematical activity. I claim that this is so central to good mathematics teaching that many other features of teaching, such as promoting a positive atmosphere, using ICT, communicating with parents, and keeping marking records, which are often considered to be the principal criteria for good teaching, become subsumed within it. Good mathematics teachers engage with mathematics themselves and engage all their students in mathematics. This focus shines a light on how learners are thinking and what they are doing, so that teachers understand more about how people might think, and how to support and develop their thinking in mathematics. When this becomes the main part of the job, good teachers can step outside the normal expectations of curriculum coverage and predicted grades – we see this in Molly and Susan and also in the teachers in Chapter 8. Differentiation becomes something that the learners do through their different kinds of engagement, rather than something teachers do to learners. Teaching becomes a subversive activity in which norms are overturned, 'lower' groups overtake 'higher' groups, and get grades they 'should not' be getting.

I would like to be able to say all this with certainty, but Adam Bede's approach challenges this: it would be possible to have all the qualities I have just described but, through the best of intentions, to lock some students into excited engagement with easier mathematics than they can really handle. To be really 'good', teachers may need to abandon expectations, schemes of work, targets and predictions, and to offer students the hardest mathematics they can possibly imagine, rope them in, care about them and ignite their thinking, and to do this with a passion and effort that ensure it works.

References

Adhami, M. (2001) Responsive questioning in a mixed-ability group, *Support for Learning,* 16(1): 28–34.

Adhami, M., Johnson, D. and Shayer, M. (1998) Does CAME work? Summary report on phase 2 of the Cognitive Acceleration in Mathematics Education, CAME, Project, *BSRLM Informal Proceedings,* 17(3): 26–31.

Ahmed, A. (1987) *Better Mathematics.* London: HMSO.

Ahmed, A. and Williams, H. (1992) *Raising Achievement in Mathematics.* London: West Sussex Institute of Higher Education/Department for Education and Science.

Ainscow, M. and Tweddle, D. (1979) *Preventing Classroom Failure: An Objectives Approach.* Chichester: Wiley

Ainscow, M. and Tweddle, D. (1988) *Encouraging Classroom Success.* London: David Fulton.

Anderson, J. and Schunn, C. (2000) Implications of the ACT-R learning theory: no magic bullets, in R. Glaser (ed.) *Advances in Instructional Psychology: Educational Design and Cognitive Science,* Vol. 5, pp. 1–33. Mahwah, NJ: Erlbaum.

Anghileri, J. (2000) *Teaching Number Sense.* London: Continuum.

Anghileri, J. (2006) A study of the impact of reform on students' written calculation methods after five years' implementation of the National Numeracy Strategy in England. *Oxford Review of Education,* 32(3).

Askew, M., Brown, M., Johnson, D., Millett, A.M., Prestage, S. and Walsh, A. (1993) *Evaluation of the Implementation of National Curriculum Mathematics at Key Stages 1, 2 and 3.* London: School Curriculum and Assessment Authority.

Avital, S. and Barbeau, E. (1991) Intuitively misconceived solutions to problems, *For the Learning of Mathematics,* 11(3): 2–8.

Bauersfeld, H. (1988) Interaction, construction and knowledge: Alternative perspectives for mathematics education, in D. Grouws, T. Cooney and

D. Jones (eds) *Perspectives on Research on Effective Mathematics Teaching*, pp. 27–46. Mahwah, NJ: Erlbaum.

Bell, A. and Wheeler, D. (1968) *Examinations and Assessment*. Leicester: Association of Teachers of Mathematics.

Bernstein, B. (1990) *The Structuring of Pedagogic Discourse*. London: Routledge.

Bills, C., Bills, L., Watson, A. and Mason, J. (2004) *Thinkers*. Derby: Association of Teachers of Mathematics.

Bjorkqvist, O. (1997) Some psychological issues in the assessment of mathematical performance, in E. Pehkonen (ed.) *Proceedings of the 21st Conference of the International Group for the Psychology of Mathematics Education*, Vol. 1 pp. 3–17. Lahti: University of Helsinki.

Black, P. and Wiliam, D. (1998) Assessment and classroom learning. *Assessment in Education: Principles, Policy and Practice*, 5(1): 7–73.

Blease, D. (1983) Teacher expectations and the self-fulfilling prophecy, *Educational Studies*, 9(1): 123–35.

Blease, D. (1995) Teachers' judgements of their pupils: broad categories and multiple criteria, *Educational Studies*, 21: 203–16.

Boaler, J. (1997) *Experiencing School Mathematics: Teaching Styles, Sex and Setting*. Buckingham: Open University Press.

Boaler, J. (2002) *Experiencing School Mathematics: Traditional and Reform Approaches to Teaching and Their Impact on Student Learning* (revised and expanded edition). Mahwah, NJ: Erlbaum.

Boaler, J. and Wiliam, D. (2001) 'We've still got to learn!' Students' perspectives on ability grouping and mathematics achievement, in P. Gates (ed.) *Issues in Mathematics Teaching*, pp. 77–92. London: RoutledgeFalmer.

Boaler, J., Wiliam, D. and Brown, M. (2000) Students' experiences of ability grouping – disaffection, polarization and the construction of failure, *British Educational Research Journal*, 26: 631–49.

British Broadcasting Corporation (2005) Black Boys Separate Classes Idea. www.news.bbc.co.uk/1/hi/education/4323979.stm (accessed 5 August 2005).

Broadfoot, P. (1979) *Assessment, Schools and Society*. London: Methuen.

Brophy, J. and Good, T. (1974) *Teacher–Student Relationships: Causes and Consequences*. New York: Holt, Rhinehart and Winston.

Brown, A. (1992) Design experiments: theoretical and methodological challenges in creating complex interventions in classroom settings, *Journal of the Learning Sciences*, 2(2): 141–78.

Brown, L. and Coles, A. (1999) Needing to use algebra: a case study, in O. Zaslavsky (ed.) *Proceedings of the Twenty-Third Annual Conference of the International Group for the Psychology of Mathematics Education*, Vol 2, pp. 153–60. Haifa: Technion.

Brown, M., Askew, M., Millett, A. and Rhodes, V. (2003) The key role of educational research in the development and evaluation of the National Numeracy Strategy, *British Educational Research Journal*, 29(5): 655–72.

Burton, L. (2004) 'Confidence is everything' – perspectives of teachers and students on learning mathematics, *Journal of Mathematics Teacher Education*, 7: 357–81.

Butler, R. (1987) Task-involving and ego-involving properties of evaluation, *Journal of Educational Psychology*, 79: 474–82.

Chazan, D. (1996) Algebra for all students, *Journal of Mathematical Behavior*, 15: 455–77.

Christiansen, B. and Walther, G. (1986) Task and activity, in B. Christiansen, A. Howson and M. Otte (eds) *Perspectives on Mathematics Education*, pp. 243–307. Dordrecht: Reidel.

Coard, B. (1971) *How the West Indian Child Is Made Educationally Subnormal in the British School System: The Scandal of the Black Child in Schools in Britain*. London: New Beacon.

Coard, B. (2005) Why I wrote the 'ESN book'. www.education.guardian. co.uk/racism/story/0,10795,1406216,00.html (accessed 7 August 2005).

Cockcroft, W.H. (1982) *Mathematics Counts: Report of the Committee of Inquiry in the Teaching of Mathematics in Schools*. London: HMSO.

Coffield, F., Moseley, D., Hall, E. and Ecclestone, K. (2004) *Should We Be Using Learning Styles?* Learning and Skills Research Centre, www.lsrc.ac.uk (accessed 5 August 2005).

Cooper, B. and Dunne, M. (1998) Social class, gender and equity and National Curriculum tests in mathematics, in P. Gates (ed.) *Proceedings of the First International Mathematics Education and Society Conference*, pp. 132–47. Nottingham: Centre for the Study of Mathematics Education, University of Nottingham.

Cooper, B. and Dunne, M. (2000) *Assessing Children's Mathematical Knowledge: Social Class, Sex and Problem-Solving*. Buckingham: Open University Press.

Cooper, P. and McIntyre, D. (1996) *Effective Teaching and Learning: Teachers' and Students' Perspectives*. Buckingham: Open University Press.

Damasio, A. (2000) *The Feeling of What Happens: Body and Emotion in the Making of Consciousness*. London: Heinemann.

Dearing, R. (1994) *The National Curriculum and its Assessment*. London: School Curriculum and Assessment Authority.

Denvir B. and Brown M. (1986) Understanding of number concepts in low attaining 7–9 year olds, *Educational Studies in Mathematics*, 17: 15–36, 143–64.

Department for Education and Employment (2001) *Key Stage 3 National Strategy Framework for Teaching Mathematics: Years 7, 8 and 9*. London: DfEE.

Dowker, A. (2005) Numeracy recovery: a pilot scheme for early intervention with young children with numeracy difficulties, in A. Watson, J. Houssart and C. Roaf (eds) *Supporting Mathematical Thinking*, pp. 28–38. London: David Fulton.

Dreyfus, T. (1991) Advanced mathematical thinking processes, in D. Tall (ed.) *Advanced Mathematical Thinking*, pp. 25–41. Dordrecht: Kluwer.

Dunne, M. (1994) The construction of ability: a critical exploration of mathematics teachers' accounts. Unpublished PhD thesis, University of Birmingham.

Dweck, C. (1999) *Self-Theories: Their Role in Motivation, Personality and Development*. Philadelphia: Psychology Press.

Ellerton, N. (1986) Children's made up mathematics problems: a new perspective on talented mathematicians. *Educational Studies in Mathematics*, 17: 261–71.

Ernest, P. (1991) *The Philosophy of Mathematics Education*. London: Falmer.

Fairchild, J. (2001) *Transition from Arithmetic to Algebra Using Two-Dimensional Representations: A School Based Research Study*. Oxford: Department of Educational Studies.

Feuerstein, R. (1980) *Instrumental Enrichment: An Intervention Program for Mathematics Education*. London: Croom Helm.

Fielding, M. (2001) Students as radical agents of change, *Journal of Educational Change*, 2(3): 123–41.

Fischbein, E. (1987) *Intuition in Science and Mathematics: An Educational Approach*. Dordrecht: Reidel.

Gardner, H. (1983) *Frames of Mind: The Theory of Multiple Intelligences*. London: Heinemann.

Gates, P. (ed.) (2001) *Issues in Mathematics Teaching*. London: RoutledgeFalmer.

Gillborn, D. and Youdell, D. (2000) *Rationing Education: Policy, Practice, Reform and Equity*. Buckingham: Open University Press.

Gipps, C. (1992) National Curriculum assessment: a research agenda, *British Educational Research Journal*, 18(3): 277–86.

Goffman, E. (1959) *The Presentation of Self in Everyday Life*. Garden City, NY: Doubleday.

Gramsci, A. (1949) *Gli intelletuali e l'organizzazione della cultura*. Turin: Einaudi.

Gramsci, A. (1971) *Selections from the Prison Notebooks*. London: Lawrence and Wishart.

Hadamard, J. (1945) *An Essay on the Psychology of Invention in the Mathematical Field*. Princeton, NJ: Princeton University Press.

Haggarty, L. and Postlethwaite, K. (2003) Action research: a strategy for teacher change and school development? *Oxford Review of Education*, 29(4): 423–48.

Hallam, S. and Toutounji, I. (1996) *What Do We Know about Grouping Pupils by Ability? A Research Review.* London: Institute of Education.

Harries, T. (2001) Working through complexity: an experience of developing mathematical thinking through the use of Logo with low attaining pupils, *Support for Learning,* 16(1): 23–7.

Hart, S., Dixon, A., Drummond, M., McIntyre, D. (2004) *Learning without Limits.* Maidenhead: Open University Press.

Hiebert, J., Carpenter, T., Fennema, E., Fuson, K., Wearne, D., Murray, H., Olivier, A. and Human, P. (1997) *Making Sense: Teaching and Learning Mathematics with Understanding.* Portsmouth, NH: Heinemann.

Hiebert, J., Gallimore, R., Garnier, H., Giwin, K., Hollingsworth, H., Jacobs, J., Chui, A., Wearne, D., Smith M., Kersting, N., Manaster, A., Tseng, E., Etterbeek, W., Manaster, C., Gonzales, P. and Stigler, J. (2003) *Teaching Mathematics in Seven Countries: Results from the TIMSS 1999 Video Study* (NCES 2003–013). Washington, DC: National Center for Education Statistics.

Holt, J. (1964) *How Children Fail.* Harmondsworth: Penguin.

Houssart, J. (2001) Rival classroom discourses and inquiry mathematics: the 'whisperers', *For the Learning of Mathematics,* 21(3): 2–8.

Houssart, J. (2004) *Low Attainers in Primary Mathematics: The Whisperers and the Maths Fairy.* London: RoutledgeFalmer.

Independent (1998) Some schools believe that their experiments in teaching single sex have improved boys' performance, *The Independent,* 26 November. www.literacytrust.org.uk/Research/ressinglesex.html#Some%20schools (accessed 11 January 2006).

Ingenkamp, K. (1977) *Educational Assessment.* Slough: NFER.

Ireson, J, and Hallam, S. (2001) *Ability Grouping in Education.* London: Sage.

Jaworski, B. (1996) *Investigating School Mathematics.* London: RoutledgeFalmer.

Key Maths (1998) *Foundation,* Revised Edition. Cheltenham: Nelson Thornes.

Krutetskii, V.A. (1976) *The Psychology of Mathematical Abilities in School Children.* Chicago: University of Chicago Press.

Lerman, S. (2004) Being schooled in school mathematics: Learning how to be in the mathematics classroom, in B. Clarke, D. Clarke, G. Emanuelsson *et al.* (eds) *International Perspectives on Learning and Teaching Mathematics,* pp. 339–50. Gothenburg: National Centre for Mathematics Education.

Lincoln, Y.S. and Guba, E.G. (1985) *Naturalistic Inquiry.* Newbury Park, CA: Sage.

Lorenz, J.H. (1982) On some psychological aspects of mathematics achievement, assessment and classroom interaction, *Educational Studies in Mathematics,* 13: 1–19.

MacNamara, A. and Roper, T. (1992a) Attainment target 1 – is all the evidence there?, *Mathematics Teaching,* 140: 26–7.

MacNamara, A. and Roper, T. (1992b) Unrecorded, unobserved and sup-
pressed attainment — can our pupils do more than we know?, *Maths in
Schools*, 21: 12–13.

Marton, F. and Saljö, R. (1976) On qualitative differences in learning: 1.
Outcome and process. *British Journal of Educational Psychology*, 46: 4–11.

Marton, F., Runesson, U. and Tsui, A. (2004) The space for learning, in
F. Marton and A. Tsui (eds.) *Classroom Discourse and the Space of Learning*.
(3–40) Mahwah, NJ: Erlbaum.

Mason, J. (1988) *Learning and Doing Mathematics*. London: Macmillan
Educational.

Mason, J. (2002) Generalisation and algebra: exploiting children's powers,
in L. Haggerty (ed.) *Aspects of Teaching Secondary Mathematics:
Perspectives on Practice*, pp. 105–20. London: RoutledgeFalmer.

Mason, J., Burton, L. and Stacey, K. (1982) *Thinking Mathematically*. London:
Addison-Wesley.

Mason, J., Graham, A. and Johnston-Wilder, S. (2005) *Developing Thinking in
Algebra*. London: Sage.

McDermott, R. (1993) The acquisition of a child by a learning disability, in
S. Chaiklin and J. Lave (eds) *Understanding Practice: Focus on Activity and
Context*, pp. 269–305. Cambridge: Cambridge University Press.

Mendick, H. (2006) *Sex by Numbers: Exploring the Relationship between
Mathematics and Masculinity*. Maidenhead: Open University Press.

Michener, E. (1978) Understanding understanding mathematics. *Cognitive
Science*, 2: 361–83.

Morgan, C. (1996a) Language and assessment issues in mathematics education, in L. Puig and A. Gutiérrez (eds) *Proceedings of the 20th Conference
of the International Group for the Psychology of Mathematics Education*,
Vol. 4, pp. 19–26, Valencia: University of Valencia.

Morgan, C. (1996b) Teacher as examiner: the case of mathematics coursework. *Assessment in Education*, 3(3): 353–75.

Morgan, C. (1998) *Writing Mathematically: The Discourse of Investigation*.
London: Falmer.

Morgan, C. and Watson, A. (2002) The interpretive nature of teachers'
assessment of students' mathematics: issues for equity, *Journal for
Research in Mathematics Education*, 33(2): 78–107.

Morrison, A. and McIntyre, D. (1969) *Teachers and Teaching*. Harmondsworth:
Penguin.

Nash, R. (1976) *Teacher Expectations and Pupil Learning*. London: Routledge
& Kegan Paul.

Norton, S., McRobbie, C. and Cooper, T. (2002) Teachers' responses to an
investigative mathematics syllabus: their goals and practices,
Mathematics Education Research Journal, 14(1): 37–59.

Ofsted (1994) *Science and Mathematics in Schools: A Review* London: HMSO.

Ofsted (2002) *Mathematics in Secondary Schools: School Subject Reports 2001/02.* www.ofsted.gov.uk/publications/index.cfm?fuseaction=pubs.summary &id=2875 (accessed 5 August 2005).

Ofsted (2004) *The Key Stage 3 Strategy: Evaluation of the Third Year.* www.ofsted.gov.uk/publications/index.cfm?fuseaction=pubs.summary &id=3601 (accessed 5 August 2005).

Ofsted (2005) *Mathematics in Secondary Schools: School Subject Reports 2003/04.* www.ofsted.gov.uk/publications/index.cfm?fuseaction=pubs.summary &id=4061 (accessed 5 August 2005).

Ollerton, M. (2002) *Learning and Teaching Mathematics without a Textbook.* Derby: Association of Teachers of Mathematics.

Ollerton, M. (2003) *Getting the Buggers to Add Up.* London: Continuum.

Ollerton, M. and Watson, A. (2001) *Inclusive Mathematics 11–18.* London: Continuum.

Peterson, C., Maier, S. and Seligman, M. (1993) *Learned Helplessness: A Theory for the Age of Personal Control.* New York: Oxford University Press.

Pimm, D. (1987) *Speaking Mathematically: Communication in Mathematics Classrooms.* London: Routledge.

Pitt, A. (2002) Mathematical thinking? *Mathematics Teaching*, 181: 3–5.

Pólya, G. (1962) *Mathematical Discovery: On Understanding, Learning, and Teaching Problem Solving.* New York: Wiley.

Postlethwaite, T. (1999) Overview of issues in international achievement studies, in B. Jaworski and D. Phillips (eds) *Comparing Standards Internationally: Research and Practice in Mathematics and Beyond*, pp. 23–60. Oxford: Symposium Books.

Prestage, S. and Perks, P. (2001) *Adapting and Extending Secondary Mathematics Activities: New Tasks for Old.* London: David Fulton.

Pring, R. and Walford, G. (eds) (1997) *Affirming the Comprehensive Ideal.* London: Falmer Press.

Programme for International Student Assessment (2004) *Learning for Tomorrow's World: First results from PISA 2003.* Paris: Organisation for Exonomic Co-operation and Development; www.pisa.oecd.org (accessed 2 August 2005).

Qualifications and Curriculum Authority (1999) *The National Curriculum: Handbook for Secondary Teachers in England.* London: DfEE/QCA.

Qualifications and Curriculum Authority (2001) *Standards at Key Stage 2: English, Mathematics and Science: A Report for Headteachers, Class Teachers and Assessment Coordinators on the 2000 National Curriculum Assessments for 11-year-olds.* London: QCA.

Rawls, J. (1972) *A Theory of Justice.* Oxford: Clarendon Press.

Rawls, J. (2001) *Justice as Fairness: A Restatement.* Oxford: Oxford University Press.

Revell, P. (2005) The government espouses the theory of learning styles with scant regard to the evidence. http://education.guardian.co.uk/ egweekly/ story (accessed 4 June 2005).

Roaf, C. and Bines, H. (1989) Needs, rights and opportunities in special education, in C. Roaf and H. Bines (eds) *Needs, Rights and Opportunities.* London: Falmer.

Romberg, T. (1993) How one comes to know: models and theories of the learning of mathematics, in M. Niss (ed.) *Investigations into Assessment in Mathematics Education*, pp. 97–111. Dordecht: Kluwer.

Rosenthal, R. and Jackson, L. (1966) *Pygmalion in the Classroom: Teacher Expectation and Pupils' Intellectual Development.* New York: Holt, Rinehart and Winston.

Ruthven, K. (1987) Ability stereotyping in mathematics, *Educational Studies in Mathematics*, 18: 243–53.

Ruthven, K. (1994) Better judgement: rethinking assessment in mathematics education, *Educational Studies in Mathematics*, 27: 433–50.

Schagen, I. and Schagen, S. (2001) *The Impact of Selection on Pupil Performance.* Slough: NFER.

Schoenfeld, A. (1985) *Mathematical Problem Solving.* New York: Academic Press.

Schools Examination and Assessment Council (1989) *A Sourcebook of Teacher Assessment.* London: HMSO.

Senk, S. and Thompson, D. (eds) (2003) *Standards-Based School Mathematics Curricula: What Are They? What Do Students Learn?* Mahwah, NJ: Erlbaum.

Sfard, A. (2002) Learning mathematics as developing a discourse, in R. Speiser, C. Maher and C. Walter (eds), *Proceedings of 21st Conference of PME-NA*, pp. 23–44. Columbus, OH: Clearing House for Science, Mathematics, and Environmental Education.

Sierpinska, A. (1994) *Understanding in Mathematics.* London: Falmer.

Silver, E. and Stein, M. (1996) The QUASAR project: the 'revolution of the possible' in mathematics instructional reform in middle schools, *Urban Education*, 30: 476–521.

Sinclair, N. (2004) The roles of the aesthetic in mathematical inquiry, *Mathematical Thinking and Learning*, 6(3): 261–84.

Skemp, R. (1976) Relational and instrumental understanding. *Mathematics Teaching*, 77: 20–6.

Slavin, R.E. (1990) Achievement effects of ability grouping in secondary schools: a best evidence synthesis, *Review of Educational Research*, 60(3): 471–99.

Smith, A. (2004) *Making Mathematics Count: The Report of Professor Adrian Smith's Inquiry into post-14 Mathematics Education.* London: Stationery Office.

Smith, E. and Gorard, S. (2005) Putting research into practice: an example from the 'Black Box', *Research Intelligence*, 91: 4–5.

Southern Examining Group (1988) *ATM/SEG Syllabus in Mathematics GCSE for the 1989 Examination*. Guildford: SEG.

Sternberg, R. (1998) Abilities are forms of developing expertise, *Educational Researcher*, 27: 11–20.

Sukhnandan, L. and Lee, B. (1998) *Streaming, Setting and Grouping by Ability: A Review of the Literature*. Slough: NFER.

Swan, M. (2005) *Improving Learning in Mathematics: Challenges and Strategies*. Sheffield: Department for Education and Skills Standards Unit.

Tahta, R. (1980) About geometry, *For the Learning of Mathematics*, 1(1): 2–9.

Tall, D. (ed.) (1991) *Advanced Mathematical Thinking*. Dordrecht: Kluwer.

Tanner, H. and Jones, S. (1995) Teaching mathematical thinking skills to accelerate cognitive development, in L.Meira and D. Carraher (eds) *Proceedings of the 19th International Conference for the Psychology of Mathematics Education*, Vol. 3, pp. 121–28. Recife, Brazil: Universidade Federal de Pernambuco.

Thompson, I. (1999) *Issues in Teaching Numeracy in Primary Schools*. Buckingham: Open University Press.

Tversky, A. and Kahneman, D. (1982) Judgement under uncertainty: heuristics and biases, in D. Kahneman, P. Slovic and A. Tversky (eds) *Judgement under Uncertainty. pp.* 3–20. Cambridge: Cambridge University Press.

Tymms, P. (2004) Are standards rising in English primary schools? *British Educational Research Journal*, 30(4): 477–94.

Vergnaud, G. (1997) The nature of mathematical concepts, in T. Nunes and P. Bryant (eds) *Learning and Teaching Mathematics: An International Perspective*, pp. 5–28. London: Psychology Press.

Vygotsky, L.S. (1978) *Mind in Society: The Development of Higher Psychological Processes*. Cambridge, MA: Harvard University Press.

Watson, A. (1995) Evidence for pupils' mathematical achievements, *For the Learning of Mathematics*, 15: 16–21.

Watson, A. (1996a) Teachers' notions of mathematical ability in their pupils, *Mathematics Education Review*, 8: 27–35.

Watson, A. (1996b) Problematising confidence: is it a helpful concept?, in *Proceedings of British Society for Research into Learning Mathematics*, pp. 57–62. London: Institute of Education.

Watson, A. (1997) Coming to know pupils: a study of informal teacher assessment of mathematics, in E. Pehkonen (ed.) *Proceedings of the 21st International Group for the Psychology of Mathematics Education*, Vol. 4, pp. 270–7. Lahti: University of Helsinki.

Watson, A. (1998) *An Investigation into How Teachers Make Judgements about What Pupils Know and Can Do in Mathematics*. Unpublished DPhil thesis, University of Oxford.

Watson, A. (1999) Paradigmatic conflicts in informal mathematics assessment as sources of social inequity, *Educational Review*, 51(2): 105–15.

Watson, A. (2000) Going across the grain: mathematical generalisations in a group of low attainers, *Nordic Studies in Mathematics Education*, 8(1): 7–20.

Watson, A. (2001a) Changes in mathematical performance of Year 7 pupils who were 'boosted' for KS2 SATs. Paper presented at BERA Conference, University of Leeds, September.

Watson, A. (2001b) Low attainers exhibiting higher-order mathematical thinking, *Support for Learning*, 16(4): 179–83.

Watson, A. (2002a) Teaching for understanding, in L. Haggarty (ed.) *Aspects of Teaching Secondary Mathematics*, pp. 153–63. London: RoutledgeFalmer.

Watson, A. (2002b) What does it mean to understand something and how do we know when it has happened?, in L. Haggarty (ed.) *Teaching Mathematics in Secondary Schools*, pp. 161–75. London: RoutledgeFalmer.

Watson, A. (2002c) Instances of mathematical thinking among low-attaining students in an ordinary secondary classroom, *Journal of Mathematical Behavior*, 20: 461–75.

Watson, A. (2002d) Use of unison responses in mathematics classrooms, in J. Winter and S. Pope (eds) *Research in Mathematics Education Volume 4: Papers of the British Society for Research into Learning Mathematics*, pp. 35–49. London: BSRLM

Watson, A. and De Geest, E. (2005) Principled teaching for deep progress: improving mathematical learning beyond methods and materials. *Educational Studies in Mathematics*, 58: 209–34.

Watson, A. and Mason, J. (1998) *Questions and Prompts for Mathematical Thinking*. Derby: Association of Teachers of Mathematics.

Watson, A. and Mason, J. (2005) *Mathematics as a Constructive Activity: Learners Generating Examples*. Mahwah, NJ: Erlbaum.

Watson, A., DeGeest, E. and Prestage, S. (2003a) Thinking in ordinary lessons: what happened when nine teachers believed their failing students could think mathematically, in S. Dawson, B. Dougherty and N. Pateman (eds) *Proceedings of the 27th annual conference of the International Group for the Psychology of Mathematics Education*, Vol. 2, pp. 301–8. Honolulu: University of Honolulu.

Watson, A., De Geest, E. and Prestage, S. (2003b) *Deep Progress in Mathematics: The Improving Attainment in Mathematics Project*. Oxford: Department of Educational Studies. University of Oxford. www.edstud.ox.ac.uk/people/academic3 (accessed 5 August 2005).

Wiliam, D. and Bartholomew, H. (2004) It's not which school but which set you're in that matters: the influence of ability grouping practices on student progress in mathematics, *British Educational Research Journal*, 30(2): 279–94.

Wiliam, D. (1994) Assessing authentic tasks: alternatives to mark-schemes, *Nordic Studies in Mathematics Education*, 2(1): 48–68.

Windle, B. (1989) Closing address – Afterword: A personal view. In E.R. Perkins (ed.) *Affirmation, Communication and Cooperation: Papers from the QSRE Conference on Education, July 1988*. London: Quaker Home Service.

Author index

Contents index